National Fictions

Australian Cultural Studies
Editor: John Tulloch

NATIONAL FICTIONS

Literature, film and the construction of Australian narrative

Second edition

GRAEME TURNER

LONDON AND NEW YORK

For Chris and Holly

First published 1986 by Allen & Unwin

Published 2020 by Routledge
2 Park Square, Milton Park, Abingdon, Oxon OX14 4RN
605 Third Avenue, New York, NY 10017

Routledge is an imprint of the Taylor & Francis Group, an informa business

© Graeme Turner 1986, 1993

All rights reserved. No part of this book may be reprinted or reproduced or utilised in any form or by any electronic, mechanical, or other means, now known or hereafter invented, including photocopying and recording, or in any information storage or retrieval system, without permission in writing from the publishers.

Notice:
Product or corporate names may be trademarks or registered trademarks, and are used only for identification and explanation without intent to infringe.

National Library of Australia
Cataloguing-in-Publication entry:

Turner Graeme.
  National fictions: literature, film and the construction of Australian narrative.

  2nd ed.
  Bibliography.
  Includes index.
  ISBN 1 86373 504 6.

  1. Australian fiction—History and criticism. 2. Motion pictures, Australian. 3. Motion pictures and literature—Australia. 4. Discourse analysis, Narrative. 5. Australia—Civilization. I. Title. (Series: Australian cultural studies).

A823.009

Set in 10/11lf2 pt Plantin

ISBN-13: 9781863735049 (pbk)

General editor's foreword

Nowadays the social and anthropological definition of 'culture' is probably gaining as much public currency as the aesthetic one. Particularly in Australia, politicians are liable to speak of the vital need for a domestic film industry in 'promoting our cultural identity'—and they mean by 'cultural identity' some sense of Australianness, of our nationalism as a distinct form of social organisation. Notably, though, the emphasis tends to be on Australian *film* (not popular television); and not just *any* film, but those of 'quality'. So the aesthetic definition tends to be smuggled back in—on top of the kind of cultural nationalism which assumes that 'Australia' is a unified entity with certain essential features that distinguish it from 'Britain', the 'USA' or any other national entities which threaten us with 'cultural dependency'.

This series is titled 'Australian Cultural Studies', and I should say at the outset that my understanding of 'Australian' is not as an essentially unified category; and further, that my understanding of cultural is anthropological rather than aesthetic. By 'culture' I mean the social production of meaning and understanding, whether in the inter-personal and practical organisation of daily routines or in broader institutional and ideological structures. I am *not* thinking of 'culture' as some form of universal 'excellence', based on aesthetic 'discrimination' and embodied in a pantheon of 'great works'. Rather, I take this aesthetic definition of culture itself to be part of the *social mobilisation of discourse* to differentiate a cultural 'élite' from the 'mass' of society.

Unlike the cultural nationalism of our opinion leaders, 'Cultural Studies' focuses not on the essential unity of national cultures, but on the meanings attached to social difference (as in the distinction between 'élite' and 'mass' taste). It analyses the construction and mobilisation of these distinctions to maintain or challenge existing

vi *National Fictions*

power differentials, such as those of gender, class, age, race and ethnicity. In this analysis, terms designed to socially differentiate people (like 'élite' and 'mass') become categories of discourse, communication and power. Hence our concern in this series is for an analytical understanding of the meanings attached to social difference within the *history* and *politics* of discourse.

It follows that the analysis of 'texts' needs to be untied from a single-minded association with 'high' culture (marked by 'authorship'), but must include the 'popular' too—since these distinctions of 'high' and 'popular' culture themselves need to be analysed, not assumed. Graeme Turner's *National Fictions*, reprinted here in its second edition, engages with both 'high' and 'popular' culture directly. It is the first book in Australian studies to analyse seriously the cultural construction of narratives in both 'high' literature and 'popular' film; and this has been fundamental to the book's success since its first publication in 1986. As Turner says in his new Preface, the 'book deals with both media in order to lead readers across the disciplinary divide towards new angles of inspection and, hopefully, new knowledge'.

Culture, as Turner argues, is the primary subject of this book rather than film or literature in themselves, and this is because 'narratives are ultimately produced by the culture; . . . they generate meanings, take on a significance, and assume forms that are *articulations* of the values, beliefs—the ideology—of the culture'. Given the view that texts are the productions of culture, Turner focuses here more on 'the similarities than the differences between individual texts––in other words with the common or dominant forms and meanings in Australian culture'. This approach does not, however, homogenise 'common meanings' in some nationalistically essentialising way: 'the focus upon Australian narrative is not an exercise in nationalism but an enquiry into those determinants of narrative which are culturally specific'. Above all, the emphasis here on cultural specificity rejects the naturalistic representation of 'society as a trap' (as Raymond Williams put it). Turner examines in this book a series of social 'alibis' that have been reproduced repeatedly within Australian narrative texts on behalf of the status quo—in, for instance, the bush myth, and in the representation of convictism. 'The context becomes one in which the bush and the prison offer the same limited range of possibilities for the individual: the environment is tough, but survivable if one accepts its basic domination over the self.' Images of nature—such as the harsh Australian landscape—thus become at the same time images of culture because they suggest that 'survival is all, resistance is futile, and ideals are to be tempered by contingency'. Together, the dominant themes of a colonial Australia construct a pattern of acceptance, accommodation and assent, 'posing as the "natural" structure of existence within an Australian context'. In this way, Australian narrative fictions have worked too often in a consensualising way, 'to obscure differences and divisions that may well need to be recognised and addressed'.

At the end of the book Turner warns us—in reviewing possibly oppositional elements within Australian narratives—that we should not remember only the 'dominant patterns' and 'monistic conclusions'. In some narratives, 'the realist depiction of non-consensual views of life which constructs the identification between the viewer and the characters living that life may well be interrogative, proposing rather a critical analysis of Australian society'. In other cases, formal breaks with naturalism can have 'the potential for dislodging the viewer from a comfortable position of knowing and accepting'. Still, in the end even these 'resistive' tendencies are 'contained within the general framework of meanings of the culture ... which still strives to appropriate these groups' expression as its own'. Turner follows Levi-Strauss, Will Wright and others in seeing narrative as a symbolic resolution to social contradictions; he insists on the construction of culture out of social divisions, and examines ways in which national myth 'serves to override and silence the less powerful voices in the culture'. On the other hand, though, he emphasises the need to look constantly for signs of 'renovation or resistance'. The enduring value of his book is in articulating that tension through the texts of Australian 'high' and 'popular' culture. As he says in his new Preface, if 'our narratives *do* make it easier for us to accept our social powerlessness or for us to overlook the inequities and divisions within our society, then this *is* a cause for concern'.

Culture, as Fiske, Hodge and Turner say in *Myths of Oz*, grows out of the divisions of society, not its unity. 'It has to work to construct any unity that it has, rather than simply celebrate an achieved or natural harmony.' Australian culture is then no more than the temporary, embattled construction of 'unity' at any particular historical moment. The 'readings' in this series of 'Australian Cultural Studies' inevitably (and polemically) form part of the struggle to make and break the boundaries of meaning which, in conflict and collusion, dynamically define our culture.

JOHN TULLOCH

Contents

Illustrations	x
Acknowledgements	xi
Preface to the second edition	xiii
Introduction	1
1 National fictions: *film, fiction and national culture*	13
2 The Australian context: *nature and society*	25
3 The self in context	54
4 Characterisation and individualism	87
5 Representing the nation	107
6 Complications and conclusions	128
Afterword	146
References	156
Index	166

Illustrations

For the Term of His Natural Life (1927)	*xii*
Frederick McCubbin's 'Lost' (1886) oil on canvas, 114.3 × 72.4 cm, Felton Bequest, 1940	*27*
Caddie (1976)	*39*
Caddie (1976)	*40*
For the Term of His Natural Life (1927)	*55*
Stir (1980)	*63*
Stir (1980)	*67*
The Chant of Jimmie Blacksmith (1978)	*72*
Tom Roberts' 'Shearing the Rams' (1890) oil on canvas on board, 121.9 × 182.6 cm, Felton Bequest, 1932	*112*
Sunday Too Far Away (1975)	*113*
Breaker Morant (1980)	*116*
Man of Flowers (1983)	*134*

Acknowledgements

Some of the material in this book has been published in earlier versions in *Overland*, *Australian Literary Studies*, and the *Australian Journal of Cultural Studies*. Illustrations have been provided by the National Film and Sound Archive, The Film House, The NSW Film Corporation, Film Victoria, the South Australian Film Corporation, Anthony Buckley, Paul Cox, and the National Gallery of Victoria. Their assistance is gratefully acknowledged.

George Fisher as Rufus Dawes in 'For the Term of His Natural Life' (1927). (Courtesy of the National Film and Sound Archive)

Preface to the second edition

In preparing this second edition of *National Fictions*, I have resisted the temptation to revise. While there is certainly more I would like to say, I remain in agreement with the book's arguments and am content to allow them to stand as they are. What I have done to bring the book up to date is add a substantial Afterword which alerts the reader to significant changes in the critical context since 1986 (when *National Fictions* was first published) and reviews some contemporary developments in fiction and film.

National Fictions argues that there are formal and ideological patterns in Australian narratives that cut across representational forms and media. These patterns are the product of those myths and meanings which have been culturally constructed as Australian: they are the 'national fictions' of the title. So, while it is in no way a nationalistic study, the book deals with the ways in which 'the nation' is constructed through its stories.

When *National Fictions* was first published, this was not a particularly fashionable undertaking; the idea of 'the nation' has not been popular with liberal or left intellectuals in Australia for the last two decades, and has been even less popular elsewhere. In Australia, the idea of the nation is tainted by an old left romanticism organised around mythologies of the bush and a masculinist ethic of work-based solidarity. Elsewhere, it is discredited by the reactionary nationalisms which seem in inexhaustible supply within European histories, for instance, and displaced by the increasing acceptance of the globalisation of culture: the projected abolition of national boundaries in favour of more localised structures of community on the one hand, and a multi-nationalised global economy on the other. It is easy to characterise an interest in 'the nation' as the anachronistic invocation of an essential national character which misunderstands the constructedness of national identity. Elizabeth Jacka has, for instance, represented what I call an 'Australian accent' in our national fictions as such a position. However, I maintain that the idea of an 'Australian accent' does not necessarily make any essentialising assumptions of a naturally expressive, organic Australianness speaking through our narratives. An accent is not a sign of an organic national character; rather it is a socially and historically produced marker of differences which speak generically and variously of locality, of region and of nation. As such, it still seems an appropriate metaphor to use when describing the object of this study.

However, resistance to the idea of the nation is well-founded; as we shall see in the following pages, it serves to override and silence the less powerful voices in the culture. There is the danger, in a project such as *National Fictions*, of claiming too much for large, determining, structures and of burying individual differences beneath national similarities. Nevertheless, it still seems to me that thinking about how Australian stories construct our sense of our selves is as worthwhile an exercise now as it was in 1986. Indeed, if I were to alter anything in this book, it would be my remarks at the end of chapter 6 which suggest that the conclusions I draw—since they were not meant as a prescription for a more progressive Australian narrative—should cause no social anxiety. This perhaps took the formalism of the exercise a little too far. If, as I hope to persuade the reader, our narratives *do* make it easier for us to accept our social powerlessness or for us to overlook the inequities and divisions within our society, then this *is* a cause for concern. To the extent that our repertoire of definitions of the nation facilitate such processes, they must be exposed to analysis and criticism.

What follows is an attempt to describe a major epistemological field within our culture—the way we construct Australian experience through stories. It is selective in that it maps the prevailing topography of the area. However, it is far more inclusive than any single disciplinary study since its arguments are produced through the analysis of two very different representational regimes—literary fiction and film—while drawing at times on further examples from fine art, poetry and popular culture. I would encourage readers not to succumb to the temptation of only reading those parts of the book to which their disciplinary preferences direct them; concentrating on the literary or the filmic will miss the point of the comparisons made between the two. The book deals with both media in order to lead readers across the disciplinary divide towards new angles of inspection and, hopefully, new knowledge.

Graeme Turner
Brisbane, 1993

Introduction

> The narratives of this world are numberless... Able to be carried by articulated language, spoken or written, fixed or moving images, gestures, and the ordered mixture of all these substances; narrative is present in myth, legend, fable, tale, novella, epic, history, tragedy, drama, comedy, mime, painting ... stained glass windows, cinema, comics, news items, conversation. Moreover, under this almost infinite diversity of forms, narrative is present in every age, in every place, in every society; it begins with the very history of mankind and there nowhere has been a people without narrative. All classes, all human groups, have their narratives, enjoyment of which is very often shared by men with different, even opposing, cultural backgrounds. Caring nothing for the division between good and bad literature, narrative is international, transhistorical, transcultural: it is simply there, like life itself.
>
> Roland Barthes

This book is about narrative, about the forms and meanings constructed through Australian storytellers. It is based on the conviction that narratives are ultimately produced by the culture; thus they generate meanings, take on significances, and assume forms that are *articulations* of the values, beliefs—the ideology—of the culture. The approach is interdisciplinary, examining the relationships between examples of two narrative forms, literary fiction and the feature film.

This procedure is adopted in order to gain a fuller picture of Australian narrative than is available by concentrating on one medium. The results of this book, therefore, focus upon culture as the primary subject rather than upon either literature or film. Although it does work within the discrete disciplines of literary or film studies at numerous points (and hopefully it will make many judgements of interest to those disciplines) this book can thus more accurately be seen as a contribution to the developing discipline of Australian cultural studies.

While interested in, and largely drawn from, the study of specific texts, the argument of the book is inevitably more concerned with the similarities than the differences between individual texts—in other words with the common or dominant forms and meanings in Australian narrative. As the culture produces its texts it prefers certain meanings, thematic structures and formal strategies. Within these preferred forms and meanings we find the ideology of the culture: the way it makes sense of itself and infers meaning onto its institutions and practices. In studying some of these preferences, this book aims at providing more than a critical, thematic survey of a range of Australian texts; it examines a number of the ways in which the Australian culture creates meaning in its narratives in order to suggest not only what an Australian narrative *is*, but also what it *does*.

This enterprise takes place within a complicated context. The study of Australian literature has been dominated by the search for the definition of 'Australian' literature, and has been especially concerned with problems of standards: specifically, by which standards—local, or universal—are Australian texts to be 'judged'.[1] An important political provocation for this preoccupation was the need for Australian literary studies to legitimate their area of interest in comparison with, and in terms of, the more traditional area—English literature. Until quite recently, Australian literary studies has had a predominantly evaluative cast. Its most positive productions have been eager to represent Australian literature as a body of writing that included writers of stature comparable to the greats in the English literary canon. This enterprise has not been entirely successful, but it does give some extra-literary clues to the preference for Patrick White, for example, over Frank Hardy.

Behind the arguments about standards, of course, lurked philosophical and ideological positions which were informally proposed as appropriate ones within apparently disinterested arguments and debates. This aspect of the battle for the control of the definition of Australian literature is the subject of John Docker's *In A Critical Condition*.[2] Docker sees the dominant model of Australian literary criticism, the 'metaphysical ascendancy', as one which looks for the 'best' examples of Australian writing—those which are 'universal' in quality and metaphysical in implication—and which attempts to draw lines of influence between them in order to establish a tradition. The opposing, subordinate tradition, that of the radical nationalists, interests itself instead in writers for their direct relevance to Australian society, and it has a preference for a more political, critical, and socially concerned fiction. The debate between these two camps, according to Docker, occupies a major area in Australian literary criticism.

Docker's account, while recognisable in most respects, does simplify overmuch, drawing the divisions too neatly and overlooking differences and contradictions. Further, his outlining of the ideological function of critical positions implicitly discredits the attempt to propose some kind of coherence in our literary tradition. Despite this implication, however, it *is* possible to list a significant number of studies whose attempts to explain the dominant ways of making meaning out of Australian experience through literary fiction have provided us with useful insights and provisional patterns for a preliminary theory of Australian prose narrative. For example, Brian Kiernan's *Images of Society and Nature*,[3] while the subject of much revision and amendment, offers in its last chapter a coherent model of the predicament of the individual within Australian fiction. H. P. Heseltine's 1962 *Meanjin* article[4] (updated in Kiernan's work) still holds benefits for the contemporary reader. Veronica Brady's neglected *A Crucible of Prophets*[5] is a source of many insights into the problems of a particular realm of meaning—the spiritual—in Australian writing. And rigorous treatments of discrete areas or periods of writing—such as Ian Reid's *Fiction and the Great Depression*[6]—are resonant with implications about the determinants of the larger tradition.

However, while Australian criticism has become increasingly sophisticated over the last decade, the work of defining the nature of 'Australian-ness' in literary fiction is still incomplete. The most adventurous studies in recent times have been discussions of particular texts or writers, or contributions to the general field of the relationship between literature and history—enlarging and complicating the context within which literary studies situates its subject matter. In important ways, this present study is a contribution to this latter area.

While there has been a proliferation of discussion of specific texts in literary criticism—since the evaluation of the particular text has been the first step in acts of exploration and colonisation of the Australian literary territory—this is not the case in Australian film studies. The first efforts at Australian film studies were historical, their approach 'excavatory, celebratory and polemical'.[7] Even quite recent and apparently authoritative studies, such as Pike and Cooper's annotated filmography *Australian Film 1900–1977*,[8] belong within this mode of film history. There has been a radical change in the last ten years, however, leading to the reconstruction of Australian film history.[9] Due especially to the work of John Tulloch,[10] the contextual, ideological, and industrial aspects of film production as well as the cultural significance of the meaning of individual narratives have become central concerns of contemporary academic accounts of Australian film. Unlike fiction, film generates widespread popular interest and discussion in the popular press as well as in more specialist journals such as

Cinema Papers; and it is even the subject of coffee table books such as Murray's *The New Australian Cinema* or David Stratton's *The Last New Wave*.[11] Theoretical debate of any complexity is carried on through such journals as the *Australian Journal of Screen Theory*, *Filmnews*, and more recently the *Australian Journal of Cultural Studies*. To date there is not a large body of academic criticism of Australian films, nor a wide spread of analysis of individual films outside the review pages of the popular or industry press. Having gained respectability only recently, film studies are thus still to emerge from the marginalised position which they have held in Australian academia.

Further, Australian film—even more so than Australian literature—is often seen to be beneath consideration when compared to the work of European or Scandinavian film-makers. The location of film studies within English Departments has been a dominant feature of the discipline's institutional history—and this has had, as Noel King argues,[12] a number of consequences on the success which film studies may or may not have enjoyed in representing itself as a separate, legitimate area of study. Among the consequences which concern us here is the preference which has developed for the articulation of a general film theory over the more literary exercise of establishing a body of orthodox readings of individual texts; and the specific way in which these theoretical influences have shaped the new discipline. The roots of contemporary Australian film theory and criticism are not as predominantly evaluative as in literary criticism. The early influence of cultural historians provided assistance in the establishment of an interest in the film industry itself, so context is rarely as completely ignored in studies of Australian film as it is in many studies of Australian fiction. As the influence of semiotics provided theoretical support for film studies' interest in popular culture, and as theories of representation focussed attention on the film text as a particular discursive practice rather than as an aesthetic production, the cultural function and significance of film narrative did become an important item on the new discipline's agenda.

There is a complication, however—and it lies in the marxian suspicion of studies which are nationalist in ideology. So the category of 'Australian film' is itself often seen as problematic. The environmental determinism which dominates so much of Australian literary and historical studies as a means of explaining the development of an Australian cultural tradition is explicitly attacked by contemporary film theorists;[13] and this dramatises the difference between the theoretical traditions within which the two areas of study have developed. Further evidence of the difference is the lack of attention given to proposing the importance of certain 'seminal' film texts. Structuralist in that similarities are held to be more interesting than differences, semiotic in that texts are seen as signifying structures interesting for what they reveal about signification in film texts in general, film theory in Australia has devoted comparatively little time to arguments about particular texts or particular directors. Even the productions of the revival of the seventies (from which the majority of my examples will come) are not usually provided with more attention than is possible within a review or survey article. Tulloch's first book on Australian film production in the 1920s and 1930s, *Legends on the Screen*, does provide us with the major sources of close and detailed analysis of particular films and film-makers; but this work has not yet fostered similar treatments for the films of the 1940s, 1950s, or for contemporary cinema—although a number of such works are in press at the moment.[14]

Although departments of film studies have often grown out of (or are attached to) literature departments, this has not created a close relationship between them. Indeed, the very fact of an institutional dependence—even if only an initial one—on literary studies has made film studies mark out its area in opposition to that of literature. This demarcation often takes the form of a theoretical position which denies the category of high art, and which attacks what is caricatured as the poverty of theory in literary studies. Consequently, while comparisons between film and fiction are frequent they are usually informal rather than proposed in any systematic way. The work of Colin McCabe in the United Kingdom,[15] problematic as it is, does not have an equivalent in Australia. A limited exception to this is, once again, John Tulloch's *Legends on the Screen*, where much use is made of literary constructions of the bush myth and the Australian legend—although the legend is not as problematised as it normally is in literary studies. The only book to make a systematic connection—Brian McFarlane's account of Australian fiction made into film, *Words and Images*[16]—is a reading of a collection of texts which examines the translation of one medium into another from an essentially evaluative position, one that is intrinsically literary. No conclusions are drawn by McFarlane from his study—and even if there were they would be conclusions about the translation of novels into film, which is a different matter from relating the meanings articulated in our film tradition to those articulated in our literary tradition. It is perhaps not surprising, then, that the work which this book sets out to accomplish has not been done elsewhere. The recognition that Australian literature and film are both narratives produced by the culture can be seen in Tulloch's and Sylvia Lawson's work,[17] but it is not argued by any literary critic. The two disciplines of film and literature studies, it seems, do require a degree of theoretical mediation before the benefits of either one can be shared with the other.

That mediation is occurring elsewhere. Developments in narratology reveal that the study of narrative has the potential of providing a framework within which such a two-pronged study can be undertaken. The study of narrative today is 'no longer restricted to poetics' but has become 'an attempt to describe fundamental operations of any signifying system'.[18] British and European cultural studies of representation, using discourse analysis and semiotics, also examine the way in which meaning is produced through the representation of reality in all forms of communication. Stuart Hall talks of representation as the 'active labour of making things mean' through a complicated system of regulation and exclusion which operates through language and discourse.[19] The methods developed by narratology and cultural studies offer useful ways of establishing narrative as a mediating category, of theorising the relationships between different narrative forms, and of relating the conclusions of such a study to the ideology of the culture which produces them. The opportunity offered by theories of narrative is thus one which this book sets out to exploit, and it produces different analyses of texts to those normally found in either film or literary studies.

This study is therefore text-based. It draws from a range of narratives in film and fiction (occasionally verse) a number of common structures which are then traced back into the culture. Apart from admitting the existence of important differences between the conditions of production of film and fiction, there is no attempt to present an analysis of those conditions. I recognise that a full account of Australian narrative would require this, but I do not attempt to be comprehensive in this study. To provide a full analysis of the organisation of industrial, institutional, representational and discursive determinants of narrative would involve a very different exercise, one that I do not feel competent to undertake, and one which does not serve the more limited objectives of this book.

This book has a number of objectives. First, since my own background is literary, it is aimed at widening the field of discussion of literary fiction by revealing how the patterns which dominate the Australian literary tradition also shape film narrative in this country. This does not mean that I attempt to construct a 'great tradition' of Australian film to match that great tradition enshrined in the *Oxford History of Australian Literature*;[20] indeed, qualitative, evaluative and hierarchical judgements play little part in the book or in the methodology that organises it. The notion of value, particularly in its application to Australian literary studies, operates so as to colonise and to privilege certain kinds of discourse. From this study's point of view, the cultural importance of the 'elected' texts is their privileged nature rather than their intrinsic value—or lack of it. By viewing literary fiction as narrative it is argued that literary production proceeds from sources within the culture which are related to those which generate other kinds of cultural production; and although literary fiction is formed in different ways and asks for different kinds of reception, its relation to the culture is no less direct, no less mediated by historical forces outside the author's control.

A second objective of the study is to continue the work done by Tulloch in proposing some shape for the Australian film tradition. For the films which were made during the 1920s and 1930s the work has largely been done already; films made since that time, despite the amount of attention which the 1970s revival has received, are generally not so well served. Again, this proposition of a 'tradition'—a word tainted with prescriptive overtones, but for which there is no suitable alternative—does not involve the hierarchising of various texts, but rather the drawing of parallels, the constructing of homologies between the forms which are used and the meanings which are generated by film texts. While I do refer to films made outside the 1970s and 1980s, this period is my main source of examples. I see the films of the revival as being continuous with the body of film which precedes it, despite the customary polemical arguments about the destructive effects of the long hiatus in Australian feature film production.

I have not included television productions as items of analysis, nor would I expect my conclusions to automatically apply to television. While film and fiction do share important similarities as narrative forms and also a craft-like industrial structure, the television narrative industrially and structurally (at the textual level) seems crucially different. As John Ellis points out in *Visible Fictions*,[21] the dominant narrative form in television is the series or the serial rather than the discrete, closed narrative. To have included television within this study would have involved so much qualification and exception as to render it unwieldy.

The third objective of the book is to establish those kinds of meanings which are preferred, the forms in which they are articulated, and their ideological function within Australian culture. An inevitable consequence of this is the concentration on a particular set of meanings, and thus the creation of an apparently monistic model of form and meaning in Australian narrative. In carrying out the business of describing the dominant set of meanings I have made no attempt at prescription, by ruling out aberrant forms in favour of those which seem to fit the pattern. The wider suggestiveness of the result is the justification, hopefully, of the method.

The book is designed as an application of theory. So the examples cited are simply that, rather than comprehensive surveys of the full range of possible applications of the theory—and it is for readers to judge how far one can apply the models proposed. But the examples have been drawn from a whole range of locations, from those accepted within the literary canon to those excluded, from populist film to the 'quality' films of the revival, in an attempt to establish the commonality of their sources and function within the culture.

The attempt to find points of synthesis between literary theory, film theory and cultural studies theory means that there are a large number of assumptions that need to be named. Most of these assumptions will emerge during the course of later chapters, and the major theoretical connection between film and fiction is dealt with specifically in the first chapter. Some assumptions, however, need to be named at this point. To begin with, the model of culture from which this study proceeds draws on marxian, structuralist and anthropological concepts of culture. Consequently, the important assumption here is that the concentration on Australian narrative is none other than an examination of the cultural specificity of meaning: the universality of narrative is admitted, and so the focus upon Australian narrative is not an exercise in nationalism but an enquiry into those determinants of narrative which are culturally specific. The enquiry, however, is not extensively comparative, in that references are made to the narratives of other cultures purely as a result of the need to maintain the key focus of the argument—and so they are as often rhetorical as they are systematic. This is not to deny the value of comparative methods. But to make extensive use of such methods would be to write a different book. I acknowledge, in short, that Australia is only physically an island and that its history is enclosed within a larger, western history—so that the examination of the cultural specificity of our narratives is not in any way an argument for their uniqueness but rather for a kind of Australian accent which is audible and distinctive when placed in relation to that of other English speakers.

My use of essentially synchronic methodology also needs to be noted. I have not provided developmental models of narrative in either film or fiction (although the history of both film and fiction does occupy many of the theoretical paragraphs). Primarily I have seen our *langue* of narrative—the cultural inventory of myths, of associations and of the meanings which they support—as the object of analysis which is best understood by artificially 'freezing' it, and by including within it the full range of narratives available, from the beginnings to the present. In doing this I am working within a post-Saussurean semiotic tradition, one which tends to describe a linguistic system by isolating its elements and their internal relationships in order to examine their function within the total system.[22] If language is a relational system, the relevant and available relations are those which obtain at the present time, and the analogy I draw between language on the one hand and the language of narrative on the other hand makes this approach the most appropriate.

The study of narrative as a means of studying the 'ways of seeing' of a culture is not new. Levi-Strauss' analysis of myth is a landmark in this area,[23] and most contemporary theories of narrative acknowledge its enclosure within the structures of meaning of the culture. We have long been happy to accept a view of the novel as, in Culler's words, 'the model by which society conceives of itself, the discourse in and through which it articulates the world.'[24] The referential dimension of the novel, its continual advertence to real life, is responsible for the novel becoming the major literary form of the modern era. Even more so the feature film: the referential dimension of realist cinema is so great that it can appear transparent, unmediated. The feature film is the twentieth-century storyteller, and much more than the contemporary novel it is the 'model through which we articulate the world'. Thus the study of film and fiction narrative as the product of culture eventually—and necessarily—becomes a study of representation, for narrative then also has a cultural function of making sense of experience, of filling absences, of resolving contradictions (and generally, of filling the role ascribed to it by Levi-Strauss as analogous to myth). This makes an analysis of the discourses through which Australian experience is represented all the more essential. As our study progresses, therefore, this aspect takes on greater importance.

The organisation of our chapters requires some summary. Following the introduction to the theoretical connections between film and fiction in Chapter 1, Chapter 2 examines the meanings given to the Australian context, both natural and social. The customary opposition between the country and the city is denied, in favour of a more unitary view of the Australian context which uses the harshness of the natural environment as an alibi for the powerlessness of the individual within the social environment. In this chapter there is wide reference to film and fiction, as well as extended analyses of *Caddie*, *Wake in Fright*, *Ultima Thule*, and *Landtakers*. Chapter 3 looks at the role of the individual within the context outlined in the previous chapter—as the protagonist in narrative. Two main ideas are examined: the first traces the image of the individual which is encapsulated in the fact and in the metaphor of convictism; and the second looks at this image as the representation of a particular metaphysical or existential stance. The version of the individual which emerges has the Australian protagonist responding to a secularised and alienated environment by admitting the withdrawal of meaning and value, but without inventing a replacement for which he may accept responsibility. Behind this metaphysic there is an ideological proposition that negates the value of individual action and legitimates powerlessness and subjection. The range of texts is again wide, but close attention is paid to *Stir*, *For the Term of His Natural Life*, *The Getting of Wisdom*, *The Devil's Playground*, and *Bring Larks and Heroes*.

Describing the image of a powerless and defeated selfhood constructed through the representation of the Australian protagonist reveals one set of information; examining the modes of characterisation employed in our narratives reveals another. The range of modes of characterisation in our narratives is narrow—and it reveals certain preferences about what constitutes the individual. Although we have heroes in our verse narratives, in the more realist forms of prose and film such highly individualised characters are rare. Chapter 4 examines the ideological implications and motivations of this phenomenon through, among others, the stories of Henry Lawson, the films of Peter Weir, and *Sunday Too Far Away*. Increasingly, then, this chapter touches upon the problems of representation; and so Chapter 5 looks at the dominance of certain modes of representing Australian nationalism in film and fiction. The thematic and political postures of acceptance and defeat as outlined earlier are now actively celebrated through nationalist constructions such as the battler and the larrikin. Texts examined are the films *Breaker Morant*, *The Man From Snowy River*, *Gallipoli* and *Phar Lap*.

Since the book gives an account of one dominant field of meaning, the concluding chapter—Chapter 6—therefore begins by reviewing other, possibly contradictory, developments within Australian narrative for their oppositional or ameliorative potential. There is some discussion of new formal directions in contemporary film and fiction (such work as Hayden Keenan's *Going Down* and Peter Carey's *Bliss*) which is then followed by the general conclusions.

I would like to acknowledge assistance in the preparation of this work from several colleagues in the School of English at WAIT. Delys Bird has offered the intellectual and personal support of a model colleague; John Fiske has been a challenging and important source of ideas and information; while Jon Watts, Robert Dixon and Don Grant have been helpful and sympathetic readers of work in progress. I am grateful for the generous and useful responses that this work has received from Brian Kiernan, John McLaren, Laurie Hergenhan, and, particularly, my editors, Judy Benson and John Tulloch.

I would also like to thank the University of Western Australia for the provision of a research fellowship which allowed me to work in a peaceful and congenial environment, as well as the members of the English Department at UWA—particularly Veronica Brady, Bruce

Introduction 11

Bennett and John Hay—for their interest and support during my time there. My students of Australian Studies at WAIT, who have been the testing ground for the ideas put forward in this book, receive affectionate acknowledgement and thanks; their discussions have been a major influence on the development of my work. To my wife I owe thanks for her patience and for her understanding of the utterly arbitrary sacrifice of private time demanded by this study. Finally, I owe thanks to my typist, Rae Kelly, for the unflagging excellence of her work.

NOTES

1. Brian Kiernan, *Criticism* (Australian Writers and Their Work series) (Melbourne: Oxford University Press, 1974), p.3.
2. (Ringwood: Penguin, 1984).
3. (Melbourne: Oxford University Press, 1971).
4. 'The Australian Image: The Literary Heritage' reprinted in Clement Semmler (ed.) *Twentieth Century Australian Literary Criticism* (Melbourne: Oxford University Press, 1967), pp.86–101.
5. (Sydney: Theological Explorations, 1981).
6. (Melbourne: Edward Arnold, 1979).
7. Stuart Cunningham, 'Australian Film History and Historiography', *Australian Journal of Cultural Studies*, Vol.1, No.1, p.123. This article is the source of a number of the general comments on Australian film criticism which follow.
8. (Melbourne: Oxford University Press, 1980).
9. Cunningham, p.125.
10. *Australian Cinema: Industry, Narrative and Meaning* (Sydney: George Allen and Unwin, 1982); *Legends on the Screen: The Narrative Film in Australia 1919–1929* (Sydney: Currency Press, 1981).
11. (Melbourne: Nelson/Cinema Papers, 1980); (Sydney: Angus and Robertson, 1980).
12. 'Changing the Curriculum: The Place of Film in a Department of English', *Australian Journal of Cultural Studies*, Vol.1, No.1, 1983, pp.47–55.
13. See Cunningham op. cit. as well as 'Australian Film' in the *Australian Journal of Screen Theory*, Nos. 5 & 6 (1978) pp.46–47.
14. Amongst these are Susan Dermody and Elizabeth Jacka's *The Screening of Australia*, and Albert Moran and Tom O'Regan's *Australian Film Reader*.
15. I have in mind his work on the classic realist text, making comparisons between the novel and cinema: 'Realism and the Cinema: Notes on some Brechtian Theses' first published in *Screen* (Vol.15, No.2) and reprinted in Tony Bennett, Susan Boyd-Bowman, Colin Mercer and Janet Woollacott (eds) *Popular Film and Television* (London: BFI, 1981) pp.216–35.
16. (Richmond: Heinemann, 1983).
17. Sylvia Lawson, 'Towards Decolonisation: Film History in Australia', in Susan Dermody, John Docker, and Drusilla Modjeska (eds) *Nellie Melba, Ginger Meggs and Friends*, (Malmsbury: Kibble, 1982), pp.19–32.
18. Shlomith Rimmon-Kenan, *Narrative Fiction: Contemporary Poetics*

(London: Methuen, 1983), p.131.
19 'The Rediscovery of "ideology": The Return of the repressed in Media Studies', in Michael Gurevitch, Tony Bennett, James Curran, and Janet Woollacott (eds) *Culture, Society and the Media*, (London: Methuen, 1982) p.64.
20 Leonie Kramer (ed.) (Melbourne: O.U.P., 1981).
21 (London: Routledge and Kegan Paul, 1982), pp.1–3.
22 Jonathon Culler, *Saussure* (London: Fontana, 1976), pp.29–35.
23 'The Structural Study of Myth' in Richard and Fernande DeGeorge (eds) *The Structuralists from Marx to Levi-Strauss*, (New York: Doubleday/Anchor, 1972), pp.169–94.
24 Jonathon Culler, *Structuralist Poetics: Structuralism, Linguistics and the Study of Literature*, (London: Routledge and Kegan Paul, 1975), p.189.

1 National fictions: *film, fiction and national culture*

The limitations on the comparative analysis of literary fiction and the feature film are dominated by the socio-political situation of the two forms and the disciplines which examine them. Literary fiction is an elite, privileged form,—one which is legitimated by its commitment to an objective of excellence, however that is defined; while the feature film is produced by a commercial industry which is unable to survive without creating a popular audience. Although there is government support for both forms, only with film is commercial success a major consideration. The discomfort of the literary critic with popular cultural forms has a long and distinguished history, where all sorts of arguments have been advanced about the survival of 'minority culture' against the threats of 'mass civilisation' right from Matthew Arnold, through Leavis and Eliot,[1] to the pundits of today. Similarly, film studies' recognition of its situation as an area which has to establish its respectability has produced a jealous wariness of the imperialism of other disciplines—the literary appropriation of *auteurs*, for instance—as well as a dominant interest in theorising the medium in order to establish both its essential nature and the discipline's academic rigour. So the limited degree of intercourse that occurs between the two disciplines has to deal with suspicions of elitism and imperialism on the one hand, and accusations of 'trendiness' on the other.

As pointed out in the introduction, film criticism does largely originate in the extension of English studies into mass cultural forms, even though this was often (and paradoxically) accompanied by an elitist rhetoric which denied sympathy with such forms. The increasing interest in film which occurred during the 1960s is traceable to the expansion of the concern of literary critics with the modernist narratives of film-makers such as Godard, Fellini and Bergman. The trend has generally been one way, that of literary critics moving into film. It is still the norm for film theorists to possess a strong literary background, while the reverse is not generally true. This has a number of consequences not only on the kind of interrelationships that are usually examined—the establishment of the study of the 'novel into film',[2] for instance—but also on the kinds of analysis to which film is normally subjected by people from outside film studies. Usually dominated by essentially literary assumptions, film analyses which arise from outside the discipline often substantiate the film theorists' case for the special nature of their area. (It should be noted that there are cases, although more rare, of film theorists crossing into literary areas. The results there are similar. For example, Colin McCabe's discussion of realist cinema, for all its importance, contains an argument about the typicality of *Middlemarch* as a classic realist text and about George Eliot as an acceptable voice for bourgeois nineteenth-century 'truths' about reality that many literary critics would find hard to accept. Eagleton's account of Eliot in *Criticism and Ideology* reveals, by comparison, the unexamined nature of McCabe's view.[3]) Analyses of film made by literary critics, and by psychologists or sociologists, often see film as an unproblematic medium. They ignore the necessity of enquiring very deeply into its structures in order to understand what a specific film, or film generally, might do.

The problem of making links between film and fiction, then, is not usually that of persuading film theorists to take literary fictions seriously as a separate narrative form. Not only do film theorists usually tend to have a literary background; but also they are inevitably involved either in problems of language and communication (problems which take *all* communicative acts seriously) or in areas of film theory which bear some direct philosophical relation to literary theory (for instance, the area of characterisation). Rather, the problem lies in the fact that, historically, film has been 'systematically mistaken for literature', and that it has been treated as a literary text.[4] Arguments about translations of novels into film, for instance, usually examine the two formulations of the 'same' narrative for differences of quality and effect.[5] This type of approach intuits an 'ideal' version of the literary source, a narrative which is independent of its medium and which it is (a) film's task to materialise. It therefore tends to privilege the literary text—by valorising those of its functions which are difficult to duplicate on the screen. Consequently, we cannot address this particular problem and introduce the theoretical connections between film and fiction before first looking at the difficulties inherent in the application of literary criticism to the analysis of film. Only then can we suggest ways in which film and fiction can be interrelated without overlooking their formal differences; and only then can we go on to discuss the formal and ideological determinants of Australian film and fiction as products of a specific national culture.

The obstacle which lies before literary critics who want to respond to their interest in film is that film and fiction are two different forms. The temptation is to ignore this by articulating film's structures and language in terms of those of fiction. Noel King has argued that most treatment of film in English departments in Australia simply substitutes the film text for the literary text without altering the critical practice at all; as he puts it, 'new object, same old discourse'.[6] Implicit in King's criticisms is the proposition that literary training provides one with a set of assumptions and techniques which are exactly wrong for the study of film. Gerald Mast has talked about this in a useful and argumentative study where he develops a critique of the literary response as one inimical to film studies.[7] First, he says, film is a new art form and one to which the more traditional modes of high art criticism are not always applicable. The nomination of a text as high art places it within particular cultural contexts, within particular audiences, and within particular conditions of production and reception—most of which are not those of the feature film. John Tulloch broaches this in his opening to *Legends on the Screen*, and uses it as an argument for the category of narrative within which discussions of popular culture can be usefully framed.[8] The problem of the popularity of the form, the subsequent expansion of the role of genre and convention, and the manner in which the success of a popular art is (or is not) determined, are all aspects of film criticism which both Mast and Tulloch maintain are not easily addressed through a high art model. Further, the socio-economic placement of film is different from literary fiction; there is some truth in the proposition that those who spend their leisure time watching films occupy a different class position to those who spend their leisure time reading novels.

Both Mast and Chatman[9] have suggested that there are assumptions absorbed with a literary training that need to be recognised, because they are there and because they often operate unconsciously—as prejudice rather than judgement. For instance, literary training creates a respect for the integrity of the text that motivates resistance to translations of a text from one medium to another. In their dealing with texts, literary critics also develop a preference for the reflective, contemplative and intellectual pleasures over the more passionate, sensual and stimulating ones. This can take the form of a somewhat puritanical distrust of the senses. Film takes words out of narrative and replaces them with sights and sounds, appealing directly to the senses; in Mast's words, film offers us a 'sensuous metaphor for the experience of an event'[10] rather than an ironic or reflective understanding of its significance. An important and debilitating consequence of this preference for intellectual pleasure is the common disregard for films which are clearly conventional and which operate comfortably within the boundaries of their genre—such as virtually the entire output of Hollywood. It is this disregard for genre that prompted in the 1960s the modernist preferences of early film criticism, which was attracted to European films while American films simply attracted audiences.[11] There was a sense that genre films (such as westerns, thrillers, detective films and so on) were inherently inconsiderable because they made so few claims for their own uniqueness; and this was part of a range of attitudes which accompany a respect for the literary and a discomfort with the popular. As we shall see in a later chapter, the gulf which divides the critical responses on the one hand and the popular responses on the other hand to such films as *The Man From Snowy River* and *Gallipoli* is comprehensible within this framework. In many cases, the discomfort with the popular is a theoretical blind spot: the distinction between the literary and the popular is invoked rather than analysed, and there is little understanding of the different ways in which the various modes construct their meanings. So the literary preference for a greater illusion of ambiguity and a multiplicity of reading positions, and its valorisation of the idiosyncrasies of the individual text is used to privilege the literary form over that of film.

There are, of course, *real* differences between the forms—they are not all the perjorative inventions of the literati: film does not use narrative point of view in the same way that fiction does. Visually, irony is difficult to achieve while symbol is difficult to avoid. The clearly asserted description of scene and of setting which is customary in the novel gives way to a more generalised depiction in the cinema: the camera's proliferation of information creates a problem of focus as a result of highlighting those aspects of setting which are crucial to the film's meaning. Moreover, character in film is radically different in its construction; while some may deplore the star syndrome, film stars do have an important ontological function in film. As Richard Dyer points out, stars are semiotic systems—signs—and carry a detailed and precise range of meanings with them.[12] They present an important advantage to the film-maker in that they provide a reservoir of significances which can be drawn upon in the representation of particular types and values. Further, the film-maker has the advantage of presenting a concrete, physical presence which can then be overlaid with nuances and accretions of meaning—whereas the novelist starts in the reverse position, building collections of traits, features and values in the hope of eventually establishing a concrete-like physical presence for the character. Even if this is achieved, there is not in fiction that physical particularity in our reception of character; hence the disagreements in translations of novels into films which occur about the casting, disagreements where the choice of actor or actress fails to mesh with our mental image of the character as drawn from the prose. This disagreement is a legitimate one, because the face of the star is *part* of the characterisation and not separable from it: the Phillip Marlowe played by Humphrey Bogart is not the same character as the Phillip Marlowe played by James Garner or Robert Mitchum.[13]

The genuine problem of formal comparisons is often exacerbated by discussions of film as possessing a visual 'language' which is more or less comparable to verbal language. Unfortunately, while this is a helpful metaphor in explaining the way film communicates in a *general* way, film language is not analogous in any *detailed* way to verbal language. Despite Eisenstein's assertion that the shot is equivalent to the word, it is not. There have been films compiled with as few as twelve shots, and some shots in conventional films can last for many minutes; this suggests that shots relate more accurately to the sentence or paragraph rather than the word. The most we can say with any certainty about the grammar of film language is that two successive shots are clearly related in some way. And the understanding of this connection—which can be various—is more akin to understanding a poetic trope than understanding a word or a sentence of prose.[14] Some attributes of verbal language—metaphor, irony—seem to be intrinsically literary and are difficult to reproduce in film, certainly within the dominant mode of realism. Metaphor in film becomes symbol or convention, and filmic irony tends to occur through dialogue or dramatic structure rather than in the manipulation of the camera's narrative point of view. The effects of verbal irony *can* be duplicated by visual means—by the manipulation of identification through close-ups and reaction shots, for instance—but the verbal complexity of an ironised narrative voice in the novel would be almost impossible to achieve by other than verbal means in film without departing from the realist mode.

This brief glossing of some of the differences between film and fiction is partly to shoot down some fallacies still airborne, but primarily it is to establish the inadequacy of regarding film innocently as fiction with pictures. The relation between literary fiction and film is interesting but not uncomplicated, and we are not justified in feeling that we can move easily between the two forms without making some adjustments to our approach. In other words, we need to make the connection between film and fiction a theoretical as well as a practical one.

To start at the most rudimentary level, what film and fiction have in common is that they both tell stories—they are narrative forms. And developments in the study of narrative provide us with a rich body of theory that can assist us in our attempts to explore the interrelation between film and fiction. The work of the Russian Formalists and of various structuralists and structural anthropologists such as Claude Levi-Strauss provide us with ways of reading narrative that do not depend entirely upon a literary or visual orientation. To simplify a very disparate group of theories (and for essentially introductory purposes at this point) the salient feature common to all these schools is the examination of narrative through its most primitive forms as a particular use of language; simply, narrative as a culture's way of making sense of itself. Narrative is argued to serve the same functions in all cultures; the studies of folk tales, of myths and legends in Propp and in Levi-Strauss[15] lead towards the articulation of a universal grammar of narrative that structures all story. Levi-Strauss underlines the universality of narrative structures, but he also insists on the cultural specificity of this or that particular structure in each culture. While narrative may perform the same function in all cultures, the specific manner in which any one narrative is articulated is determined by its particular culture. Since the role of narrative in primitive cultures is to resolve contradictions within experience, to explain the apparently inexplicable, and to justify the inevitable,[16] and since there are many different manifestations of contradiction, inexplicability and inevitability, there is always the need for the culture's narrative to deal explicitly with those specific aspects of experience which are meaningful to that culture.

In general these are useful concepts, although in my opinion there is a limit to the applicability of such theories—about the function of myth, legend and folk tale in primitive societies—to mass-produced filmed and printed narrative in developed industrialised societies. The fairy tale and the film, for instance, enjoy a different status as texts. The fairy tale's plot is primary—the story itself is central and will survive a number of different storytellers. In film and in prose fiction, however, the way in which the story is told (point of view, setting, characterisation, lighting, form in general) or its range of discourses becomes more important. We do not think of the film or of the novel as simply plot; and the total conjunction of plot with other formal characteristics in the novel has become one of the most widely held *dicta* among those who deal with the more sophisticated narrative forms. Reducing the novel or the film to its most basic plot structure does establish the universality of that structure and does tell us something about the work accomplished by narrative. But it will not necessarily help us in the work which we are preparing to do in this study. And the reason for this is that the analysis of a nation's film and fiction inevitably interests itself also in the features of individual texts, considered as culturally specific transformations of universal structures. The cultural specificity, the Australian-ness, of Australian texts lives in the recurring principles of organisation and selection as applied to the universal narrative structures. Australian texts employ a particular language in that they draw on those myths, connotations and symbols which have currency in the Australian culture; and they also reveal what formal preferences—the encouragement of certain genres, conventions, and modes of production—are exercised in that culture. In the patterning of such influences, then, we can see which meanings are most easily articulated within the culture, which meanings are preferred by it, and which are seen to be the most significant for it.

One of the most useful propositions deriving from post-Saussurean linguistics is that we do not make our meanings by inventing fresh concepts as the need arises (by inventing names as new objects materialise) but by making new constructions out of material already provided for us by the culture. Levi-Strauss' concept of the *bricoleur*[17] (one who makes the best he can out of the materials at hand) is one that still fits the role of the storyteller even in such potentially idiosyncratic forms as the novel. The materials for the story, its detailed and individualised representation of life, are drawn from the narrative *langue* of the culture. (Here I am making metaphoric use of Saussure's distinction between *langue*, the system of forms that is the language, and *parole*, the speech acts made possible by selection and combination within the language.)[18] This *langue* is not only linguistic in the narrow sense, but also ideological. The nation's narratives are defined not so much by factors such as the birthplace of the author or whether a text was written in Sydney or London, but rather by the bank of ideologically framed myths, symbols, connotations and contextual associations upon which they draw. The Australian, for instance, 'sunbakes', while the English 'sunbathes': this difference does not simply imply that you are more likely to be rained on at an English beach; it invokes instead a whole battery of ideological positions towards nature that is inscribed into the language of the two cultures. English nature is under control; it is orderly, and one may abandon oneself to it. Australian nature, on the other hand, is harsh, hostile; and the enjoyment of it depends on proving that one can survive its worst excesses (just as one can prove one's Australian-ness by having a bronze tan during the summer). The language of narrative is 'bathed in ideology', in Althusser's phrase, and the formal and thematic structures of narrative seem to be too. The way in which a culture's narratives represent the type of the hero, for example, reveals much about the ideology of the individual and his or her place in the society. A comparison between Australian and American heroes would surely highlight important variants in the values and beliefs governing individual behaviour in the two countries as well as variants in their traditional representations.

So far, we have briefly considered two broad ways of looking at narrative. The first approach depends on the argument that all narratives possess a deep structure which is independent of their medium and ultimately universal. It stresses the similarities between narratives, the lack of individuation at this deep structural level. The second approach is the one we are most interested in here and the one in which we find the greatest possibilities for a study of film and fiction within Australian culture. This second approach focusses on the specifically Australian articulation of these universal structures. It examines what is 'national' about the narratives by tracing the activity of the culture's own sets of values and beliefs and the ways in which it reproduces these values and beliefs in the individual text. The texts examined are not then seen simply as the natural and organic products of our emerging national character—but rather as cultural constructions, as 'national fictions'.

Put as baldly as this, the practical application of this theory may seem obscure or undetermined. But before moving from theory to practice, there are a number of theoretical assumptions which this approach challenges and which need to be nominated. There is, to begin with, the preference for the individual perceptions of the novelist or film-maker as being intrinsically more interesting and important than those cultural perceptions which transmit themselves *through* the novelist or film-maker—a preference which here is clearly discounted. The balance of power between the text and context is reorganised in this study in ways that reduce the valorising of the individual text. (There are many strands of pure literary theory which do this too.) The role of the author therefore becomes much less important here; and although this does not imply a denial that there are individuals who write or make films, it does deny that the character of their writing or their films is entirely determined by the subjectivity of these individuals. The high art preference for the 'novel' (the unconventional) discriminates constantly against film by precluding the recognition that narratives working within conventional boundaries may still retain significance. And also, the assumption that literature is prior to and therefore superior to film as an art form is deliberately dismissed. This assumption inevitably distorts comparisons and is an obstacle to the analysis of film's contribution to the theory of narrative.

There are more positive ways than these of describing the opportunities offered by the study of narrative, however. Laurie Hergenhan in *Unnatural Lives*, for instance, gently castigates our unnecessarily prescriptive use of value judgements so as to articulate our literary tradition around only those works which are seen to be 'the best'. The regrettable result has been the excision of the typical, the simply realist, the political and the conventional as lacking in any cultural or contextual importance for creating the conditions in which all our fiction—good, bad or indifferent—is written. This has created an impression of Australian literary traditions as consisting of a 'broken chain of waterholes'.[19] John Docker's attack on the exclusion of a rich and important body of Australian writing from critical consideration is relevant here too.[20] From what we know of the ways in which a culture produces its stories, the intertextual links between fictions on the one hand and the conditions of production on the other hand are not proscribed solely by distinctions of quality—any more than they are proscribed solely by the national culture, as if it operates in isolation from any wider narrative traditions. Dorothy Green quotes Patrick White's observation that he owed a great deal to the Anthony Horderns catalogue and to the novels of Ethel M. Dell. As Green says, 'readers who have only a moderate enthusiasm for White may well imagine that; but if you are an enthusiast, the point remains the same'.[21] Any comparative study of Australian narrative must have the objective of widening the field of enquiry onto the study of culture. Unlike the parodical critic Simon Lascerous in his article *The Pooh Perplex* (entitled 'Another Book to Cross off Your List') I endeavour here to enlarge the sense of context and to widen the scope of the interrelations which we can trace between national fictions and national culture.

This larger sense of context is immediately appreciable to anyone who has applied themselves to either Australian fiction or film—or both—and their respective bodies of criticism. The multiplicity of connections in both areas is illuminating. The same arguments go on, the same perceptions circulate in Australian film studies as in Australian literary studies. At all levels of critical discussion, students of Australian literature can find accounts of the film tradition which immediately strike familiar notes. An example would be the orthodox account of the plight of the individual in Australian narrative. This is articulated in our literary criticism by way of the story of the battler trying to survive 'life's grim hardships' which are 'met by a stoic invincibility of character', in one formulation; or of the post-romantic nihilist stranded between the opposing poles of a Society which is 'dehumanising in its demands' and a 'Nature that offers no refuge for the solitary', in another.[22] But so it is in the Australian film. Tom Ryan, in Scott Murray's *The New Australian Cinema*, compares Australian and American cinema:

> [Australian films] are far more modest, preferring to define the individual as a battler against overwhelming odds which cannot be defeated even if they are confronted head-on, but which will allow survival if he/she suffers the indignities without asserting resentment. This individual is a victim, a consumer of history, rather than a participant in its course.[23]

Again, in Australian fiction there is the widespread use of the fact, theme, and metaphor of imprisonment (the subject of Chapter 3), and this has already been noticed by Reid, Hergenhan and Kiernan. The metaphor surfaces once more in Australian film—hence Bob Ellis's description of the Australian star in the movies: 'while American stars look as if they are Superman on furlough, our actors look like crims on parole.'[24] This particular metaphor, with its sardonic suggestion of the precariousness of freedom, is quite familiar to students of Australian literature—where the 'double aspect' of freedom and exile has considerably helped shape the representation of the possibilities of the land. At times, the use of such essentially literary terms as the quest motif (in Susan Dermody's discussion of Australian cinema)[25] immediately reveals the need for an acquaintance with media other than film. This clearly indicates the usefulness for both disciplines to visit each other's bibliographies from time to time, but the more important point is that many of the patterns found in our fiction recur, or are seen to recur, in precisely analogous ways in our films.

And as these patterns—thematic, formal and ideological—surface in both media, this provokes questions about their currency within the culture as a whole. The fact is that the meanings formulated in both media are enclosed within a still larger system of meanings and signification. Consequently the generation of meaning in film and fiction does not take place within an exclusively literary or filmic context; rather, the narratives are particular transformations of the myths of the culture. The discussion of the bush legend, for instance, has largely been confined to a literary context, even by historians. Yet the bush legend operates in advertising, sport, television, and a multitude of other contexts; and it also dominates in early Australian film in the same ways that it did in early Australian fiction—something which is made clear in *Legends on the Screen*. While there are separate studies of particular aspects of the legend which are carried out in each discipline, the separation of approach has so far prevented us asking if the different formulations of the legend might not be produced by the same cultural forces.

In asking such questions we go beyond our goal of widening the context for either literary or film studies; we establish in fact a new area of study, one which simply draws upon these two disciplines for its material. In short we begin, through our analysis of the common properties of narrative in film and in fiction as well as in their respective critical literature, to arrive at a definition of the character and function of narrative in Australia. We have seen that any correspondence between the work done by narrative in both forms will not be accidental.

Film, fiction and national culture   23

So the way in which they perform their similar functions—the area of representation—and the end to which those functions are aimed—the work of ideology—is what the following chapters will go on to examine. Our aim is to expand and illustrate the interrelationships which we have introduced in this chapter so as to reach the dominant and defining structures of Australian narrative. We begin by examining the framing of the Australian context, natural and social, within narrative.

NOTES

1 There are numerous accounts of the 'high culture' argument; one of the most recent occurs in the opening chapter of Terry Eagleton's *Literary Theory: An Introduction*, (Oxford: Basil Blackwell, 1983).
2 George Bluestone's *Novels into Film* (Berkeley: University of California Press, 1967) is still the major example of this.
3 'Realism and the Cinema: Notes on Some Brechtian Theses'; Terry Eagleton, (London: Verso, 1978), pp.110–29.
4 Noel King, 'Changing the Curriculum', p.49.
5 Brian McFarlane's *Words and Images* falls into this category.
6 p.48.
7 'Literature and Film' in Jean-Pierre Barricelli and Joseph Gibaldi (eds) *Interrelations of Literature* (New York: MLA, 1982), pp.278–306.
8 p.19.
9 Seymour Chatman. 'What Novels Can Do That Films Can't (And Vice Versa)' in W. J. T. Mitchell (ed.) *On Narrative* (Chicago: University of Chicago Press, 1980), pp.117–35.
10 p.281.
11 The present generation of critics has reversed this, to some extent. Genre is now a key concept in film criticism. See, for example, Stephen Neale's *Genre* (London: BFI, 1980) and Thomas Schatz' *Hollywood Genres* (New York: Random House, 1981).
12 'Stars as Signs' in Bennett et al. *Popular Film and Television*, pp.236–69.
13 Mast, p.292.
14 ibid. p.299.
15 Vladimir Propp, *The Morphology of the Folk Tale*, (Austin: University of Texas Press, 1975); Claude Levi-Strauss, 'The Structural Study of Myth'. The benefits of this approach have influenced studies of literary narrative (Seymour Chatman's *Story and Discourse*, for example) as well as accounts of popular film—see William Wright's *Six Guns and Society* (Berkeley: University of California Press, 1975).
16 Levi-Strauss, ibid.
17 *The Savage Mind* (London: Wiedenfeld and Nicholson, 1966), pp.17–33.
18 Ferdinand de Saussure, *Course in General Linguistics* trans. Wade Baskin, (London: Peter Owen, 1960), pp.13–14.
19 (St. Lucia: University of Queensland Press, 1983), p.13.
20 *In a Critical Condition*.
21 *The Music of Love: Essays on Literature and Life* (Ringwood: Penguin, 1984), p.149.

22 A. A. Phillips, *The Australian Tradition* (Melbourne: Longman Cheshire, 1958), p.61; Brian Kiernan, *Images of Society and Nature*, p.181.
23 p.125.
24 Quoted in Sue Matthews *35MM Dreams* (Ringwood: Penguin, 1984), p.268.
25 'Action and Adventure' in *The New Australian Cinema*, pp.79–80.

2 The Australian Context: *Nature and Society*

It has become customary to talk about the representation of the Australian context as divisible into two separate and opposing terms; these appear variously as the country versus the city, rural versus urban, nature versus society. While each of these pairs differs from the others in certain respects, they are all attempts to label the perceived split between life within an Australian urban, social environment and life which takes place within, and is thus determined by the demands of, the landscape. Discussion of this perceived split has been dominated by three connected arguments, of which only the third is specifically generated by the Australian context. First, there is the proposition that there is a basic opposition between the city and the country; second, it is stipulated that this is essentially a Romantic opposition between Society and Nature, an opposition which is resolved in favour of the search for some harmony with Nature; and third, it is proposed that the search so initiated is usually fruitless because of the hostility, vastness, indifference or cruelty of the Australian version of Nature. The influence of both Brian Kiernan and H. P. Heseltine is strong in this formulation, but it is very widely held and relies heavily on what Judith Wright has called the 'double aspect' of the Australian version of nature—its dualistic ability to simultaneously represent both the 'reality of newness and freedom' and the 'reality of exile'.[1]

The third proposition, the duality of the promise of Australia, is the one I wish to examine. The hesitation before the reality of Australia is manifest in early colonial writing and painting; and such hesitation qualifies even the most romantic of nineteenth-century fictions—for instance Boldrewood's *Robbery Under Arms*. The duality is also central to Vance Palmer's nationalist account of the legend of the 1890s; despite Palmer's own commitment to the fundamental role of the land in forming the national character and the national literary tradition, he still reminds us that 'even the most patriotic spirits' in the late 1880s 'thought of Australia as a lean, unlovely mother, denied the teeming richness of happier lands.'² Nevertheless, Palmer goes on, 'this strange earth that made such exacting demands . . . gradually imposed a loyalty on those born to it'—and Australia would easily provide the opportunity for a creative response if only Australian writers could 'let the spirit of its wild earth steal into their hearts or affect their imaginations.'³

The binary pattern shapes most formulations of an Australian tradition: it provides the preference for the country over the city in the radical nationalist position; it orders the description of the Australian imagination in Heseltine and Kiernan; and it is implicated in the two traditions of Australian literary criticism outlined in John Docker's work.⁴ Both the radical nationalist position and Docker's 'metaphysical ascendancy'⁵ see the land as offering a threat as well as a promise. The definitions of the duality do vary however, in that what one tradition sees as the threat of isolation and the promise of freedom the other tradition sees as the threat of banality and spiritual starvation, and the promise of harmony and metaphysical transcendence. Ross Gibson's *A Diminishing Paradise*, too, deals with the problem of the two images of the Australian context and argues that one of the images, paradise, gradually fades away as its illusory character becomes accepted.⁶

The positing of this dichotomy is understandable, since even a cursory glance at our narrative and representational traditions makes it seem basic to a wide range of Australian texts. We can find it in Lawson, Paterson, Furphy, Richardson, Herbert, White, Stow and in a host of contemporary writers. In Australian poetry, coming to terms with the landscape is perhaps the pre-eminent subject. The growth to maturity of Australian artists is also customarily seen in terms of the painters' coming to grips with the physical representation of the land in the first instance—the Heidelberg School—and discovering its abstract, metaphysical or mythic properties in the second instance—Sydney Nolan. (The parallel here with Docker's 'nationalists' and 'metaphysicals' in literature is suggestive.) In all cases, the country is preferred to the city as the authentic location for the distinctive Australian experience. This does not rule out, however, the characteristic ambivalence about the bush. The meaning that the land can take on may vary widely: Clarke's 'weird melancholy' and Lawson's ending for 'The Bush Undertaker' foreground isolation, madness and death, while the assertion of the spirituality immanent in the land structures White's treatment of the country in *Voss* and Stow's treatment of aboriginal myths in *To the Islands*. The use of Aboriginals as a metonym for the indigenous version of nature is conventionalised, and the combination of mysticism and Romanticism in their representa-

Coming to terms with the landscape: even the Heidelberg School emphasises its dominance and isolation in Frederick McCubbin's (1855–1917) 'Lost' (1886), an image that inevitably recalls the art direction in 'Picnic at Hanging Rock'. (*National Gallery of Victoria*)

tion in our narratives derives just as much from an uncertain response to the landscape as to the Aboriginal race itself.

While Vance Palmer (and later, Tom Inglis Moore[7]) assumes that the interest in the landscape is produced by the land itself, it does not matter in fact what colour the land takes on in Australian narratives. The investigation of its possibilities—slim though they often are—is provoked not by the land's virtues but rather by disappointment in Australian society. Voss becomes a scourge of Australian mediocrity, and it is his need for something beyond the material benefits of Australian society that links him with Laura. Stow's Heriot wants to destroy everything that he has built at the Aboriginal mission in a gesture of repudiation of the very social values which he has imposed on the blacks in his charge. In both novels, the only attention which is given to the social world is to establish it as deserving of contempt, suspicion or regret, and as a sufficient provocation for the Romantic search for the self in Nature. Despite the differences between White and the nationalists, both White and Palmer see Australian society as crippled by a stultifying suburban conformity. And despite the important rash of urban, social realist novels during the period between the wars that Ian Reid documents,[8] there were still comparatively few Australian writers before World War II who presented us with intrinsically interesting urban social worlds. There was a strong preference for the 'organic community' presented in Lawson's stories and in the orthodoxy of *The Legend of the Nineties*, where the distinctiveness of Australian life is represented by the most extreme example—the pioneer in the bush.

In the pattern of representation that critics have detected in our fiction (to briefly summarise the positions of Kiernan, Heseltine and others) the keynotes are those of the harshness and indifference of the land, and thus the difficulty of surviving on it; the compensations lie in the assertion of a unique natural beauty, in the discovery of a certain spirituality in communion with the land, or in the mastery of the stoical, pioneering virtues of endurance and acceptance. Noticeably, there is a greater sense of challenge and thus a more heightened sense of life in narratives of the bush than those set in urban environments, (denoted in fiction by a romantic contemplation of the land's aesthetic qualities and in film by blinding vistas of space and light); and it is this which seems to justify the orthodox literary critical view of the land as an alternative to, and an escape from, an unsatisfying society.

In film, the same points can be made; the same preference for the rural over the urban has been maintained. While the discussion of this tradition in our film has been less extensive, the work of John Tulloch and of Sylvia Lawson has already established the thematic and physical domination of rural subjects and rural locations since film began in

Australia.[9] John Tulloch's *Legends on the Screen* argues that the 'key' opposition in early Australian cinema was that between the organic, natural world of the country and the class-ridden, urban-industrial society of the city. Tulloch places the bush legend at the centre of his discussion of silent and early sound cinema in Australia. The legend (and the period from which it is derived, the 1890s) is one to which our film industry has continually turned to produce images of Australia for both local and overseas consumption. Certainly it is clear that our film-makers, just like our writers and painters, see the Australian landscape as more distinctive, more of a cinematic exotic, and thus they present more of it on the screen.

Films such as *The Mango Tree* (1977), *The Irishman* (1978) and *All the Rivers Run* (or, as the popular mini-series was called by American viewers, *All the Rivers Walk*) exist for almost no other purpose. But in many films, such as *Picnic at Hanging Rock* (1975), *The Chant of Jimmie Blacksmith* (1978), *Sunday Too Far Away* (1975), *Wake in Fright* (1971), or *My Brilliant Career* (1979), the land takes on a narrative function beyond that of mere setting. As in the fiction of White, Herbert, Stow or Keneally, the land operates as a source of meaning, offering a kind of spirituality or significance that is explicitly absent from society. The opening of *Picnic at Hanging Rock* presents a slow pan across a landscape which is gradually losing its veil of fog, the camera moving from the natural majesty of the rock to the presumptuous imposed order of the Ladies' College. As the opposition between these two entities is established visually, it is punctuated and emphasised by the sudden introduction of the flutes in the soundtrack. The basic conflict of the film is established even before the titles have concluded. And the resolution of this conflict leaves the rock impervious and victorious; the society is routed and the film-maker, Marlow-like, asks us not only to see this occurrence as 'one of the mysteries' but also as some intimation of the innate and obdurate strength and hostility of this world. Such deference to the land and its imperatives is at least equivocal (as indeed it is in Clarke and Lawson) in that the land is not a considerate host.

This immediate assertion of the conflict between Australians and their natural environment occurs in a surprising number of films made during the 1970s revival. *Sunday Too Far Away* opens with Jack Thompson's Foley driving his FJ along a dirt road through featureless country. Lulled to sleep by the monotony, he crashes; his personal affinity with the land—symbolised by his work as a shearer—is manifest in the philosophic manner in which he takes his water bag and hikes off to continue his journey. The opening of *My Brilliant Career* has Sybylla concentrating over her pen as a dust storm threatens to envelop the house; her family rush in, closing windows and doors to lock the forces of nature out, and the opposition between the signifiers of civilisation and society on the one hand and those of the landscape and nature on the other is established.

In both film and fiction, then, the texts seem to invite us to accept that the land is central to a distinctively Australian meaning. As both Docker and Kiernan have pointed out, literary critics have been especially glad to entertain this proposition. Taine's history of English literature, with its Darwinian theory of cultural development, exerts a considerable influence on historicist attempts to trace the developing relationship between Australia's evolving culture and the natural environment.[10] Taine's nineteenth-century ideas (defining the three elements which comprise the *Zeitgeist* or the spirit of the age—race, epoch and environment) live well beyond the nineteenth century in the discussion of Australian writing. Implicit in Palmer, they are explicitly invoked as late as 1974 in Tom Inglis Moore's *Social Patterns in Australian Literature*. Moore sees the land as the essential progenitor of meaning: 'our literature', he says, 'is ultimately born of the land'.[11] The concept of the land producing its literature as a kind of natural, relatively unmediated expression of itself does tend to permeate Australian literary criticism; and it has made the occasional appearance in Australian film criticism, too.[12]

The best work within the literary orthodoxy does move beyond Taine. But it still sees the nature/society opposition as definitive. As he pursues Heseltine's suggestions about the influence of Neitszche and post-Romantic thought in general on Australian writing, Brian Kiernan in the closing chapter of *Images of Society and Nature* describes the Australian literary representation of society as effective in that it entraps and controls, but as unacceptable in its failure to provide the compensating 'organic' benefits of a community. Kiernan's account of the protagonists' dilemma in Australian fiction has them alienated, transplanted and rejecting Australian society in favour of pursuing— without much hope of success—harmony with nature. The relation between society and nature in this formulation is polar: they are opposite to and exclusive of each other. The individual's plight, then, lies not so much in attempting to reconcile the conflict but in choosing as a Romantic to search for his place in Nature. The double bind for the heroes that Kiernan describes is not that they are unable to perceive the goal to which their lives should be directed, but that they are unable to achieve this goal because of its particular character. The Romantic desire to find oneself spiritually in Nature has in Australia to deal with a material version of nature that is antithetical to Romanticism: inverted in season, in mood and meaning, the Australian landscape as mirror to the soul reflects the grotesque and the desolate rather than the beautiful and the tranquil. Stow's Heriot sees this reflection and recognises it in his closing remark: 'my soul is a strange country'.[13]

Heriot's pursuit of death in Nature is a nihilistic response to the frustration of the Romantic ideal. Exile from Europe also disenfranchises the subject from certain European philosophical assumptions, and the Australian finds himself in a context where the 'normal' metaphysical possibilities are closed. Keneally's Halloran, in *Bring Larks and Heroes*, marries in secret because there are no priests—his religious condition is that of a castaway. Trapped at the 'world's worst end', he feels abandoned by God, gulled by his King; and he faces death with questions of existence still tumbling from his lips. The nihilistic response to existence that Kiernan and Heseltine describe is a result of the Australian protagonist being stranded between the two poles of nature and society.

Australian fiction's thematic preference for the rural over the urban is taken rather literally by many critics, and is in fact inflated by the critics' own preference for examining the representation of the land— with its greater metaphysical possibilities—rather than urban society. Ian Reid is right to point out as he does in *Fiction and The Great Depression* that if there is a 'double aspect' to the land as Judith Wright claims, then the amount of equivocation and ambivalence in the treatment of urban society suggests that there is also a 'double aspect' to the representation of society.[14] That urban society *is* a subject for our writers Reid establishes convincingly. Since the Depression, he argues, Australian novelists have talked more about the familiar, distinctive features of the urban environment; and they have evolved a language which distances them from, say, Lawson and his tradition of social-realist urban melodrama. Certainly post-war fiction has gradually appropriated for itself the topic of the nature of Australian urban and suburban society, and its manner of representing it reveals anything but a simple unanimity of rejection. The work of contemporary writers such as Robert Drewe, Peter Carey, Frank Moorhouse, and Murray Bail pushes contemporary urban experience right into the foreground in order to explore a basic ambivalence that has within it the dual possibilities of criticism and celebration.

This dual pattern is familiar; it is the same one we find in the treatment of the land. This suggests that the 'choice' being made between the society and nature is *not* the most basic choice. If the 'double aspect' infects the treatment of both the land and the city—and it is the *same* double aspect (the reality of freedom countervailed by the reality of exile, which in urban terms often articulates itself in terms of substance versus banality)—then it would seem that the city/country dichotomy is itself produced by something more basic. It is the controlling opposition, the 'doubleness' of the view of the Australian context that we need to examine, and not just the features of Australian experience onto which it projects itself.

The structure of the opposition, rather than its content, demands attention as we notice that the two poles are held apart. Judith Wright, again, complains that there is no middle ground, no ground in which the city and country could occupy 'their proper place, each complementing the other'.[16] The individual is left in limbo, unable to comfortably accept either polar position but forced to accept the dilemma as a fact of existence. A number of critics have noted the way in which accounts of fiction have themselves maintained this rigid dichotomy; and this suggests that it is just as much part of those critics' system of belief as it is part of the texts. Ian Reid argues for a more dialectical analysis, one which accounts for change and which resists the polar alternatives, by examining the relations which he insists exist between them.[17] He has an unlikely supporter in G. A. Wilkes, whose *The Stockyard and The Croquet Lawn* set out to complicate what he saw as a too glibly dichotomised version of Australian literary culture.[18] Wilkes' evidence does support the contention (although it is not necessarily one that he himself would have made) that any ability to settle happily for the centrality of the bush tradition in Australian narrative depends on the activity of myth and ideology rather than on any 'objective' history.

The preoccupation with the land and its communities is so strong in Australian narrative as to be remarkable. The trend infects accounts of Australian film as well as fiction, even in studies of the national film form which examine the productions of the industry at regular intervals in an attempt to describe the Australian film in terms of its social content and visual style. Given the basic inappropriateness of the bush legend and the iconography of the bush to contemporary Australian existential realities, the congruence of interest and focus on these pastoral myths requires explanation. The longevity of the pastoral ideal, surviving as it does Australia's urbanisation and suburbanisation, suggests that its survival is due to its ideological and mythic function rather than to its close relation to historical conditions at any point or series of points in Australia's past or present.

This possibility has not received much attention in accounts of narrative, although it has informed sociological and historical studies of nationalism and hegemony.[19] In studies of fiction, any view of the myth of the land as an ideological product comes a distant second to the common assumption that our view of the land emerges naturally from a response to it. It is a 'natural', 'real' and 'accurate' picture that is not a myth—either in the sense of being untrue, or in the semiotic sense of being an ideologically motivated transformation of history.

Yet it is probably unexceptionable to say that any concept of nature received by a culture cannot be 'natural'. The concept of nature produced by a culture and represented in its narratives is just that—a product of culture. This is not always recognised in discussions of context. It is naive, for example, for a literary critic to exclaim that 'the image of nature presented in art may depend at least as much on the artist's preconceptions and theoretical convictions as on the qualities of what is being portrayed'.[20] (In addition to the 'preconceptions' and 'convictions' of the artist, one could add, among other considerations, the general ideology of the culture, the artist's biographical insertion into it, the mode of production of the artwork itself, and so on.) Eagleton's *Criticism and Ideology* and Macherey's *Towards a Theory of Literary Production*[21] may not provide us with perfect models but they do take us sufficiently towards an understanding of the processes of cultural production, so that we quickly become very wary of talking about 'the qualities of what is portrayed', the 'real' rather than the artistic representation—as if in any case one can easily make the distinction. The image of nature depicted in art is essentially ideological, and the most important relation it bears is not to the 'real' qualities in nature, for example, but to an ideological formation of nature in the culture.

Of course, the ideological production of the culture's view of nature has not gone completely unrecognised, even if all the consequences of this recognition have not been approached. While only a few critics are happy to perceive the contemporary view of nature as a construction (by drawing on myth and ideology in its version of history) more do find it possible to look backwards and see how our perceptions of the land have been generated by forces other than direct exposure. M. B. and C. D. Schedvin in *Intruders in the Bush*, for instance, argue that the distinctive character of the convict culture—so important to Russell Ward's *Australian Legend*—actually derived from conditions applying in Britain rather than developed in response to Australian conditions.[22] Brian Kiernan begins *Images of Society and Nature* by referring to Coral Lansbury's claim that the stereotype of the working-class settler in Arcady, and the vision of society as a victimising mechanism, derive as much from the perceptions and ideology of the urbanised masses in England as from the specific experience of Australian society and landscape.[23] Richard White also argues this in *Inventing Australia*, adding that the vision of the landscape which we now accept as natural and which crystallises in the decades around Federation was essentially an urban production, the 'city-dweller's image of the bush': 'a sunlit landscape of faded blue hills, cloudless skies and noble gum trees, peopled by idealised shearers and drovers'.[24] Like Wilkes, White clearly sees how urban are the values of a Lawson or a Baynton, or the Heidelberg painters, and how those values were imposed upon the bush in order to 'invent' the real Australia. White's reference to the 'idealised shearers and drovers' reminds us, too, that for a writer such as Paterson (even Lawson), and for many of our early film-makers, the depiction of the bush was also the location for the romanticising of an authentic 'natural' community, the invention of a social structure in which the positioning of the individual in the network of loyalties and responsibilities was valorised as the antithesis to the town. The representation of the bush in such nationalist fictions is as much an invention of another model of social organisation, an alternative model of *culture*, as it is of nature.

In discussions of film, similar connections are drawn. In her discussion of nationalism in Australian film, Anne B. Hutton points to the urban basis of nationalist myths—in this case the importance of the rural in the Australian experience.[25] Her analysis of *Newsfront* (1978) points to director Phil Noyce's dramatisation of just this process in the section where the Cinetone management, under pressure from American competitors, decide to forgo their international and 'hard news' coverage in order to concentrate on 'the real Australia'. The head of the company tells his staff that this means more emphasis on rural life, even though they all know it is *not* the real Australia. In Hutton's view, Noyce's film makes a 'strong point about the perpetuation of Australian nationalism':

> ... the decision to promote the outback as a primary leitmotif was an economic and socio-political reaction to the encroachment of American values in urban Australia. Without making too much of a simplification, it is the result of urban conflicts that promote the imagery of idealisation and nostalgia for the rural lifestyle and values.[26]

Newsfront does not always stand at such a distance from ideology; it offers a more naive nationalist point of view in Len Maguire's response to the American offers at the end. Nevertheless, the film reminds us that our view of the country is not created by history in any simple way. Rather, it is produced by the culture's mythologising of its history.[27]

Given such arguments, Tom Inglis Moore's appropriation of Taine's *Zeitgeist* or John Carroll's discussion of the national trait of scepticism[28] are clear examples of what film theorist Stuart Cunningham calls 'geography as epistomology'—of the habit, that is, of seeing meaning or knowledge as something which emerges organically from a physical location rather than as a product of the signifying systems of a culture. In an article attacking the category of 'Australian film' (which he sees as a naturalising one) Cunningham lists the assumptions that go with this way of talking about Australian film; they will seem just as familiar to those used to accounts of Australian prose and include the 'return to natural order', the centrality of the landscape, and the 'ambience of country/city'. He goes on:

> This is a reversion to a version of nineteenth century pastoralism—knowledge is in nature and only the correct sensitivity and awareness will unlock its secrets. [This theorisation] of Australian film fixes it at the level of the elision of culture into nature.[29]

In Marxist theory, the elision of culture into nature is the classic bourgeois use of ideology, and it converts the contingent and interested actions of men and history into the inevitable and disinterested processes of the natural order of things. Its most important effect is that it pre-empts calls for change by removing it from the agenda—one cannot change nature. Seeing the Australian context in terms of a hostile and intransigent nature, therefore, does allow social discontent to be displaced, to be projected onto a set of conditions in which the individual is 'naturally' impotent. The representation of the structures of the culture as natural occurs through an inscription of ideology onto history, and this transformed history then becomes a powerful controlling fiction—one which proscribes the range of meanings that, for instance, can be seen as Australian. The fact that structural oppositions between city and country in our narratives are resolved in favour of nature—given Australia's inhospitable version of nature—suggests a great deal about the large transformations that have been required to produce the preference for the natural.

Our versions of nature and of society are, then, fictions which prefer certain meanings, generate certain myths, and produce certain ideological results. Cunningham quotes Marx's assertion that 'particular modes of producing the past were constantly reconfirming people in an imaginary relation to the present'.[30] In order to see those 'particular modes' clearly we do need to accept the, at least provisional, possibility that our relation to the present is 'imaginary'. We need to see the received idea of the Australian context as myth or fiction, with certain attributes and ideological functions. The task then is not to try and decipher the 'truth' about history. Rather, it is to examine the myth of the culture that emerges from the dialectical relationship between nature and society in specific texts—as ideologically produced formations that serve to reconfirm people's view of their context as natural.

Myths, according to Levi-Strauss, tend to supply absences, to play out resolutions of conflicts that in reality cannot be resolved. It involves a kind of *bricolage*.³¹ Our myth of the land is of this kind. Unarguably harsh in its extremes, bizarre in its affectation of beauty, it is just these most harsh and bizarre aspects of the land which we perversely enshrine in our image of national character. From a European point of view, it is a brazen attempt to do what Colonel Korn advises in *Catch 22* when Yossarian makes a second run on a target: 'act boastfully about something we ought to be ashamed of'—a response that could also shed some light on the mythologising of Gallipoli. More importantly, the myth has two important functions: to find within nature imaginary resolutions to conflicts which are insoluble within culture; and also to focus on those aspects of culture which most actively justify and naturalise one's position in culture—in fact, which will persuade acquiescence in hegemony.

To deal with the first, we can go some way to seeing the function of the myth of the land and of our context if we remind ourselves that, at its crudest, our image of nature is a critique of our culture: nature *is* what culture *isn't*—it is defined by difference. The attraction of the idealised bush community as the paradigm of the authentic Australian existence derives part of its attraction, one guesses, from the fact that it is in the middle of the opposition; it is an invention which is neither wholly nature nor culture, but a compromise between the two. John Tulloch, in his analysis of the bush legend in film, has argued that the bush community can be successfully idealised because it is outside culture, and therefore outside class and history. The contradictions of urban existence are displaced and resolved in the myth of the ideal, organic, non-contradictory existence in the land.³²

But Nature does not only offer a Romantic retreat from society; it offers also a withdrawal from the political, socio-economic realities of existence—into, eventually, the spiritual or metaphysical. Consequently, the rage which John Docker *et al* direct at proponents of the 'metaphysical' strain in Australian literature—notably the work of White and Hope—derives from the sense that it articulates an avenue of withdrawal from the material world. This withdrawal is only available to a certain elite, privileged, class group. Finding spirituality in a gob of spittle may be revelationary, but when it is paired with a view of ordinary people that infers their ultimate banality from their living-room decor, it may seem elitist and misanthropic indeed.

The second usage of the myth of nature is the one I want to give the most attention to. This is the representation of nature in ways that justify the individual's position within culture and within society. The double aspect here is the land's potential as both a challenger and a leveller. The problem of survival with the land establishes a myth which sets limits to personal achievement and to personal endeavour.

The threshold of transcendence is thus lowered, so that instead of mastering the land, the real heroism lies in surviving it. Living with the land is mythologised as the authentic Australian experience. The effect of this on the individual is that it also supports an ideology which depends upon the necessity of accepting personal and socio-economic limitations, and of settling for survival as the highest good. The myth of the land is a myth of the culture in that it tells us how we are to live within Australia; and it is a myth that withdraws from the individual most possibilities of change, or of the assertion of personal imperatives.

I will treat the specific problems which arise for the individual in the following chapter, but for the moment I want to look at a number of texts in order to reveal how the opposition constructed between society and nature results, not in a duality, but in the establishment of a central, unifying and accommodating myth of the Australian context. The texts, chosen for reasons which will become clear as I proceed, are the films *Caddie* (1976) and *Wake in Fright* (1971), and the novels *Ultima Thule* and *Landtakers*.

Although *Caddie* and *Wake in Fright* differ in setting, one being urban and the other rural, there are similarities in the structural, rather than the material, features of their environments. These similarities suggest that there is not a great deal of difference between the representation of the city and the country. There is, of course, a difference in the strength of the forces urging conformity in the country—less resistible forces like heat, distance, isolation. Both environments, however, are harsh and impervious to individual imperatives; one due largely to the physical sacrifices it requires in order for a community to survive in it, the other for more clearly socio-economic reasons. Both communities are ambivalently portrayed as having their crude, crass and dehumanising sides; but they are also portrayed as having a richness of texture, a complexity of ritual, and a pattern of loyalties and dependencies that signifies a substantiality of life. Both are seen as environments against which it is futile to struggle; one must adapt and accept, with humour and with an awareness of the commonality of the condition. Not without aspects of celebration (in *Caddie*'s case) or simple awe at the scale of the desolation (in the case of *Wake in Fright*) both analyses of victimhood in Australian society are ultimately extremely equivocal.

Caddie[33] is an urban film dealing with the plight of an abandoned wife and her two children during the Depression. The film begins in a middle-class suburban villa and follows Caddie's (Helen Morse) gradual journey down the class ladder into the working-class slums of Balmain. In many ways it falls into the muck-raking, naturalist formula in which melodramas of working-class life are used to vent anger on the system that allows, for instance, children to die of diphtheria. Certainly, *Caddie*'s plot is full of occurrences whose melodrama is only obscured by the fact that there are so many of them; the structure is episodic, so that high drama tends to be milked out of each incident—with the curious effect that it is possible to see much of the film as relatively realistic. Made during *International Women's Year*, it does have within it numerous references to the plight of women; and men largely get the blame.

Given such apparently political motivations, it is perhaps surprising that the film is an essay on acceptance, on finding one's place and on living within it. Caddie's pretensions to middle-class comfort and decency have to be sacrificed in order to survive; and her initial disgust at the grotesqueries of the working class (particularly evident in the claustrophobic shots of the first bar she works in—in which the six o'clock swill corrals her behind the bar, the camera fighting to pick her out through the crush of yelling patrons) gradually modulates as she becomes more acceptant of the similarity between her condition, her fate, and theirs. That is, Caddie's view of her context initially possesses some of the 'doubleness' discussed earlier, but she soon sees that only certain aspects of the culture, certain class groups, have any sense of possibility open to them. For the rest, survival is the goal.

Typically, the film persuades us to accept such a grim and dour narrative by *celebrating* just those aspects of the context which we have to accept. The depressed inner suburbs of Sydney and the pubs that Caddie works in are shot through a golden glow of nostalgia; the interiors, in particular, are given to us in realist detail but coloured vividly by the lighting in dominant tones of green, gold, and brown. The lighting is often high and bright, setting the scene below it in the haze of history; while the score—even during some of the most potentially harrowing sequences—recreates the period with affection, nostalgia and romanticism. Commentators on Australian film have noted the stylistic incongruities between the narrative and the *mise-en-scène*, and this is most noticeable in *Caddie* in the disjunction between the documentary realism of the script and the lyricism of the visuals. Further, the representation of the working class modulates gradually through the film—as Caddie moves from her first encounter with Robyn Nevin's spectacularly bruised prostitute, to the vomiting drunks of the six o'clock swill, to the archetypal little Aussie battler Josie (Jackie Weaver), whose engaging response to tribulation is 'Life's a bugger'. If Josie represents the kind of stoicism and dry acceptance which are so important to our myths of survival on the land, then the development of the urban working class as the model community—along the same lines as the idealised bush community, with loyalties to mates and neighbours—also occurs through the

Nature and society 39

Caddie (Helen Morse) preparing to descend the class ladder without shedding propriety.

relationship with Bill and Sonny, the two rabbitohs, who save Caddie's life at considerable risk to their reputations. Once we are convinced of the security of the working-class context—embattled as it is—the film is free to allow Caddie her full appropriation by the working class; and she becomes an SP bookie's tout. The visual representation of Caddie changes during this period: she relaxes physically; she sheds inappropriate middle-class modesties; and the simple act of pinning her hair back from her face and growing it longer at the back (instead of the fashionable but repressed looking little bob that she began with) appears to 'open her up'. At the end, despite her being bullied by the law over her divorce, we see her unable to dwell on her personal depression because of the irresistible pull she feels towards her children.

A relaxed, working class Caddie making arrangements with her SP boss (John Ewart). (*Stills from 'Caddie' with kind permission of Anthony Buckley*)

The film closes with a sentimental sequence of the three of them laughing on Caddie's bed—a close-knit unit just like the mother and children in Lawson's 'Drovers Wife', their closeness vindicating Caddie's struggle. As a consoling image it is qualified by the end titles which inform us that her Greek lover dies before they can be married; but underlined by the last note we see—Caddie died in 1960. Like an opening batsman, then, she seems to be judged by the length of her innings rather than by the quality of her strokes. In *Caddie* survival is both the goal and the benefit, within the context which the film depicts as urban Australia. Importantly, that context—events, social conditions, rather than personal actions—determines her fate, and what she learns during the film is to perceive it accurately so that she can adapt to it.

Like the opening of *Caddie*, which details her surroundings (albeit those she is about to leave for good), the opening of *Wake in Fright* (1971)[34] establishes the conditions in which the main character finds himself. The camera is located above the landscape, and rotates a full 360° to reveal the vast, featureless plain surrounding the two buildings which make up the town of Tiboonda—the schoolhouse and the pub, separated by the railway line which divides the screen into halves. The landscape dwarfs the buildings and those enclosed in them, making the little group in the schoolroom, waiting for the clock to terminate the last school day of the year, faintly ridiculous. As if the teacher/student separation was not a sufficient signifier of difference, the film's director Ted Kotcheff takes us through the town's slatternly little pub into the teacher, John Grant's, room. It is dark; the outside world is shut out and it is littered with reminders of the world elsewhere—university, suburban bungalow, the Harbour Bridge, the beach—as well as indicators of the only relationship that Grant can articulate with this landscape: that of the detached, superficial observer, as shown in his 'rock collection' and the predictable sketches of bleached tree trunks and the skulls of dead sheep.

Unlike Caddie, whose resistance to the environment which she must inhabit comes as much from naivety and fear as from contempt, John Grant's (Gary Bond) attitude is established (in the drink that he has with Charley at the bar while waiting for the train) as mockingly supercilious, convinced of his superiority. The screen is divided by the bar as the town is by the rail road, and John is to Charley what the school is to the pub. Charley's face dominates the scene initially, his tolerant amusement at Grant's self-assurance revealed in his ironically addressing him as 'Ned Kelly'—another indicator of Grant's distance from such indigenous myths of heroism and defeat in the bush. John Grant is eager to leave not only Tiboonda and the NSW Department of Education (to both of which he is the 'bonded slave') but also Australia. 'I'd like to get to England' he tells Janette, who seems unable to comprehend such a goal. His early dealings with Chips Rafferty's wonderfully sinister Jock Crawford, the town cop, on arriving in the 'Yabba suggest that there is a wider basis for his discontent—which is his arrogant, if innocent, assumption of his innate superiority to these country yokels. Jock sees him as different too, but not in a flattering way: 'you clever blokes never stay in one place for long' he says, and the implication that Grant misses is that this is both a privilege of the educated and a failure to adapt—weakness. Kotcheff manages to align the audience with Jock, to a degree; Rafferty's performance with the beer is presented humorously and affectionately, allowing the audience to find Jock a richer character than Grant does. Since Jock 'draws' the camera and dominates the scene, Grant's patronising treatment of him seems ungenerous, less tolerant than the behaviour of the 'Yabba yokels whom he despises. In retrospect, of course, the film's ending discloses how little John Grant has to feel superior about.

There are many signifiers of difference separating Grant from his context: his accent, his insistence on wearing his jacket (which singles him out at the two-up game—'Where's the bloke with the jacket?')

and his intellectual pretensions. The film does not support his assumptions of superiority even while it presents those to whom he feels superior in a mercilessly objective manner. Frustrated by the 'arrogance of stupid people' (the friendly insistence of every one that Grant meets in the 'Yabba that it is the best place in Australia) Grant overhears Doc Tydon utter what he presumes are similar sentiments in the cafe at the back of the two-up school. 'All the little devils are proud of hell' mumbles Tydon. Grant's vigorous attack on the kindness of Crawford and others is repulsed by Doc, however. Once again the film refers the human possibilities to the contingencies of their context, and it has Doc imply that there is little one can expect from an environment such as this. Not only does Doc accuse Grant of perceiving his outsider status as a privileged rather than an ignorant position (by reminding him that 'discontent is the luxury of the well-to-do') but he also accuses him of bald stupidity: 'It's death to farm here and it's worse than death in the mines. Do you want 'em to sing opera as well?' Doc becomes an important voice in the film, one who understands both sides and has learnt how to survive within this world without discontent.

The remainder of the film exposes Grant to the rituals of initiation into the community. The losses at the two-up game, the need to depend on 'mates', the obligatory sharing of drink and drunkenness, the definitively male character of the world—all these are demonstrated to him in scenes that are rich and full of life, but also sinister and threatening. The two-up scenes overwhelm the viewer as the game does Grant, their values and behaviour providing glimpses into a way of life that is complex and arcane. Grant, however, still maintains his conviction of superiority even while most in the game's grip; it is as if he thinks he is exploiting the simplicity of the game in ways that the locals are too ignorant and unsophisticated to understand. He fits into the paradigm of the immigrant to the country who exploits its simplicity for personal gain while, like Cabell and Mahony in the novels dealt with next, despising the culture that proffered the opportunity. It is not until he loses that he is forced to take the culture on its own terms. The loss of his money, his books, his jacket, his ticket out, is also the loss of his difference, his privilege, and his privacy; the rest of the film is taken up with breaking those constructs down in order to prove just how fragile this structure of difference is.

In the notorious kangaroo hunt the audience's repulsion is directed at a number of sources. Grant is not seen, finally, as separate from the ritual despite his personal motives for entering into it. The similarity of the use of lighting on the kangaroo's terrified, and John Grant's panic-stricken, faces places them both in the role of victim—thus generating some sympathy for him. Like Dick and Joe, however, he is concerned with being seen to be a man; whatever the ordeal involved, he is still vulnerable to this challenge. When he proves his 'manhood', he ironically establishes that he is no better than Dick or Joe, with the same potential for cruelty and brutality. Proving his manhood 'levels' him, and explodes his assumptions of superiority.

Since the film is placed so precisely within the culture, it does make certain propositions about the necessity of living in the way its people do in order to survive. Jock Crawford's prophetic reference to suicide as one way out of town is reinforced by John's failed attempt at escape and, subsequently, suicide. If the world of the 'Yabba is grotesque and repellent, the film does not deny that it has a kind of grim validity. Jock Crawford is seen as a man who knows his world and can live in it better than John Grant; the aggressive friendliness that so irks Grant also saves his life and feeds him for long periods; the wry acceptance of a Doc Tydon may be connected to the decadent, predatory figure that he becomes during the homosexual 'rape' after the kangaroo shoot, but he also 'knows more about himself than most people'. This apparent objectivity in the narrative is also present in the curiously ambivalent ending. As Grant returns to the inevitable Tiboonda like an escapee returning to gaol, the feeling of enclosure is strong; however, he is presented to us as a man who can now deal with this context in a more acceptant, less arrogant and thus less individualist, manner. In a reprise of the scene in the train leaving Tiboonda at the film's beginning, he is offered a beer by some men at the other end of the carriage. Unlike the first time, now he accepts. At this point he seems to have passed through the ordeal with a new respect for his context—which means that he understands he cannot change it—and with fewer illusions about himself. As does *Caddie*, *Wake in Fright* establishes that its protagonist's personal horizon is utterly dependent upon recognising the limitations of his context.

Moving into literary fiction, we see that both the myth of surviving within the Australian context and the definition of that context are essentially the same as it is in film—with the possible exception that the consequences tend to be more costly for the literary protagonists (the resistance to the inevitability of the context can be very destructive). Like *Caddie*, Brian Penton's *Landtakers*[35] is a mixture of social realist recreation of history and episodic melodrama. Cabell, though, is not likeable in the way that Caddie is. He is a reluctant settler in Australia; and, like John Grant, he continually yearns to return to England and his home. He expresses a strong antipathy to Australian society and to the land, seeing himself unfairly imprisoned within it. However, Penton's narrator feels some sympathy for Cabell's plight:

Settling [Australia] was quite a different matter from settling Africa and America. The story is not at all the same. There was nothing spectacular in the country to break the dead monotony and loneliness of the life—no tigers, as Peppiott put it. A man just had to learn to wait—or go mad. Really all these early settlers were just slightly off their hinges: not, as one generally conceives them, simple people, simple honest backwoodsmen. Loneliness, ennui, and impatience took strange psychological shape in them. And they were not ordinary men. The time and the circumstances bred enormous hatreds, enormous greeds, and their struggles with the incredible land, even allowing that the romantic mists of time magnify all things, were saga-like. (17)

The narrator makes clear in this passage that the battle is against nature and circumstance rather than the self, and much of Cabell's story supports this. Flood, fire, drought—all figure importantly in the narrative as the catalysts for sequences of events about which Cabell can do nothing. Yet, the comparison between the main character and the convict, Gursey, reveals weaknesses in Cabell: Gursey has the ability to 'wait' (mentioned above) which Cabell lacks. Much of Cabell's personal frustration results from his habit of putting notional limits on the time which he will allow himself in order to make his fortune and escape. These periods of time lengthen, as it becomes increasingly clear to the reader that Cabell will never reach the end of his self-imposed servitude. His yearning for escape rules out, too, any possibility of adaptation or of deriving benefit from his struggle. Gursey, in an outburst which seems more consistent with the thematic interests of the author than with the convict's character, attacks Cabell for his attitude to the country. Cabell sees Australia as a mine for future riches but he is unwilling to invest his own resources in order to make it a decent place for free men to live:

> Cabell laughed, but in a forced, mechanical way. 'Ach,' he said quickly to change the subject. 'What kind of a new nation could you make, anyway, with nothing but convicts in chains?'
> 'It's only convicts in chains could make a new nation', Gursey said slowly, sadly. 'It's only them who want one.'
> Cabell laughed again.
> 'Laugh', Gursey told him bitterly. 'You might laugh on the other side of your black face one day. It's a long way from your merry old England out here, and it's a very funny sort of place, where nothing happens like it should. Christmas comes in the middle of summer. The north wind's hot and the south wind's cold. Trees drop their bark and keep their leaves. The flowers don't smell and the birds don't sing. The swans are black and the eagles white. You burn cedar to boil your hominy and build your fences out of mahogany. 'Aye,' he sneered, 'it's not the same as the Old Country at all.' (56)

Like John Grant, and Richard Mahony, Cabell is also blinded by irrelevant snobbery and social pretension. His 'release' in the marriage to Emma is short-lived, spoiled irrevocably by the single fact of her convict past.

While Cabell does spend most of the novel resisting the inevitable results of his location, he does experience occasional moments of harmony in which he sees the land with hope and contentment. It is in this mood that we find him at the end of the novel:

> 'I'm rich. I've got a fine property. I'm not old, yet. I'm sound as a bell. Nine men in ten would give half their lives to be in my shoes. I can sit back now and take it easy.'
>
> The picture of himself, standing in the garden at Overbury one spring night twenty three years before, flashed across his mind again. He was looking up at the stars, gripped suddenly by the magnificent promise of life. In the certainty of youth's inexplicit hopes he had dedicated himself to deeds as vague and inglorious as the Milky Way.
>
> The picture faded slowly into the vast panorama of waving grass. He shook his head slowly and repeated, 'I'm satisfied. To be what I am. Where I am.' (360)

This mood is undercut by the fact that he has just ripped himself free of McGovern and that his sight has been both literally and metaphorically restored. Like all of Cabell's moods, it is wrought of passion and self-regard rather than self-knowledge. The reader cannot forget the frequent references to 'Her Majesty's gaolyard, Australia' and Cabell's continual depiction of his own plight as one of imprisonment. Setbacks have caused him to feel as though 'cold stone walls were closing in and crushing him' (188), postponing incrementally his escape from this 'prison within a prison' (3). So the substance of the narrator's intrusion at the end, immediately following the passage quoted above, comes as no surprise to the reader:

> As though Life the sorceress could be so easily disarmed! He did not know what temptations she was laying out for him in the future of a land of opportunity. The lodes of gold and silver still uncovered—the prosperous towns that would spring out of the bush—the wealth they would shower on him through no will of his own, at once awakening old dreams and forging stronger ties. In his present mood of contentment he could not foresee the time when he would look out on this same scene with disillusioned eyes, rich beyond any limits he had ever imagined but possessed once more by doubt and disappointment—How even then, when he had thought he had learnt for good and all the futility of hoping, new mirages would rise to wring a few more years of living and struggling out of him. (360)

Clearly, the 'futility of hoping' is the lesson which Cabell has failed to learn and the one which makes it impossible for him to be content in his environment. Cabell resists his fate as if it depends upon his own action despite the overwhelming proof of the indifference of nature towards his griefs, his struggles and his ambitions. In part, Cabell's characteristics are sufficiently individualised to displace his saga slightly, to make it one of his own making and thus one that would occur no matter what the location; but he does provide us with a detailed paradigm of the Australian who cannot live in Australia because he cannot accept it as an environment.

Similar arguments are made, of course, about Richard Mahony in *Ultima Thule*,[36] and the two careers have much in common. D. R. Burns' discussion of Richard Mahony in *Directions of Australian Fiction 1920–1974* is entitled 'A Statement of Limits'. Burns articulates the proposition that 'in this environment' Henry Handel Richardson teaches us that 'human existence is something to be borne rather than enjoyed'.[37] Brian Kiernan, too, talks of the 'unresolved conflict between his [Richard's] temperament and the world in which he finds himself';[38] but then Kiernan goes on to argue that this is a feature of Mahony's character which has little to do with the particularity of the world. Rather than worrying at this—and it has become something of a perennial debate—we will follow Burns' suggestions and compare Richard's and Mary's dealings with the world. Burns claims that the 'solution' to the material problems of living in *Ultima Thule* is seen to lie in the 'simple and unremitting efforts of the Mary Mahonys'.[39] There is indeed a structural contrast between Richard's failed attempts at surviving common existence in Australia and Mary's own grim achievements. Notwithstanding the oscillation in our responses to Mary as a psychological construct, the Mahonys provide us with opposing responses to circumstances, and opposing versions of the conception of the self upon which the circumstances act. Mary, for instance, is materialist, practical, and ultimately selfless, prepared to subdue her needs and hopes in order to support those of her husband and family. Richard however is a much more complex, and a much more individualistic, character. Like Cabell and John Grant, Richard insists on his own difference; a major part of his tragedy derives from his sense of being superior to his condition—and that 'condition' includes his social and ethical environment as well as his reduced financial status. Like Cabell he rails at those forces which keep him from realising his dreams, and from wrenching himself 'free' from other people, from debt, from work, and ultimately from Mary herself—who becomes his moral goad and, in a sense, his gaoler. Again, like Cabell, all this reaction and resistance on his part only brings discontent and an exacerbation of his already severe isolation from others and from his context:

> These infamous people! Why, oh why had he ever set foot among them ... ever trodden the dust of this accursed place! A man of his skill, his experience, wilfully to put himself at the mercy of a pack of bush-dwellers ... Chinese coolies ... wretched half-castes!

—And, striding ever more gallantly and intolerantly, he drove his thoughts back and salved his bleeding pride with memories of the past.
  He saw himself in his heyday, in Ballarat, famed alike for his diagnoses and sureness of hand; saw himself called in to perform the most delicate operations; robbed of his sleep by night, on the go the livelong day, until at last, incapable of meeting the claims made by him, there had been nothing left for him to do but fly the place. And spurred by the exhilaration of these memories, he quickened his steps till the sweat poured off him. (115)

Cabell, while prone to such dreaming too, is more physical than Richard and does deal with the material world effectively. Richard uses the considerable resources of his deteriorating mind—it has a talent for abstracting itself from the real in order to explore areas of self-justification or to enjoy self-pity—to fence off the realities he needs to deal with until he finally parts company with reality altogether. As this occurs, the novel's focus gradually withdraws from Richard, transferring it to Cuffy and then to Mary. This permits the reader to see Mahony's plight, finally, as pathetic:

Now he was dismayed . . . by his own solitude. To rehearse the bare facts: wife and children were a hundred and fifty miles away; his other little child lay under the earth; even the servant had deserted; with the result that there was now not a living creature anywhere within hail. This miserable lagoon, this shrunken pool of stagnant water, effectually cut him off from human company. If anything should happen to him, if he should be taken ill or break a limb, he might lie where he fell till morning, his calls for help unheard. And the thought of this utter isolation, once admitted, swelled to alarming proportions. His brain raced madly—glancing at the fire . . . murder . . . sudden death. Why, not a soul here would be able even to summon Mary back to him . . . no one so much as knew her address. Till he could bear it no longer: jumping out of bed, he ran to the surgery and wrote her whereabouts in large letters on a sheet of paper, which he pinned up in a conspicuous place. (101)

His failure to deal with his hardships, the fear of desertion here, is almost childish; and his vulnerability to melodramatic imagination does not allow his feelings to have any dignity.
  Mary, however, is anything but pathetic. She is not likely to see her difficulties as emerging from the coarseness of texture of Australian society. Richardson informs us that Mary finally takes over the reins of her own life. On being offered a post office job she 'straightway telegraphed acceptance' and 'becomes a member of the working class' (228). With real sympathy for Mary (although with little understanding of what a 'working class' might be other than a group of people who work every day) the novel details the humiliation and embarrassment which she undergoes in her relations with other members of her new class: 'they jostled her, failed to apologise, kept their hats on in her presence, lolled and lounged, bandied private jokes, laughed and

talked openly in disregard of her.' (229) While this section of the novel has a privileged naivety that makes Katherine Susannah Pritchard's dislike of Richardson utterly predictable, Mary is seen to survive exactly the kind of humiliation which Richard went to most lengths to avoid. The principles underlying their dealings with their difficult situations are open to inspection when we compare the novel's treatment of Richard's move to Barambogie to Mary's move to Gymgurra. Richard's relocation is handled in letters of wildly oscillating moods, dubious practicalities, and contradictory descriptions of what he sees. When May moves to Gymgurra—altogether a worse situation—she is, firstly, able to see it as it is. This is something which Richard was not able to do in Barambogie:

> ... all around her what seemed to her the flattest, barest, ugliest, country she had ever had the misfortune to see. Not a tree, not a bit of scrub, hardly so much as a bush broke the monotony of these plains, these immeasurable, grassy plains ... to Mary, lover of towns, of her kind, of convivial intercourse, the scene struck home as the last word in loneliness and desolation. (237)

'Mastering her dismay', the narrator tells us, Mary 'pinned back her skirts and fell to work' making life bearable there. To do this she had to accept that she is in no way special or unique, and recognise her commonality with others by fulfilling her functional role in the community as the Post Mistress. Her full acceptance of her conditions is supported, as being the only appropriate response to them. This acceptance is preferred to Cuffy's continuing embarrassment with, and dissociation from, his surroundings:

> ... fiercely Cuffy hated the gaunt, untidy yard; the unfinished back of the house ... Somewhere there had been straight black trees like steeples, that swept their tops about when the wind blew; lawns with water spraying on them; hairy white strawberries that somebody made you open your mouth to have popped into. And vague and faint as those memories were, as little to be caught and held as old dreams, they had left a kind of heritage, in the shape of an insurmountable aversion to the crude makeshifts and rough slovenliness of colonial life. (240)

While there is considerable ambivalence in her nostalgia for England, in comparison to Cuffy (a true son of Richard) Mary appears to be a paragon of pioneering self-sacrifice. Her compensation, as with Caddie, is the 'natural' one—the validation of her convictions of the importance of her family—and through this she is given some hints of transcendence:

> There came moments when she could understand and condone the madness of the mother who, about to be torn away, refused to leave her little ones behind. For, to these small creatures, bone of her bone and flesh of her

flesh, links bound Mary that must, she felt, outlast life itself. Through them and her love for them, she caught her one real glimpse of immortality. (243)

In the contrast between Richard's self-destruction and Mary's dogged survival there is thus a representation of the response to the Australian context that is characteristic of our narratives. This representation is produced by a myth which depends heavily on notions of acceptance, upon the tolerance of frustration, and on the recognition of the levelling nature of Australian experience; and which also exposes the essential weakness and destructiveness of any resistance based upon assumptions of uniqueness, of superiority of class, of intelligence or destiny. The Australian rural environment is defended in terms of its authenticity; and it is seen as capable of wearing all such assumptions down. Thus Mary is left in her Post Office and Richard in his grave. They have been reduced not dramatically by a malevolent, vindictive force—but inevitably by the continent's callous indifference to their hopes.

It is worth digressing briefly to admit that there are more positive representations of the basic myths of existence in Australian narrative—ones which allow the central individual a kind of spiritual revelation as a compensation for isolation and personal failure. In such narratives, however, the social world is just as unacceptable as it is in *Landtakers* or *Ultima Thule*, forcing the protagonists into nature to find a metaphysical alternative. *Voss*, *To the Islands*, *The Tree of Man*, *The Chant of Jimmie Blacksmith* are all of this kind, but it is important to note that in all these cases the function of the spirituality which has been discovered in nature is to enable one to face death rather than to enrich life.

The other major mode of representation of *living* within the Australian context which is constructed around a positive version of experience is to be found in the narrative ballads emerging from the nationalist peaks of the 1880s and 1890s. However, while the romantic ballads of Paterson, for example, do mythologise the life of the land without a hint of equivocation yet there is still no sense of the individual overcoming or subduing the land—as there is, for instance, in American balladry. Looking briefly at both the poem and the film *The Man From Snowy River*, we can see that the myth which produces both is one of learning to deal with the land in an unequal partnership. It is the land that sets the terms for co-existence. The 'hero' is never given any special powers other than a humility of perception (selflessness) that provides access to the land's quality. (This assumption of an instinctive communion with the land's substance is not confined to Romantic ballads, either; it also surfaces in Stan Parker's relation to the land in *The Tree of Man*, and in White's endowing of his simpleminded characters—Harry Robarts in *Voss*, and Bub Quigley in *The Tree of Man*—with supra-normal perceptions.) Even in the film, where the man from Snowy River is particularised by the image of the actor on the screen and by his acquisition of a personal history, the 'hero' is not seen as personally extraordinary in any way. What distinguishes him, as in the poem, is the fact that he is 'mountain-bred'—he is of the land.

The poem actually spends very little time describing the man from Snowy River himself, but it spends a great deal of time on the horse:

And one was there, a stripling on a small and weedy beast;
    He was something like a racehorse undersized,
With a touch of Timor pony—three parts thoroughbred at least—
    And such as are by mountain horsemen prized.
He was hard and tough and wiry—just the sort that won't say die
    There was courage in his quick impatient tread,
And he bore the blade of gameness in his bright and fiery eye,
    And the proud and lofty carriage of his head.[40]

There is a transfer of characteristics between the man and his horse, typing them equally as products of the land rather than as creatures of the society. Calling the man simply by his regional origin places him in nature rather than culture. When he takes off on his legendary ride down the mountain, the disconnection between the man and society and the oneness between man and beast is emphasised as he 'lets the pony have his head'; and the connection with nature is dramatised by the image of their racing down the mountain 'like a torrent down its bed'. The result is not to ennoble the man, or even a breed of horse, but to celebrate a land that presents a sufficient challenge to produce such spectacles. As a portrait of the 'man who' (in Clancy's words) 'could hold his own' and who is therefore 'good enough', it is proudly nostalgic; it manages to achieve this effect by intimating a humility and ordinariness in the men involved in such deeds, while simultaneously expressing a sense of awe and wonder for the natural environment in which they have been privileged to find a place. The film too does exactly this—its enormous vistas of the high country dwarfing human affairs even as it takes Jim and Jessica to its craggy bosom.

The impulse that enables *The Man From Snowy River*, in the case of both the film and the ballad, to celebrate Australia derives partly from specific causes. It is dependent upon a nationalist motive which will be discussed in a later chapter and which is more generally countervailed by less celebratory perspectives. The dominant myth of the Australian context sees the imperatives of the self surrender to the exigencies which are imposed by the environment, and this is true regardless of whether the myth is rural or urban in application, or articulated in a celebratory or critical mode. Regardless of whether that environment is a 'natural' one or a 'naturalised' one, there seems to be little that the individual can do to affect or change his condition. This may result in so-called national traits—a sense of defeat, a limited faith in social action, a respect for solitariness that also accompanies a suspicion of community or groups. In narrative the result is most often the construction of the condition of enclosure, restriction and entrapment. Even a parable of a kind of transcendence like *To the Islands* is prefaced by a section of Marston's *The Malcontent*, depicting the body as a cell in which the soul is imprisoned. *Voss, The Vivisector,* and *Bring Larks and Heroes* also employ this image.

This condition of entrapment can assume a variety of literal or metaphoric forms. We have the fixing of social horizons and personal possibilities in the imprisoning concepts of race in *Capricornia* and *The Chant of Jimmie Blacksmith*; the function of institutions in convict fiction, *Three Cheers for the Paraclete, The Unknown Industrial Prisoner, Woman of the Future, The Devil's Playground* and *Stir*; gender in *Caddie, My Brilliant Career, The Man Who Loved Children, The Commandant, The Getting of Wisdom,* and the stories of Barbara Baynton; the workings of capitalist systems in a brace of Depression novels including *Seven Poor Men of Sydney* and *Power Without Glory, Sunday Too Far Away, Mouth to Mouth, Newsfront, Between Wars*; and the physical surroundings in the works of Lawson. Over this range of material, the metaphor of the prison and convictism is notable for its recurrence. I have already referred to it in *Landtakers* and *To the Islands*. Brian Kiernan notes its importance in *Bring Larks and Heroes,* and Ian Reid traces it through a cross section of Depression novels in *Fiction and The Great Depression.*[41]

If the representation of the context is as unequivocal as I suggest through the metaphor of imprisonment, the 'double aspect' seems now to have disappeared under inspection. Indeed, there does not seem to be such a strong Romantic interest in 'freedom' in our narratives as Judith Wright and others have suggested. Rather, 'freedom' occurs as simply the other side of the coin of entrapment and bondage; it gives point to the sense of exile and loss by representing what has been lost. It is a mythic construct which smooths over the contradiction between the promise and the reality which Australia offers—whereby the Australian version of nature is to Nature what the prison is to Society. Some doubleness resides, still, in the fact that the myth of Australian context is a controlling, limiting one, which derives its main symbols and meanings from the twin sources of its version of nature and of society—but while the sources may be two

52 *National fictions*

the meaning is one. The rigours and difficulties of the natural landscape together with the social system of convictism provide compelling images of Australian existence and have a centrality to our narratives that is not sufficiently explicable by their basis in historical fact. They provide us with the alibi that we need to accept the status quo in a society where there are strong physical, social and hegemonic reasons for doing so. Within both the pioneering myth of the land, and the submissive myth of the convict system, the difficulty of survival becomes the justification for failing to do more than that. The context becomes one in which the bush and the prison offer the same limited range of possibilities for the individual: the environment is tough, but survivable if one accepts its basic dominion over the self.

Veronica Brady, in an interesting and revealing comparison of American and Australian colonial myths through the novels *Voss* and *Moby Dick*, suggests that the duplicity of the Australian promise has been misunderstood; the 'new beginning' is not one of romantic possibilities at all:

> Australia offers a new beginning not because it is a kind of paradise, but, on the contrary, because it is purgatorial, the place of the ordeal which reveals the possibilities which may emerge from the pain and the mastery which may emerge from submission.[42]

The ascetic possibilities which Brady suggests apply more, perhaps, to *Voss* than to most other fictions, but her central idea that Australia represents a place of purgation is useful. After all, a penal colony is precisely the secular equivalent of purgatory.

NOTES

1 *Preoccupations in Australian Poetry* (Melbourne: Oxford University Press, 1965), p.xi.
2 *The Legend of the Nineties* (Melbourne: Melbourne University Press, 1954), p.29.
3 ibid., pp.49, 56.
4 H. P. Heseltine, 'The Australian Image: The Literary Heritage'; Brian Kiernan, *Images of Society and Nature*; John Docker, *In a Critical Condition*.
5 *In a Critical Condition*, Chapter 4.
6 (Sydney: Sirius Books).
7 *Legend of the Nineties*; Moore, *Social Patterns in Australian Literature* (Sydney: Angus and Robertson, 1974).
8 *Fiction and The Great Depression*.
9 Tulloch, *Australian Cinema*; *Industry, Narrative and Meaning*; *Legends on the Screen*; Lawson, 'Towards Decolonisation: Film History in Australia'.
10 See Docker's outline of historicism in the chapter on 'The Australian Background' in *A Critical Condition*, and Kiernan's *Criticism*.

Nature and society   53

11 op. cit. p.320.
12 See Jack Clancy 'Parents and Orphans', *Cinema Papers* No.42, (1983) pp.50–2.
13 Randolph Stow, *To the Islands*, rev. edn (Sydney: Picador, 1983), p.126.
14 p.34.
15 p.19.
16 *Preoccupations*, p.xvii.
17 *Fiction and The Great Depression*, p.xii.
18 (Melbourne: Edward Arnold, 1981), p.55.
19 See the work of Tim Rowse, R. Connell, and Terry Irving, in particular Rowse's *Australian Liberalism and National Character* (Melbourne: Kibble, 1978).
20 Andrew Taylor, 'Bosom of Nature or Heart of Stone' in C. D. Narasamhaiah (ed.) *An Introduction to Australian Literature* (Brisbane: John Wiley, 1982), pp.144–56.
21 (London: Verso, 1978); *Towards a Theory of Literary Production* (London: Routledge and Kegan Paul, 1978).
22 ed. John Carroll (Melbourne: Oxford University Press, 1982), pp.82–108.
23 p.2.
24 (Sydney: Allen and Unwin, 1981), p.85.
25 'Nationalism in Australian Cinema' *Cinema Papers*, No.26, (1980), pp.97–100, 152, 153.
26 p.153.
27 Tim Rowse's book, cited earlier, is an exhaustive examination of this process.
28 *Intruders in the Bush*, p.211.
29 'Australian Film' *Australian Journal of Screen Theory*, Nos.5 & 6, (1978) p.37.
30 p.42.
31 Levi-Strauss, C., *The Savage Mind*, p.17.
32 *Australian Cinema*, p.193.
33 Directed by Donald Crombie.
34 Directed by Ted Kotcheff.
35 First published in 1934 (Sydney: Angus and Robertson, 1972). Further page references to this novel will appear in parentheses in the text.
36 Henry Handel Richardson, (Harmondsworth: Penguin, 1972) first published in 1929. Further references to this novel will appear in parentheses in the text.
37 (Melbourne: Cassell, 1975), p.13.
38 *Images of Society and Nature*, p.45.
39 p.13.
40 A. B. Paterson, *The Man From Snowy River*, (Sydney: Angus and Robertson, 1973), p.1.
41 *Images of Society and Nature*, p.148; *Fiction and The Great Depression*, pp.119–25.
42 'The Novelist and the New World: Patrick White's *Voss*' (1979). *Texas Studies in Literature and Language*, Vol.21, No.2, p.179.

3 *The Self in Context*

Readers of Docker's *In a Critical Condition* may feel that they recognise the account of the dilemma of the individual within the Australian context which is given at the close of the preceding chapter. The account could be seen to be a recycling of the 'gloom thesis', that subgenre of the 'metaphysical ascendancy' which Docker locates within the hegemonic construction of the tradition of Australian literature. The 'gloom thesis' is recognisable by its explicit pessimism, its stress on the keynotes of 'terror, alienation, doubt, suffering and misery',[1] and Docker rightly attacks the political principles which lie behind it. He argues that the gloom thesis recognises only a narrow range of representations of Australian experience as either 'Australian' or 'literary'. The preference for this monistic view of Australian literature, for restricting it to one dominant pattern of form and meaning, is according to Docker unexamined, contradictory and imperialistic. Docker places the preference within a political context, in which the history of Australian culture is being rewritten as an anti-democratic and regressive narrative and in which the privileging of the 'civilised', the metaphysical and the 'universal' in literature is employed to discount writing that is clearly political or social in its interests.

There seems little to disagree with in Docker's point about the essentially political nature of a denial of the political and the social in literature. Jameson reminds us that 'even the most formalising kinds of literary or textual analysis carry a theoretical charge whose denial unmasks it as ideological';[2] and Catherine Belsey's account of 'commonsense criticism' also maintains that there is 'no practice without theory, however much that theory is suppressed, unformulated, or perceived as obvious'.[3]

Further, and at the level of textual analysis, there seems room for argument with Vincent Buckley's proposition of the centrality of 'terror' to our writing, or H. P. Heseltine's assertion that 'Lawson's most compelling response to the Australian landscape is one of

A study in the melodrama of isolation: Rufus Dawes (George Fisher) in Norman Dawn's 'For the Term of His Natural Life' (1927). (*Courtesy of the National Film and Sound Archive*)

horror',[4] key elements in the metaphysical account of Australian literature. Motifs of acceptance and resignation are as common in our literature as those of despair, yet they are not responses to 'horror' or 'terror'.

Nevertheless, behind Docker's critique one hears a nagging, if unspoken, question: if the gloom thesis, for example, is not an accurate assessment of the tradition, what is? Despite the dangers of oversimplification, of smoothing over contradictions, or manufacturing a single consensual model where there are in fact numerous conflicting models, there *is* some point to examining the way in which a culture prefers and determines dominant ways of representing the plight of the individual within its context. Geoffrey Dutton once divided Australian writing into an Age of Gloom and an Age of Wit, his analysis resting on the remark that 'gloom or good humour in a writer is, of course, partly a matter of temperament. Some writers are just naturally cranky.'[5] But as long as we perceive some coherence—be it thematic, formal, political or metaphysical—in the body of narrative produced by the Australian culture, such a remark cannot be taken seriously. The ways of seeing and representing a culture in its narratives are indeed various, but the role of the author's subjectivity is no longer given the kind of privileged position which was once bestowed upon it by Romanticism. In fact, many accounts of the subjectivity of the author now see it as a mechanism that reveals the *culture's* meanings more than the *author's* individuality. Ian Reid describes it in this way:

> ... the subjective factor in a writer's representation of the actual has much the same effect as a staining liquid rubbed into wood, modifying the original material but usually in such a way that the grain, the social fibre, is all the more evident.[6]

Even in a tradition as individualistic as the American, it is quite possible to see *Moby Dick* or *The Scarlet Letter* as the products of a particular culture with its own myths and meanings rather than as the mysterious expression of the pathology of a Melville or a Hawthorne. The pathology of a Melville or a Hawthorne is not created out of whole cloth, but is a product of their particular history within a culture that works on and through them by shaping even the most idiosyncratic and distinctive of subjectivities. It is thus necessary to examine how often certain structural arrangements, certain patterns of image or representation, recur in our narratives to reveal the nature of the culture's specific selection and generation of meanings and significances.

The problem with the orthodoxy which Docker describes lies not so much in its attempt to formulate an Australian tradition, but in the hidden assumptions behind the choices made and in the invocation of literary values in order to legitimate those choices. Although this book is not interested in the hierarchising processes implicit in such criticism, and although it is no part of its argument to defend the gloom thesis as such, many of the thesis' perceptions seem valid. There are moments of overlap between its position and the model proposed in this chapter; the differences lie in the conclusions and inferences drawn, the model of culture from which the accounts proceed. In any case, Docker's account of the hegemony is in danger of monism itself, attempting to 'disprove' the case put by his metaphysical opponents.

Although he argues that the work of Heseltine, Buckley and Wilkes is as much cultural product as cultural analysis, he doesn't follow this through in his own position. Both the way in which literature organises its meanings, and the way in which that organisation and meaning is received, are overdetermined by the culture. There *is* no 'true' objective pattern to be described, simply attempts at description—which are no less interesting for that. Docker seems convinced that there is a Real, an object external to its representation, and his castigation of other critics seems motivated by his adjudgment of their separation from that ideal.

It is important to establish whether there is a wider field of discussion than Docker acknowledges—one in which many of the patterns which he describes recur and resonate, reflecting important agreements about the nature of Australian experience represented in narrative. If we move outside the enclosed walls of Docker's 'prison house of criticism' into more populist, more industrialised, less elitist areas, and widen our field of enquiry to include film narrative, this then becomes evident. Significantly, in doing this we move outside Docker's own 'regime of truth' in the university English department—to a less comprehensively colonised and less Eurocentric discursive field, the reception of Australian film.

The gloom thesis is echoed in accounts of Australian film, although it is given very different significances there. Accounts of the narrative tradition in film tend not to be tinged with the same longing for a more positive, humanistic tradition; and they tend to view the thematic patterns proposed as political rather than metaphysical. This neatly turns the gloom thesis on its head, arguing for a discussion of the particularity of the Australian condition rather than its universality. Film criticism in Australia, as suggested in the *Introduction*, may have grown out of literary criticism but it has developed in different theoretical directions; its dominant theoretical influences are post-modernist, materialist, marxian and structuralist. So it is interesting to see how often, despite this difference, the major components of the orthodox accounts of Australian literature recur in accounts of Australian film. Discussions of texts both within and without an incipient Great Tradition of Australian feature films employ the same kinds of descriptions which we find in literary criticism. These include the foregrounding of the sense of alienation and isolation; the individual's disaffection from Australian society; and the ambivalent representation of the landscape, which is perceived as offering the twin possibilities of freedom and defeat. Given the materialist politics of much film criticism, the place of the individual in society is reworked as the place of the individual in history—as a response to the preponderance of period drama during the revival—and becomes an important topic. A typical account is Tom Ryan's:

> Perhaps the most significant recurring narrative pattern is that which locates the characters in a position of powerlessness in relation to the movement of the historical periods in which they are placed ... Australian narratives ... are peopled by characters who are governed by forces beyond their control, and who are shown to be in a position of defeat at the close of the film.[7]

On the subject of the central protagonist's relation to the Australian context, Ryan maintains that the 'individual, and those with whom he/she is likely to come into contact, can play no part in the construction of history'.[8] His description of the 'preferred' version of the alienated individual is similar to the literary versions referred to in the preceding chapter—and although it has been quoted earlier, it bears repeating in this context:

> [Australian narratives prefer] to define the individual as a battler against overwhelming odds which cannot be defeated even if they are confronted head-on, but which will allow survival if he/she suffers the indignities without asserting resentment.[9]

Critic and screen writer Bob Ellis broaches the problem of the source of the patterns which he detects in the themes of Australian films: what 'moves', he asks, the film-maker Carl Schultz to make 'films in which young children cause beloved adults to die in multiple shipwrecks?' His answer is to place such films within the larger cultural context:

> ... they are only part of a larger national perception, so apparent in our cinema, of the pointlessness of every effort, since nothing ever changes and you end at your beginning. Aunt Edna recaptures Bazza, Judy Davis rejects Sam Neill... Don's party doesn't win the election. Petersen fails the exam. Breaker is taken away and shot. Jimmie Blacksmith is taken out and hanged. Ned Kelly is taken out and hanged. Mad Dog Morgan is shot, decapitated, and his scrotum given to Frank Thring. Phar Lap is taken out and stuffed. Richard Moir gives up looking for Anna. Jack Thompson in *Sunday* ends up broke and lonely as he began. The Man of Flowers ends up rich and lonely as he began... Mr Perceval the pelican is shot... Bill Hunter, in *Newsfront*, grim and principled as ever, loses his wife and mistress but keeps his limp.[10]

Although the description is deliberately parodic, the list of films cited in Ellis' remarks is extensive, and glosses a dominant pattern in the feature films of the 1970s. The notions of futility, dispossession or powerlessness which Ellis invokes are also traceable in such manifestations as Barry Humphries' Sandy Stone and in Humphries' own remark that Australians see themselves as 'exiles from life's feast';[11] or in a summary of the position of the Australian working man once given by Paul Hogan: 'If you have a go, you can do it. And if you can't, it doesn't matter'.[12] The second sentence is at least as important as the first.

There is a point at which such systemic connections build up a reductive momentum of their own, and one is aware of this danger. Posed against this, however, is a long history of criticism of film and fiction locating dominant patterns of meaning, features of structure, and recurrent images in our narratives.[13] While it is true (and later we will explore this in some detail) that there are a number of different ways of representing the individual within Australian narrative, there is nevertheless a central location for the exploration of this type. Where the narratives employ protagonists who are individuated and provided with an internal field of personal conflict—and where they are also constructed as the sites of contestation for external social forces and determinants—we have a model of the self in society. As we shall see, there are defining and determining features of this model in Australian narrative.

This point was raised in the last few pages of the preceding chapter, but it does need more thorough demonstration. There is, for example, the sense of disconnection between self and society in the radicalising of prisoner China Jackson in Stephen Wallace's film, *Stir*; in the cycle of invitation and rejection which structures Jimmie Blacksmith's relationship with white and black worlds in the film and the novel of *The Chant of Jimmie Blacksmith*; in the released prisoner, Tony's, remarks that the outside world is no better than being 'inside' in Esben Storm's *In Search of Anna*; in *For the Term of His Natural Life*'s radical severance of the relationship between the progressively brutalised Rufus Dawes and the 'normal' society of Richard Devine, which reaches such a point that the only possibility for Dawes' 'redemption' is after death (in the short version) or after a long period of resocialisation (in the longer version).

Colonial society's negation of the power of the individual also motivates Halloran's exploration of the possibilities of faith and revolution as a means to salvation in *Bring Larks and Heroes*; it is implicit in the all but complete absorption of personal life by the industrial system in *The Unknown Industrial Prisoner*; it motivates Laura's attempts to gain acceptance by deceit, sycophancy, and the disowning of her family in Richardson's *The Getting of Wisdom*. The representation of the barrenness of the Australian social context is also common in the 'major' novels in the literary tradition—*The Fortunes of Richard Mahony* and *Voss*, for instance—while the personal sacrifices necessary for survival on the land are documented in the short fiction of Lawson, Baynton, Rudd—and also litter the productions of the Australian film industry from Longford's *On Our Selection* (1920) to Miller's *The Man From Snowy River* (1982).

The dominance of death or total alienation as a mode of narrative closure or thematic resolution is explicit in Ellis's remarks as well as in Kiernan's book. The recurrence of death and suicide in Australian narrative is so frequent as to hardly require further demonstration. In some novelists' work, such as David Malouf's, it might seem pathological: he seals *An Imaginary Life* with the death of Ovid, *Johnno* with the death of Johnno, *Fly Away Peter* with the death of the metonyms for Australian innocence, and *Child's Play* with an assassination.

Such a survey proves little without further analysis; it is, after all, a list of components extracted from the frameworks which produce their meanings. The similarity of the components, however, parallels a similarity in structure—in the formal and thematic structures which shape the narratives, and the recurrent use of a dominant image or metaphor which directs us back to the model of the individual's dealings with the Australian context. The general thematic revolving around exile, divorce, and isolation is, as noted earlier, often articulated through the fact or metaphor of imprisonment. Many of the novels and films mentioned take place within prison, or within an institution which is explicitly compared with prison—the school in *The Getting of Wisdom*, the Puroil plant in *The Unknown Industrial Prisoner*. Imprisonment, convictism, is a rich source of imagery and meaning within Australian culture, and in its specific meanings as well as its wider application, it provides us with a central paradigm for the depiction of the self in Australian narrative.

The treatment of convictism and the related concerns of freedom, escape, subjection and alienation, are not confined to Australian fiction. As Laurie Hergenhan points out in the introduction to his study of the convict novel, *Unnatural Lives*, the expression of alienation within Romantic and Victorian responses to the industrialisation of Europe draws heavily on imprisonment or its 'corollaries' of escape and freedom. Further, since the beginning of the twentieth century, the 'prison and the madhouse have been two main foci for expressions of alienation in world literature'.[14] Foucault's establishment of the centrality of the technology of the prison as a model for social control within industrialising societies since the beginning of the nineteenth century is well known—and his thesis also depends upon a close analogy between the political structures of the prison community on the one hand and those of the wider community on the other. His argument in *Discipline and Punish* makes it less than surprising that 'prisons resemble factories, schools, barracks, hospitals, which all resemble prisons'.[15]

Convictism does have a more central place in our history, our language and thus in our patterns of representation, than in other colonial nations. The role of convictism in establishing the social structures, producing such attitudes as mateship for example, is a subject of regular controversy among historians—although assessments of its ultimate importance range from the crucial to the negligible.[16] Even accounts which agree on the importance of convictism differ widely on the precise nature of that importance. Hergenhan's account of James Tucker's novel, *Ralph Rashleigh*,[17] reveals a strong ideology of conservatism and conformism that rejects the condition of convictism while advancing the claims of the emancipist who has lived down the stigma of his origins. This contradicts Ward's assertion of a direct transfer from the egalitarian solidarity of the convict into the myth of the bush pioneers.[18] The pioneer, in Tucker's representation, is rather defined by his difference from the convict, and the successful emancipist defined by his rejection of the values of his convict origins, and his commitment to those of the pioneer.

Convictism has a complicated relationship with nationalist ideology. Initially providing a ghetto-like, subcultural myth in early Australia, it becomes a stigma to be repressed, recast, and re-interpreted as pretensions towards a more progressive, civilised nation develop. Barry Andrews argues that Clarke's *For the Term of His Natural Life* is a typical attempt to 'excuse' the convict by revealing the iniquity of the system and to renovate the myth of our beginnings by depicting the convict as innocent victim, exiled for 'stealing a loaf of bread'.[19] The relationship between the history of convictism and the meanings attributed to it by the dominant ideology oscillates vigorously. It is proudly acknowledged as the source of Ward's egalitarian Australian legend in the 1950s; it is appropriated as an image of political repression by the left-wing in the 1930s and turns up in the hands of left-wing authoritarians in Christina Stead's *Seven Poor Men of Sydney* as the 'genuine Australian heritage', the 'rebellious men, martyrs of nineteenth century Trades Union England';[20] its class connection with the subjected and dispossessed exposes it to conservative revision as an inappropriate image of Australia—hence the banning of films dealing with convictism and bushranging during the 1920s. One typical response to the proposal of filming *For the Term of His Natural Life* (1927) deplores the recovery of the 'stigma of the past', making 'capital out of the drab and sordid days of Australia'.[21]

Representations of Australia in the films of the 1970s revival evaded this problem by constructing a view of our history which sees the *land* as our enemy, rather than the authoritarian social and political structures initiated in the penal colony. So, convictism has been seen alternately as the genuine heritage, or as an unfortunate episode best forgotten. At present, the myth seems to have stabilised itself, so that despite the work of McQueen, Robson and others, the myth of the convict as the innocent victim—brutalised by the system and thus the source of our anti-authoritarian and democratic heritage—is established and available for appropriation by the usual range of interests (the comic use of the convict in an advertisement for long-term investment accounts by a Perth building society springs to mind here). As Barry Andrews points out, historians' attempts to challenge this view have come 'too late'; such myths are now within our language and are not open to empirical renovation. Connell and Irving's claim that the convict experience was 'sterile'[22] is arguable not only since they admit that the structures of convictism—particularly the use of assigned labour—set up the basic conditions for labour in the colony, but also because they underestimate the purchase of the image of convictism within the culture's mythology. The importance of this image is indicated by its role in narrative.

The specific representation of the convict has not changed greatly between *For the Term of His Natural Life* and *Bring Larks and Heroes*, but the currency of the image has been dramatically extended. Beyond the specificity of the image, it is the structural features of its assumptions (about the position and the power of the individual in Australian society) that provide us with a thematic and ideological model for the central characters of our narratives. It is this model that we will trace now. We begin with narratives dealing literally with convictism, then broaden out to include the more metaphoric exploration of the condition of exile and imprisonment. The initial comparison is between a social-realist film produced in the late 1970s and a melodramatic Victorian novel written in the 1870s: Stephen Wallace's *Stir* and Marcus Clarke's *For the Term of His Natural Life*.

Such a comparison may seem a little forced, but there are illustrative parallels to be drawn between the protagonists of these two narratives, Rufus Dawes and China Jackson: the parallels are those of the structure of the characters, and the thematic principles which produce that structure. Both Dawes and China are convicts. Dawes is innocent, enduring convictism for the noblest of motives. He can be seen, as Andrews suggests, as a renovation of the image of the convict as well as a focus for the indictment of the system itself. China is a criminal, although he is only 'in' for shoplifting this time, and thus *Stir*'s indictment of the system of imprisonment which he endures is more uncompromising than Clarke's. Although there is no attempt within the story line to justify China to the point of making him a romantic hero, his is still the viewpoint of the film, and the casting of Bryan Brown ensures his identification with anti-authoritarian values and Australianism. While China is clearly not an innocent, there is no sense that his criminality could in any way justify or provoke the treatment that he is given; his persecution is the product of simply being placed within the regime of the gaol.

The contemporary version of the convict: Bryan Brown as China Jackson in 'Stir' (1980). (*Courtesy of the NSW Film Corporation*)

As convicts, both characters are dramatically 'elected out of the human condition' and divorced from a normal context. Their general response is similar: China returns to prison embittered and alienated; Dawes gradually becomes that way. Both are seen as solitaries, eschewing comradeship with the other convicts and preserving a strict separation. Our first view of Dawes on the convict ship *Malabar* depicts him 'cap pulled over his brows ... hands thrust into the pockets of his coarse grey garments', 'aloof' from the 'dismal joviality' of the other convicts.[23] Although China is welcomed by several of the prisoners as he returns, he rejects the attempt to interest him in their grievances and spends most of his early conversations with other prisoners establishing his independence and his intention of also remaining 'aloof'. For Dawes this solitariness is partly protection, partly a sense of disconnection with the social context in which he has been placed; for China it is self-preservation, insurance against spending more than his allotted time in prison. For both, as the narratives progressively reveal, the maintenance of this solitariness is a benefit against which the social and moral forces around them conspire; the erosion of their separation from their setting is a loss of definition and renders them vulnerable to the society and to the dissipation of their integrity. Among the forces which render this separation more difficult is their being regarded by their fellows as tough, hardened, potential leaders—thus being given a role which would place in jeopardy not only their physical survival but also their sense of themselves as intrinsically alien in this surrounding, as 'other' than their fellows.

This surrounding is comprehensively brutal. The detailing of floggings and death in *For the Term of His Natural Life* is matched by the gratuitous assaults on the body and personal dignity in *Stir*; and a further indication of the gaol's level of sensibility in the film is the violence of the language, dominated by obscenity and exclamation, of both prisoners and warders. The shared discourse of the screws and the criminals in *Stir* is an important element in the film's successful assertion of the lack of any essential difference other than power between the two groups of men. Veronica Brady notes the lack of this distinction in *For the Term of His Natural Life*: 'Law appears as the codification of violence and those in authority in the convict society appear little different from the convicts in their charge'.[24] The novel actually asserts Dawes' 'superiority' to Frere during the castaway episode (161), and exposes Frere to Sarah's critical assessment on several occasions: confronted with Frere's morality in action, she exclaims 'and these are the men sent to *rule* us' (203). The myth of a brotherhood among prisoners only appears towards the end of Clarke's novel, and the difficulty in establishing some group solidarity preoccupies the activists in gaol for most of *Stir*. There is no consoling sense of community, as there is in the bush stories of Lawson; and incarceration is only alleviated by an alternative and temporary social contract at moments of extreme stress or provocation—for instance, the operation of the 'Ring' on Norfolk Island, and the futile rebellion at the close of *Stir*.

Both protagonists have moments when they feel that cooperation with the system is justifiable and in their own best interests. China halts a stop-work meeting among the prisoners in order to maintain peace within the gaol; and Dawes informs on Rex's planned mutiny. Both find their actions counter-productive, only rendering them more vulnerable to a system that regards cooperation as weakness or treachery. Sooner or later, China is told, one has to stop them 'walking all over ya'. Dawes takes longer to learn the lesson, even though he understands that cooperation with the social system is a 'sacrifice' of freedom and of the self (180). His experience as a castaway is represented as a re-admission of the prisoner into society and it provides him with hope of reclamation. However, becoming an 'active member of society' (157) only exposes the fact that inasmuch as society is represented by Frere, it is corrupt. Dawes' attempt to become a useful person is doomed in its apparent success: that is not what Frere wants him to be. The sardonic irony of his name underlines his antithetical relation to the concept of brotherhood.

There is one incident in each narrative which provides us with an analysis of the power relations between prisoner and warder, and where we can see marked similarities. In *Stir*, the guilt-ridden warden, Norton, explains to China that the warders only had control because 'you let us'. The prisoner's abdication of control is derived from fear—their fear of the licence provided by the law's total legitimation of the warders' power—and also from their sense that the warders' potential for the use of this power is more final and violent than their own would dare to be. Similarly, Clarke concludes his account of Frere's humiliation of the prisoner who steals his gun with the words: 'As he went out—so great is the admiration for Power—the poor devils in the yard cheered him' (303).

Powerlessness dominates both narratives. Not only are the central characters impotent, unable to change their position; they are also surrounded by servants of the very system which victimises them, who are themselves unable to instigate change. North, the drunken minister in Clarke's novel, protests and remonstrates but is thwarted by the combination of his own weaknesses and the imperviousness of the system to his complaints. Norton, the conscience-stricken warder in *Stir*, also protests and warns his superiors to no avail. He takes to drink, and eventually explodes in a rage of hate and guilt against

China, his moral goad. Attempts to enforce some accountability into the system inevitably fail: North is unable to gain justice after Kirkland's death; China's television interviews concerning the riots which occurred during his previous spell in the prison provide news but little else; Dawes' attempt to clear his name during the trial of the mutineers is futile; and even Sylvia has to recognise her impotence and leave Norfolk Island. Further, attempts at resistance also fail; Dawes' refusal to flog Kirkland results in his being flogged with him and in the lash being handed over to the bestial Gabbett, while China's refusal to stop the men rioting results in the governor deciding to send him to Grafton in the morning. Resistance is definitively solitary. Clarke's warders understand the need for isolating each man and note that 'if the prisoners were as faithful to each other as we are, we couldn't hold the place for a week' (244). Since the predicament in either narrative is such as to defy any possibility of identification between the self and its condition, there is no sense that any one of the felons could derive any consoling benefit from the commonality of his plight; each man is isolated in his own attempt to deal with his condition despite the closeness of the quarters or the mutuality of that condition.

The possibilities of amelioration, resolution, or alternatives are thus minimal. The futile attempts to make the system justify itself to those outside it underlines the complicity between the gaol and the wider social system which has brought it into existence. The comprehensiveness of the social condition is what the 'Ring' endeavours to 'escape' (396). Further, there is no metaphysical or religious alternative—despite the attempt to impose one at the end of *For the Term of His Natural Life*. Notwithstanding a number of accounts of the novel which emphasise the 'redemptive theme'[25] as a serious counterpoint to its more nihilistic implications, the ending of Clarke's novel is marked with the hoary conventionality of the melodramatic Victorian novel. This means that the reference to a redeeming God is as much weary cliché as it is a formal solution to a metaphysical problem. The fact that 'God's terrible far from Port Arthur' (288) is more convincingly demonstrated by the novel than the unimagined redemption coming to Dawes after death. Typically for convict fiction, the representatives of the Church in the novel (North and Meekin) underline its impotence, hypocrisy, and its enclosure within the values and practices of the society. For China Jackson too there are no metaphysical issues, only the material satisfaction of the successful gesture of defiance—burning the gaol to the ground.

The resolution of both these narratives is grim—ending with Dawes' death, which is complicated only by the enfolding arms of Sylvia and the hints of redemption; and with China and his fellow rioters being bussed out (presumably to Grafton), finally convinced of the total

The self in context   67

China Jackson and fellow rioters awaiting retribution in 'Stir'. (*Courtesy of the NSW Film Corporation*)

futility of hoping for any alleviation of their condition. The final words of the film acknowledge the benefits of solitary confinement, the 'slot', because there 'you're always prepared' and thus spared the illusion of hope. All that is won for China is some declaration of the self in defeat, a sense of integrity that is connected with 'having a go' despite the inevitability of failure. The example provided is one of learning how to take subjection and defeat, how to survive that condition rather than how to overcome or transcend it.

Surviving convictism is also a problem for Thomas Keneally's Halloran in *Bring Larks and Heroes*. Like Dawes, Halloran is continually seen as an exile, dispossessed, placed in the 'natural penitentiary' of Australia at the 'world's worst end'. Like *For the Term of His Natural Life*, the novel is riddled with images of hell, although Halloran is ultimately placed in a metaphorical purgatory; and thus the problem of salvation becomes crucial. Despite the wealth of religious symbolism, and the importance of faith in the novel's existential arguments, Keneally's colonial Australia is also abandoned by God. The lack of a Catholic priest to sanctify Halloran and Ann's marriage places them, Halloran argues, in the religious condition of the 'castaway'.[26] Halloran accurately sees, too, how God is used to justify and legitimate the system; God is 'conscripted' like the rest of the soldiers. As Halloran is forced to discriminate between the conflicting loyalties which he has contracted—to the crown, to God, to the army, to Ann—in order to remain true to himself, his beliefs disintegrate into doubt and fear. His eventual choice is to withdraw from the oaths to his King and country, and to actively participate in subversion. The result is his execution.

Throughout *Bring Larks and Heroes*, then, the problem of the separation of the individual from the social-political system in which he is placed is seen to be crucial—since one's response to the problem ultimately determines one's salvation. A collision between religion and politics occurs within the individual self as he or she must decide if the dictates of the conscience should mobilise resistance against the perceived iniquities and corruption of the society. Much later, Keneally wrote the novel which Halloran would have longed for: *Schindler's Ark*, where the gaoler actively conspires with the gaoled in order to subvert the system. There again, as the title reveals, the conflation of social/political actions with the religious problem of salvation is part of Keneally's analysis of the outsider. But in *Schindler's Ark* the individual is *not* the focus of interest—despite the immense provocation in Schindler's history. In that novel the focus is on the experience of imprisonment itself, its conditions, its degrees, its day-to-day dealing with death and survival.

The key factor in *Bring Larks and Heroes*' demonstration of the pervasiveness of the convict image is that Halloran is not a prisoner but a gaoler. He is a servant of the system who becomes progressively alienated from it, and also from the antipodean context in which he finds himself. The entrapment of those who guard the prison has been noticed elsewhere, and it occurs again in this novel; as the soldiers prepare for a skirmish with the prisoners they seek to remind themselves, says the narrator, of something that they were not sure of— 'that they were not the prisoners, and the felons were'.[27] Clarke makes a similar point in *For the Term of His Natural Life* when he places the military personnel as exiles, too—although they are exiled from a different world to the criminals (99–100). Major Vickers' response to his entrapment is similar to that experienced by the convicts, although it is much less uncomfortably enforced. Frere, of course, 'likes it' there (105). In both novels, therefore, the Australian condition is more or less alleviated by one's class position and access to power; however, the fact of being placed in the environment is seen in similar ways.

The appropriation of the myth and metaphor of convictism occurs through a wide range of fiction as a means of representing the condition of life within the Australian context.[28] Its most detailed, almost allegorical, application in narrative is possibly David Ireland's *The*

Unknown Industrial Prisoner. In this novel, modern industrial Australia is a direct descendant of the penal colony; the workers, or prisoners as Ireland calls them, still bear the 'inch-wide residual scars of chains passed down from father to son, from ankle to ankle for half a dozen generations, their legacy from the bloody and accursed empire'.[29] Taking the evolutionary view of Australian history to its extreme he maintains that little has changed in this penal colony, its laws still 'promulgated in the name of the sovereign of another country'. Like Peter Carey's *Bliss* which assumes as its ground the economic and mythic colonisation of Australia by America, *The Unknown Industrial Prisoner* describes an economic colonisation at the hands of the European combine, Puroil, in whose plant the characters are imprisoned. The first chapter of the novel is entitled 'One Day in a Penal Colony', and the analogy between modern industrial Australia and the nineteenth-century penal colony is drawn in some detail:

> The country towns had nothing to offer, no new cities were being developed or dams built in the country's dead centre; prisoners were allowed to drift jobless to the few large coastal cities from all over Australia as soon as they left school, to choose their place of detention. . . They weren't compelled by others to apply to any one place of labour, but they understood that once accepted for detention, their boss or commandant had power over them just as great and far more immediate than the government of the country. To all intents their employer was more powerful, for he was the main point of contact between government and prisoner: he deducted the prisoner's tax. Apart from this he prescribed how and when men should come and go, how they dressed, what they ate, the movements of their arms and legs, the words they spoke. There were accepted facial expressions, compulsory signs of loyalty, accepted opinions, desirable morals, compulsory attendance on pain of loss of food money, and the rule, made by employers, that the prisoners must not refuse to work no matter how unfairly they considered they were treated. . . The days of five hundred lashes were gone but in their place were strike penalties of five hundred dollars a day.[30]

Industry's appropriation of the technologies of the prison, and the application of discourses of the acceptable and the delinquent to control behaviour which Foucault charts so carefully in *Discipline and Punish*, are themes presented in imaginative form here. To the extent that Ireland manages to weave into this world recognisable pictures of everyday, ephemeral, Australian life, his analogy makes its point.

The sense of disconnection and alienation experienced by the prisoners of Puroil is dramatised by the parodical retreat set up by the Great White Father—the Home Beautiful, established in secret to provide a place where men could exist independently of the company, in an environment of their own making. This response to an alienating system—an attempt to find an alternative context—recurs in Australian narrative. It is a further widening of the desperate plight of the prisoner, who cannot accept his enclosure within the prison but who necessarily demands a community in which he *can* exist. Fred Schepisi's film, *The Chant of Jimmie Blacksmith* (1978), very deliberately employs this model of the relation between the central protagonist and his context; Schepisi explains his interest in the story of Jimmie Blacksmith in an interview with Sue Matthews; to Matthews' question 'What was it attracted you to the book in the first place?' Schepisi replied, 'The story of a man at odds with the system who just wants to be himself and get on in the system. That's probably what attracts me to most material.'[31]

This is a succinct account of the central problem for the Australian protagonist. Given the depiction of a system that will not allow any identification with it, the possibilities of the protagonist being himself *and* getting on in the system are usually seen to be mutually exclusive. *The Chant of Jimmie Blacksmith* makes this clear. In it, there is a deliberate attempt to frame the aboriginal in nature, to propose his harmony with it. Jimmie and Mort merge completely with their surroundings—making it difficult, as Schepisi says, to find them in the frame: 'I tried to construct every shot so that you had to look for the Aboriginal in the frame before you found him, because he was so much a part of it.'[32] Yet, in Schepisi's film, Jimmie is no 'noble savage'. He is given individual problems, one of which is precisely his rejection of the kind of 'harmony' that is proposed visually by the film, and another the pursuit of a place within the white social structures to frame his existence. While the Australian bush may appear to submerge him, the representation of the blacks' camps and the degeneration of tribal life make it very clear to us why harmony within that existence is unacceptable. For such as Jimmie there is no 'natural' context; what the whites see as his natural place he rejects. And in its place he puts the Nevilles' myth of assimilation through breeding, which allows him to invent the possibility of carving out a natural role among the whites. Given the character of white society, this is never a real possibility, so Jimmie is stranded between his 'natural' role among the blacks and the white world into which only *he* feels he can naturally fit.

The film positions against the sense of space in the landscape batteries of images of social enclosure: the dining room at the Nevilles, from which the camera pulls back as the hall walls crowd in on the tableau at the dining table; prison cells; the prison yard where Jimmie washes with the stripes of the convict imposed on his body by the sunlight shining through the bars; the underworld of the blacks' camps at night; the pile of bodies in the drunk tank after a night on the wine with relatives; and the image of Jimmie's mutilated face looking out of the cell at the hangman. The narrative movement of the film has Jimmie repeatedly seeking places into which he can usefully and personally fit—only to find those places corrupt, deathly and entrapping. His ticket for entry into white society, his marriage to the pregnant Gilda, is effectively cancelled by the discovery that her baby is not his after all, the marriage a sham. The job with Farrell positions him within white society, but definitively as a black. His ultimate 'declaration' of war is a statement of independence, and a register of the frustration that he has experienced in trying to find a place for himself that is not demeaning and humiliating.

The end for Jimmie, and for a large number of protagonists in our narratives, is death. Although he is unlike Richard Mahony in that his alienation is primarily produced by external forces, Jimmie nevertheless shares with Mahony the inability to accept the condition in which he has been placed. And, just like Mahony's, his attempts to resist that condition result in failure and self-destruction. The axe-murders are, as Susan Dermody points out,[33] as much suicidal as they are homicidal.

Death or conclusive defeat are not the only modes of resolution of the predicament of imprisonment in Australian narrative. Many novels, in fact, eschew a strong sense of closure at all. They set up the problem, find it essentially intractable, and leave the reader with that fact. The open-endedness of the films made since the 1970s revival has made this something of a convention. There are instances, however, of more positive conclusions. The Bruce Beresford film of *The Getting of Wisdom* (1977) presents an account of an escape from this condition: Laura's talent as a musician—like Sybylla's talent in *My Brilliant Career* (1979)—provides her with a ticket out of the social system, out of the normal role of the woman, and out of Australia. In Schepisi's first full length feature, *The Devil's Playground* (1976) (which also focusses on the plight of a protagonist who 'just wants to be himself and get on in the system') the main character, Tom, is able to renounce his vocation and leave the seminary. His departure is understood and assisted by the two most sympathetic Brothers in the seminary, and the final shot of the reflection of the sky and trees on the car window which is superimposed on Tom's expectant face provides a genuine sense of release. As in *Jimmie Blacksmith*, the basic organising opposition is that of the natural versus the unnatural. The boys are seen as naturally innocent and inquiring—while the vocation itself is accused by some of the Brothers of being 'bloody unnatural', teaching one to 'hate one's body', and producing 'fanatics'. In its depiction of the enclosed, repressed world of the seminary, the film is extremely sensitive to the ambivalence with which the Brothers treat their existence. Francine, who is particularly guilt-ridden, engages in

Jimmy Blacksmith (Tommy Lewis) loses out to white Australia yet again. Petra Graf (Liz Alexander) introduces Jimmy to his 'son' in 'The Chant of Jimmy BLacksmith'. (*Courtesy of Film Victoria and* **The Film House**)

erotic fantasies, furtive visits to swimming pool changing rooms, and finally leaves the order. Victor, who feels he 'belongs' there, reveals in his attempted flirtation with the girls in the pub how difficult and alien the 'real' world outside is for him to cope with. The generosity of Schepisi's treatment of the Brothers allows that some may find this prison-like atmosphere to their liking, but it is clear that Tom represents a kind of normality that reacts to this enclosure and repression by a basic, physical denial—hence the recurrent scenes of his bedwetting.

Beresford's *The Getting of Wisdom* is less generous, and the world of the school is seen as dark, inhuman and oppressive; the interiors are all deep polished boards, hidden corners, and over-exposed windows with light from the brilliant outside trying to penetrate. The schoolmistresses feel as trapped as their charges, paralleling the warder/ prisoner connection in *Bring Larks and Heroes* and *For the Term of His Natural Life*: 'You call this free?' asks one of them; and even the most privileged of pupils, Evelyn, talks of feeling 'walled in'. Laura's lack of fit within this surrounding is dramatically established as she is introduced to the school in the vivid farrago of a dress which her mother has lovingly made for her; in this single image the two main problems that Laura faces in integrating herself within this community—and they are never fully overcome—are instantly represented: her individuality is to be curbed and restrained by the school; and her class position—her secret vulgarity of connection and taste—is betrayed. Laura's portrait is unlike Tom's in *The Devil's Playground* in that she does not communicate a sense of an integrated self trying to enter an alien but desired environment; rather, she explores the avenues of deceit, hypocrisy and sycophancy to ingratiate herself with girls who are presented as anything but admirable, and thus she undermines her own individuality. Laura never does identify fully with her environment, nor does she assert her independence of it—despite the resounding success of her concluding piano recital. If the film is about a 'winner' as Phillip Adams has said, then her winning is curiously compromised.

The novel from which the film is drawn is much more ironic, and less sanguine about the future for Laura.[34] There is no artistic escape imagined, and the 'wisdom' which Laura acquires is really a range of techniques for subduing the self in the face of social disapproval. Richardson's Laura is the product of an education system which trains girls for the social structures that it serves. The link between the institution and the society is made abundantly clear; not only do the teachers spend much of their time training 'ladies', outlining the boundaries of the acceptable and the delinquent, but the ease with which the graduates pass into the conventional roles for women is

74 National fictions

sardonically underscored at the novel's end. The career of the two most individuated of Laura's peers is summarised with some cruelty:

> Within six months of leaving school, M. P. married and settled down in her native township; and therefore she was forced to adjust her rate of progress to the steps of little halting feet. Cupid went a-governessing, and spent the best years of her life in the obscurity of the bush.[35]

Despite Laura's exhilarating sprint out of the picture at the end of the novel, there is no social alternative to the school; its structures are those of the society. God and religion offer no comfort either. Just as in *For the Term of His Natural Life*, *Bring Larks and Heroes*, and *The Chant of Jimmie Blacksmith*, the tenets and representatives of the Church are found wanting in *The Getting of Wisdom*. After failing to get a response from God to her proposed deal over an impending history exam, Laura rejects Him: 'she could not go on loving and worshipping a God who was capable of double dealing; who could behave in such a "mean fashion"'.[36] Although this is the ironised response of an adolescent, it is of a piece with a narrative tradition which is 'bitter and agnostic' and whose determined secularity can be compared with Nietszche's madman's response: 'God seems to be dead and the Church to be his grave'.[37]

Veronica Brady's *A Crucible of Prophets* (from which this last remark is drawn) also underlines the difficulty of resolving the dilemma of Australian experience.[38] Brady looks to a spiritual resolution, but she admits that the dilemma is physical and geographical as well as metaphysical. Convictism, in her argument, entails both physical and metaphysical isolation; and it is also responsible for features of the social context which prevent it ameliorating the individual's condition. At the very least, our beginnings in convictism could be argued to have inhibited the development of a consoling cultural mythology—the enabling myth of the priority of the individual and the self which informs American narrative, for example. Instead, the Australian myth accommodates us to the inevitability of subjection. The reasons for this seem simple: America's society was established to escape from the perceived iniquities of life in Europe, while Australia was a prison established to contain some of those judged guilty of perpetrating the iniquities of Europe. To simplify further, the American's was a mission of hope, while ours was the ordeal of exile. Therefore, both excluded and disaffected, and totally without a supporting mythology to convert the predicament into either quest or revolt, the central character in our narratives is firmly trapped. It should hardly surprise us, then, that our most enduring literary and mythic image is one of imprisonment, its result death and suicide. Even in the moves towards closure which sometimes occur (in the narratives which do not employ death or suicide as final solutions) we can still follow the pattern of the prisoner's response to the gaol: we find the alternative of escape (usually to England) in ... *The Getting of Wisdom, Merry Go Round in the Sea, The Devil's Playground*, and *The Man Who Loved Children*; of identifying with the land, the prison itself, as a way of winning some peace of mind and a sense of place ... in Lawson's stories, *On Our Selection, Voss, To the Islands, Walkabout, Sunday Too Far Away*, and most period dramas in film; of moral criticism of the gaolers in order to propose the moral superiority of those incarcerated ... in *For the Term of His Natural Life, Mouth to Mouth, Schindler's Ark* and *The Fortunes of Richard Mahony*; and of a railing against the boredom, the lack of nourishment which the society of the prison offers, whereby the frustration itself acts as a relief from the pain it expresses in ... *The Unknown Industrial Prisoner, Don's Party, In Search of Anna, Winter of Our Dreams, The Savage Crows*, and a large amount of contemporary fiction from the pens of such writers as Frank Moorhouse and Peter Carey.

The patterns outlined above may seem laboriously detailed. Yet it is important to establish their existence in order to move on to the next step, which is to examine the significance of these representational patterns. To do this is not only to deal with the metaphysical, although that is a starting point. Ultimately, though, it is more important to deal with the material and ideological significance given to the construction of a particular power relation between the individual and Australian society.

In *Discipline and Punish* Michel Foucault describes the revolution which occurs in systems of punishment and control at the turn of the eighteenth century in France. As it turned from a torture of the body to the use of imprisonment and restraint, the new system of punishment aimed to provide modern society with an entire politics of social control—whereby the individual 'soul'[39] was to be constructed through the methods of imprisonment and supervision. Society was soon to be dominated by the institutions of industrialisation—the factory—and to be shaped by a more democratic, egalitarian expression of social responsibility—the school, the hospital, and the asylum—and so the new politics of punishment which Foucault describes set up a whole range of discourses to articulate specific notions of the 'normal' and of the 'delinquent'.

Australia was established as a society at a point in history which intersects with Foucault's turning points almost exactly. Although it was born out of a preceding discourse of criminality—in which criminals were seen as an alien, 'bastardised' race—the penal colony of

New South Wales would not find any amelioration of its sense of exclusion in the new discourses Foucault describes and which could probably be argued to arrive here with Lachlan Macquarie. Even as punishment alters its meaning, from expressing the vengeance of the sovereign to defending the society, the prisoners find themselves categorically opposed to the society which has incarcerated them. The powerful sense of a norm violated, a contract betrayed, no longer emerges from the felon's low caste but is individualised, personalised, and powerfully dramatised by his forcible exclusion from the society. The colonising of Australia sets up, in Foucault's terms, a society in which the majority are individualised delinquents, and in which the 'normal' is the area occupied by the powerful few. Colonisation of black Australians is accompanied by the colonisation of the souls of the prisoners, as they are constructed apart from the normal activities and relationships of society. The Australian habit of looking back to England—which has lasted for generations—is not only a looking back to the society from which our forefathers were exiled, but to a social norm unavailable in delinquent Australia.

In the relationship between the structures of social order and the 'normal' in Australian society, we can sense the traumatic condition of subjection into which the first inhabitants of Australia were thrust. It seems inevitable that this would have a profound effect on the myths and meanings articulated within the culture then and since. The position of being outside the society has an effect on our ideology of the individual, and so a more general discussion of individualism follows this chapter. At this point, however, it is sufficient to recognise the important relation that exists between the condition of white Australia's beginnings on the one hand and the kind of meanings we now give to our sense of place, our history, and our contemporary version of the self on the other hand.

In making such connections, I am partly drawing on the example of American literature, certain studies of which trace central constructions of meaning, central thematic preoccupations, and central structural parallels in its fiction. Not content with noting the wealth of prelapsarian symbolism in the representation of the American hero in fiction, or else the dominant modes of gothicism and romanticism, the work of Chase, Fiedler, and Lewis, among others, have traced these features to the beliefs and myths which seem inherent in them.[40] The myth of Adam is tied in with the motives for settling America in the first place; and it is comprehensively argued by R. W. B. Lewis to be a defining myth within American thought, one which particularly dominates its fiction. This myth is pieced together with the aid of the early colonial rhetoric as well as with patterns of plot and thematic direction in American fiction. In these patterns, moral priority is placed on the individual self, and a faith is expressed in the innocence of the American Adamic hero. Leslie Fiedler follows the themes of love and death in American fiction, and finds certain psychological and existential patterns recurring across several centuries of American writing. The profile of the individual self which emerges from such criticism has also entered accounts of American film, and such structural analysis of the western or the war film as Stephen Fore's recent essay on *Southern Comfort*[41] provides us with models which clearly reveal the ideological assumptions underlying the American notion of the hero as it occurs in film and prose narratives.

These American studies infer a direct relationship between the past and the present. They assume that meaning is determined by history through its transformation into myth. For instance, the initial myths behind American settlement provide the images upon which Lewis can base his study; and the colonial and pioneering myths related to the environment, the Indians, and the version of civilisation which America expected itself to erect, provide Fiedler with the material for *Love and Death in the American Novel* and *Return of the Vanishing American.*[42] Despite many subsequent attempts to discuss more discretely literary rather than cultural myths (such as Raymond M. Olderman's *Beyond the Waste Land*[43]) the work of Fiedler and of Lewis still has a resonance and suggestive power that transcends their relatively unsophisticated methodology. A lesson to be drawn from such studies of a colonial society's writing is the need to direct attention to the myths established in its beginnings. For while these myths may serve different functions as they are used by different interests, they do operate as the 'maps of meaning'[44] of the culture. Their meanings do not themselves change, but are rather available for appropriation or incorporation by various interests whose own meanings may thus be recast or renovated. The myths of nationalism, as we shall see in a later chapter, provide useful examples of this process.

There is an important qualification to be made here. Just as Fiedler places early romantic writing in America within a European tradition (which is dominated by Richardson's heroines and the cult of sensibility) and just as discussions of Australian film admit that the industrial domination by Hollywood must also produce a degree of ideological colonisation—so we need to accept that Australian narrative and the ideology articulated within it is also constructed within a context that is wider than the shores of the continent. Accounts of the nineteenth century in Australia make clear how much of what was once presumed to be indigenous was imported; Coral Lansbury's account of Arcady in Australia, Richard White's account of the 'American model' are two examples of this.[45] Literary studies, rightly, place our literature within a generally post-romantic context in which world literature has taken a more agnostic, more alienated course. Thus Australian images of alienation are simply particularisations, culturally specific transformations of a withdrawal from the absolute—which are usually seen to culminate in French existentialism or in the lexical playing fields of 'metafiction'. The history of our film industry, as John Tulloch has shown,[46] is also contained within certain parameters (the parameters set by Hollywood) and even the Australian film's concentration on the bush legend must be seen in relation to global economic patterns.

In an article in *Overland* in 1980[47] I proposed certain parallels in the development of Australian film and fiction, not in terms of chronology but in terms of the development of their formal attributes and their representations of Australia. The documentation of Australian life, for instance, was clearly a preoccupation of films in the 1970s and can also be seen in the films of the first twenty years of Australian film production. This is also an aspect of Australian literature—hence Frederick Sinnett's accusation during the nineteenth century that our early novels were simply 'travel books in disguise'.[48] More importantly, I discussed the pattern which is discernible in the films made during the 1970s: an open-ended, loosely structured narrative which depended for its sense of closure on the invocation of history—for instance, in the imposition of dates or in summaries of the personal fortunes of the characters at the film's end. The end-titles of *Caddie*, detailing the main character's life after the film, and the account of the shearer's strike at the end of *Sunday Too Far Away*, are examples of the method. While film-makers saw this strategy as emerging more from contemporary and world-wide trends—for less resolved, more open-ended movies—there is nevertheless a clear parallel in the kinds of resolutions found in our fiction. The strategy is also noticeable in very early films such as *On Our Selection*, made in 1920. Further, there is cultural specificity here, in the fact that it is history which provokes the open endings of our films—and not questions of existential meaning as for the *nouvelle vague* cinema as a world trend. And history *displaces* the individual, as Tom Ryan points out; it *subsumes* personal histories within the whole—thus minimising the importance of individual personalities, careers, events or circumstances. There has thus been a stylistic evasion of highly structured, crisis-oriented narratives in our films; and this seems to be an evasion of story itself. Although this is under threat at the moment (through such genre films as *Mad Max I* and *II*) it is still a noticeable feature of the Australian film tradition. Bob Ellis refers to the pattern when he admits to preferring more Australian films 'actually to come to an end':

> leaving the shearer's strike out of *Sunday*, the death of Caddie's lover out of *Caddie*, Anna out of *In Search of Anna*, Cathy's husband out of *Cathy's*

Child, the flying saucer out of *Picnic at Hanging Rock*, and the last wave out of *The Last Wave*, and replacing them all with farewell subtitles, seems to be rather over-headily artistic.[49]

Anne B. Hutton's article, 'Nationalism in Australian Cinema',[50] sees the dominance of the period film as one which gives away any hope of the film's 'argument' dominating. By argument I assume she means both a strong structural manipulation of the narrative and some sense of its claiming to do more than simply recycle the myths of Australian history—in favour of an increased 'textuality', a preference for visual style. This point is also made by Tim Burstall, who accuses Australian film-makers of possessing a distinct 'antagonism to style' in anything other than the visual sense,[51] and criticises them for their reluctance to impose more structure on the narrative. Hutton makes the additional point that the film's 'textuality' panders to essentially *literary* notions of value and that this, together with the dominance of the use of literary material for film translations, excises the 'stamp of personal consciousness of the film-maker'.[52]

While such criticisms are legitimate, they all lead to an attempt to prescribe what an Australian film *should* be. While sympathising with the irritation, say, at the dominance of period films, or at the loss of commercial nerve that sends a film-maker to a novel for his or her narrative idea, this study maintains that the pattern which emerges from these accounts is also that of Australian fiction. This suggests that we are not dealing with makers of narrative who are simply 'failing' to make their narratives properly, but rather with the dominance of particular ways of making meaning, of particular views of social and existential conflicts which are then expressed in our narratives' structures.

In literary narratives the lack of resolution, and the use of alienation and death as the mechanisms of closure for so much of our writing is—as we have seen—well established. In the last chapter I referred to Kiernan's treatment of the individual's failure to articulate a worthwhile and satisfying life within an Australian context. Although he notes the strong influence of Romanticism in the representation of nature in our literary traditions, Kiernan sees this paradigm of the individual predicament as occurring within a potentially existential, or absurdist, framework.[53] A perception of absence—'nothingness' as the more Nietszchean accounts would have it—does dominate our fiction and so invites an existential interpretation. Camus' description of the plight of the absurd man, the individual who 'finds himself in a world suddenly deprived of lights or illusions', is clearly applicable to Australian fiction's depiction of the protagonist:

> Man feels an alien, a stranger. His exile is without remedy, since he is deprived of the memory of a lost home or the hope of a promised land.

This divorce between man and his life, the actor and his setting, is properly the feeling of absurdity.[54]

The reference to the 'memory of a lost home' is the only aspect of this description that does not apply to the individual in Australian fiction; the yearning for England is still a romantic residue which our writers adopt. The term 'divorce', however, and the image of the actor deprived of his setting, admirably describes both the dilemma of the individual and the predicament of the prisoner. 'Divorce' as a term unites both the predicament and its recognition. Further, the hope of a 'promised land', as we have seen in the previous chapter, is in Australian fiction ultimately denied.

While the 'feeling of absurdity' is recognisable in Australian fiction, the 'absurd man's' response—a lived philosophical commitment to dealing with an apprehension of the absurd—is less evident. Apart from isolated trends in contemporary fiction, there is little properly absurdist fiction or absurdist film in our narrative traditions. In many ways, our narratives halt just before the feeling of absurdity, without fully accepting it; they are arrested at a 'pre-existential moment', admitting the withdrawal of meaning and value but without inventing a replacement for which they may accept responsibility. Instead of responding to an existentialist vision by evolving an existentialist mode of behaviour, the narratives tend to admit defeat. Our fictional heroes often have to be destroyed because there is nothing else for them. Rufus Dawes dies because the novel's world has offered no context wherein he could convincingly renovate his life. *Bring Larks and Heroes* too offers an unresolved and awkward dialectic between the Christian and the existential viewpoint, a dialectic which is terminated by the double barrels of, first, Halloran's alienation, and then his death. Our fiction seems more ready to imagine the death of the protagonist than to accept a manner of his survival that would imply either a philosophical or a material resolution of his separation from the context or from meaning.

The source of this may lie in the situation described at the beginning of this section. If Australia is a 'delinquent' society, if the myth of exile proposes that life does not go on here as it does elsewhere, and if there is an intuition of a society beyond these shores in which the 'norm' resides, then 'universal' philosophical solutions to the problems of existence within the society may not be convincing. Our fictions characteristically address not only the modern, 'universal', problem of meaning that has its own archaeology within world literature, but also specifically Australian physical and metaphysical problems. Metaphysically, Australia becomes a special case, since existence here is defined as being Australian as well as human. As victims of a cosmic xenophobia, we are still bailed up by the problem of being Australian as well as by (the usual) problems of inventing or discovering meaning. Far from being an indication of cultural immaturity, or of the failure of our writers' and film-makers' attempts to articulate a national identity, this is in fact a defining feature of the portrait of the individual as protagonist in Australian narrative.

At this point it is necessary to examine some of the terms that I have used in the last few pages. The concept of a narrative expressing 'universals', of there being a 'metaphysic' that is not also material and ideological, is one that is not consonant with the theory of narrative employed in this book. While this theory accepts that there are 'universals' which all narratives deal with, these are physical rather than metaphysical. As Eagleton says, 'human animals ... share a biological structure even where they do not share a direct cultural heritage. Birth, nourishment, labour, kinship, sexuality, death, are common to all social formations' and to all narrative.[55] This 'biological structure' is, however, historically mediated. The deep structure which Levi-Strauss and others insist organises all narrative may well have a universality, too—although this level of structure is not one to which this study has addressed itself. What I have been calling a 'metaphysic' may well be acceptable within more traditional methodologies; within the framework of this study, however, it needs a less mystical description.

The invocation of universals, the focussing on a metaphysic dealing with the 'meaning of life' is ideological. It bears specific assumptions, priorities and political repercussions. To the extent that criticism interests itself in metaphysics, it tends to discount the social, the political, the material. Thus it distances itself from the political world within which its judgements eventually must function. The assumption that Docker attacks in Manning Clark (that 'ideology is not ideology if it is metaphysical'[56]) can be seen as an attempt to employ the idea of universality as a means of evading the táking of issue with the world of particulars in which we live. The insistence on the importance of the metaphysical meaning of literature or of film is usually accompanied by an insistence on the comparative unimportance and ephemerality of ideology (usually dismissed as political didacticism). The work of Althusser on ideology, and of Foucault on the role of discourse in constructing reality, encourages us to see this as a discourse which privileges its terms in order to naturalise particular political realities, specific power relations, or the status quo. Often this is difficult for us to accept in contemporary situations, although it is more acceptable when applied to earlier periods or to other cultures.

82 *National fictions*

Eagleton's description of the rise of English Studies in the nineteenth century, its filling of the ideological vacancy left by the decline of religion is more or less recognisable:

> Literature was in several ways a suitable candidate for this ideological enterprise. As a liberal, 'humanising' pursuit, it could provide a potent antidote to political bigotry and ideological extremism. Since literature, as we know, deals in universal human values rather than in such historical trivia as civil wars, the oppression of women or the dispossession of the English peasantry, it could serve to place in cosmic perspective the petty demands of working people for decent living conditions or greater control over their own lives, and might even with luck come to render them oblivious of such issues in their highminded contemplation of eternal truths and beauties.[57]

If we accept, ironic as it is, Eagleton's description of the qualities of literary judgement and of its ability to displace the material, the political and the social, then this does throw into question the heirarchising patterns of judgement which characterise contemporary literary criticism at the same time as it illuminates the ideological function of those judgements. Even if we do not ask *for whom* are universals the important meanings, it still does seem reasonable to suggest that the function of emphasising the metaphysical as the most elevated of literary planes is to displace the ideological and to naturalise the conditions to which the political and the social might refer—thereby placing the ideological within the category of the polemic. There is, in this formulation, no 'position' behind the universalising practice—it is simply true, and beyond the petty details dealt with by ideology.

The concentration on universals does have an ideology, however— no matter how much it is 'exnominated'. The remarks quoted at the beginning of this chapter from Frederick Jameson and Catherine Belsey underline this. Behind the thematic paradigm of Australian narrative and its metaphysical structure as we have examined them, lie meanings which have important ideological resonances and which naturalise a particular way of seeing Australian experience. This way of seeing rests upon the withdrawal from meaning, upon a denial of the possibility of significance that affect more than one's putative relation with the cosmos. Laurie Hergenhan notes one relevant area in the conclusion to *Unnatural Lives*. In his account, the convicts are 'doubly alien' as a result of their social dispossession and their physical exile in a land depicted as hell. In the convict fiction which he examines he detects a fundamental concern with 'the possibility, or denial, of social change, a concern often linked with individual regeneration'.[58] As we have seen, the concern tends to be more often with the denial than with the possibility of social change. The resistance to social change and its implication for a sense of personal and political powerlessness (as noted in the texts which we have examined) has undoubted ideological consequences, encouraging conservatism and an unquestioning acquiescence in existing social conditions. Such acquiescence in the present is the subject of Gramsci's theory of hegemony—his description of the ways in which a subjected people can be persuaded to assent to their own domination. The success of this process in Australia can be seen in yet another aspect—which is the reluctance to enquire too closely into the structures, the experience, of life itself. John Carroll in his discussion of what he sees as a national trait—scepticism—describes its overtly political manifestations:

> Political idealism has been the exception in Australian history. There is not a convinced belief that mundane institutions and this-worldly activity can be radically transformed for the better, that idealistic passion can be translated into social progress.[59]

Similarly, Veronica Brady's 'Great Refusal' is not only a refusal of God, as she sees it, but a scepticism about meaning itself. Meaning becomes, as she describes it in Furphy for instance, a system of customs and practices which have a determined secularity and practicality, priding itself on its ability to deal with the world as it is.[60]

The reluctance to construct an individualised and potentially oppositional meaning which goes beyond the practicalities of day-to-day existence has its counterpart in the formal structure of our narratives. The episodic narrative structure in our films; the absence of Hutton's 'stamp of the film-maker's consciousness'; the dominant modes of resolution and narrative closure; the preponderance of documentary realism in film (which passes meaning over to history); and the saga form in fiction (which passes meaning over to nature)—all these constitute a withdrawal from individual analysis. Hutton understandably infers from the period film's dominance that film-makers are so 'unable to define what Australia is' that they simply restate the 'myths of what it has been'.[61]

If we accept that meaning is not immanent in the self but is socially constructed, then the function of the thematic model of the self which I have outlined clearly is to naturalise a position that undermines the individual's prospects of playing any active, individualised role within society. The type of the individual represented through the protagonist in Australian narrative clearly shows how difficult it is to give any priority to the self over the context. The result is a reiteration of the themes drawn out of the first chapter, on the Australian context: survival is all, resistance is futile, and ideals are to be tempered by contingency. The alibi is provided by the representation of the land as harsh, hostile, impervious to human endeavour—but eternal. And this alibi is convincing, even though (as I have pointed out) it is an image of culture as much as it is an image of nature. The fact is that it is much simpler to see this positioning of the individual as political against the backdrop of society than against the background of nature; this explains why nature figures so prominently to delimit and console individual experience in our narrative. However, this representation of nature is a displacement of society and its meaning is ultimately the same as if it *was* society. The only difference is the degree to which the ideological is obscured by the invocation of the natural, the timeless and the inevitable as metaphysical determinants of existence.

The pessimism which so many commentators note as a feature of Australian fiction, then, is not simply a temperamental or metaphysical position; it is also a political one, operating to naturalise an ideological view of the power relations between self and society which proposes the futility of individual action against the status quo. The battleground of the metaphysical ascendancy, the self in search of spirituality, is largely a territorial reserve set aside by ideological treaty as that area of criticism and conflict which Australian society can tolerate. While the social, the political, constitute an area that is not unexplored by our writers and film-makers, it is not an area of exploration that meets with the approval of the dominant interests in the society. And so Docker's account is as acceptable a guide to the operations of hegemony as any. The account given of the relation between the self and context within our fiction provides us with a number of concentric images—those of imprisonment, of exile and of divorce; as such, they seem suggestive and productive metaphors for Australian existence. As reproductions of an ideological positioning of the individual within Australian society they are accurate dramatisations of the way in which a politics of survival and of acceptance manages to win the assent of the culture—posing as the 'natural' structure of existence within an Australian context.

NOTES

1 p.140.
2 Fredric Jameson, *The Political Unconscious: Narrative as a Socially Symbolic Act*, (London: Methuen, 1981), p.58.
3 *Critical Practice* (London: Methuen, 1980), p.4.
4 *In a Critical Condition*, p.122.
5 'Strength Through Adversity' *Bulletin*, Centenary Issue (January 29, 1980), p.131.
6 *Fiction and The Great Depression*, p.130.
7 p.120.
8 p.125.

9 p.125.
10 *Cinema Papers*, p.61.
11 *Rolling Stone*, (11 December 1980), p.108.
12 'Peculiarly Australian—The Political Construction of Cultural Identity', Tim Rowse and Albert Moran in S. Encel and L. Bryson (eds), *Australian Society*, fourth edn (Melbourne: Longman Cheshire, 1984), p. 259.
13 'Life and Death of the Bunyip: History and the Great Australian Novel' *Westerly*, No.2 June, 1983, pp.39–44.
14 (St Lucia: University of Queensland Press, 1983), p.14.
15 Translated by Alan Sheridan, (Harmondsworth: Penguin, 1979), p.228.
16 The extremes could respectively be seen in Ward's *The Australian Legend*, (Melbourne: Oxford University Press, 1958) and Connell and Irving's *Class Structure in Australian History*, (Melbourne: Longman Cheshire, 1980).
17 *Unnatural Lives*, pp.16–30.
18 *The Australian Legend*, Chapter II.
19 'More Sinned Against Than Sinning: A Note on the Convict Legend' in C. D. Narasimhaiah (ed.) *An Introduction to Australian Literature*, pp.166–82.
20 (Sydney: Angus and Robertson, 1981) first published in 1934, p.170.
21 See John Tulloch, *Legends on the Screen*, pp.306–7.
22 *Class Structure in Australian History*, p.51.
23 *For The Term of His Natural Life* (Sydney: Angus and Robertson, 1975, first published in 1874) p.32. Further references to this work will appear in parentheses in the text.
24 *A Crucible of Prophets*, p.7.
25 See, for example, Laurie Hergenhan, 'The Redemptive Theme in *His Natural Life*', *Australian Literary Studies*, II (1956), pp.32–49; or the first chapter of Brady, *A Crucible of Prophets*.
26 (Melbourne: Sun, 1968), p.16.
27 p.128.
28 See the concluding pages of the previous chapter.
29 (Sydney: Angus and Robertson, 1979; first published in 1971), p.2.
30 pp.3–4.
31 *35MM Dreams*, p.42.
32 p.43. Brian McFarlane, in *Words and Images* (p.106) argues that this intention is not achieved. Jimmy, he says, is 'never quite at one with this unyielding landscape'.
33 *The New Australian Cinema*, p.88.
34 See McFarlane's *Words and Images* for a rather different account of the two narratives which is largely concerned with judging which is the more successful.
35 Henry Handel Richardson, *The Getting of Wisdom* (Melbourne: Heinemann, 1977, first published in 1910), p.208.
36 ibid. p.203.
37 See Ellis, p.61; Brady, *A Crucible of Prophets*, p.16.
38 p.3.
39 Foucault describes his version of the 'soul' in some detail: 'the historical reality of this soul ... unlike the soul represented by Christian theology, is not born in sin and subject to punishment, but is born rather out of methods of punishment, supervision and constraint' (p.29).

86 National fictions

40 *Love and Death in the American Novel* (New York: Dell, 1969); R. W. B. Lewis, *The American Adam* (London: University of Chicago Press, 1955).
41 'The Perils of Patriotism' *Australian Journal of Cultural Studies*, Vol.2, No.2, pp.40–60.
42 *Return of the Vanishing American* (London: Jonathon Cape, 1968).
43 (New Haven: Yale University Press, 1973).
44 Stuart Hall, 'Culture, Media and the "Ideological Effect"' in Curran, et al (eds) *Mass Communication and Society* (London: Edward Arnold, 1977), p.330.
45 *Arcady in Australia* (Melbourne: Melbourne University Press, 1970); *Inventing Australia* (Sydney: George Allen and Unwin, 1981).
46 *Legends on the Screen*.
47 'Travel Books in Disguise: The Australian Film and the Australian Novel', No.79, pp.20–4.
48 *The Fiction Fields of Australia* (ed. C. Hadgraft) (St Lucia: University of Queensland Press, 1966) p.31.
49 *Cinema Papers*, p.61.
50 *Cinema Papers* No.26, (1980), pp.97–100, 152, 153.
51 'Triumph and Disaster for Australian Films' *Bulletin* (September 24, 1977), pp.45–55.
52 Hutton, p.100.
53 *Images of Society and Nature*, p.178.
54 Albert Camus, *The Myth of Sisyphus* (Harmondsworth: Penguin, 1975), p.13.
55 *Criticism and Ideology*, pp.178–9.
56 *In a Critical Condition*, p.142.
57 *Literary Theory: An Introduction*, p.25.
58 p.167.
59 *Intruders in the Bush*, p.215.
60 See Chapter Two, *A Crucible of Prophets*.
61 Hutton, p.98.

4 *Characterisation and Individualism*

The preceding description of the role of the individual in Australian narrative is not the only version of the self represented in our fictions. If we approach Australian narrative by way of an examination of at least one other of its dominant modes of characterisation, then we can arrive at a different construction of the self. This is not one which is discontinuous with that articulated in the previous chapter but one which reveals further sources for the thematic patterns which I have already outlined. In short, there is indeed (as we have seen) a dominant mode of characterisation in Australian narrative which subordinates the individuated self to the setting which produces it; but this very same mode also enables us to expose another aspect of metaphysical scepticism and its ideological sources—an aspect which consists of a suspicion of individuality itself, of difference.

If, as I shall go on to argue, the representation of character in a culture's narratives is related to the concept of identity within that culture, then there is in Australian literary fiction in particular a mode of characterisation so prominent as to undermine all familiar assumptions about individualism being central to our literary version of national or personal identity. The literary convention of mateship ('literary', since mateship is a developed social myth and narrative convention well before film begins in Australia) depends upon a representation of character which is ideologically *opposed* to the individual. While I will extend this argument to film towards the end of this chapter, I want initially to confine the discussion to literary characterisation. The theory of character in literature in any case is both more developed than and prior to theories dealing with character in film; furthermore, it is in the stories of Henry Lawson that I wish to trace the suspicion of individuality, associated with the literary convention of mateship. First, however, a few words about the concept of character itself.

'Character' is itself a problematic term, as is the relation between theories of character and the ideology which produces them. So far, no account of the production and reception of character has received general recognition. The most powerful influences on contemporary attempts at dealing with character have been Russian Formalism and the various structuralisms, the structuralists having followed Propp's lead in seeing character as a function of plot. For structuralist theorists such as Todorov, characters are collections of traits syntagmatically combined in response to the exigencies of the plot. This revives an Aristotelian view of narrative by recovering the primacy of the plot; indeed, structuralists tend to see assertions of the independence of character as expressions of a commitment to the existence of a 'psychological essence' hidden at the core of the self, and thus to a fixedly realist view of literature or, more directly, to bourgeois individualism.[1] Contemporary Marxist and structuralist positions coincide in their rejection of the notion of character which is normally associated with the traditional nineteenth-century novel—where the rich, semi-autonomous characterisation carries attendant assumptions about the unique individual. Individual 'identity' has thus been re-theorised, so that we now talk of 'subjectivities', our view of the individual self being that of a unity which is constructed through the internalisation of external processes and not as a quasi-autonomous object which simply expresses itself. This constitutes a clear withdrawal from the individualist, romantic version of the self implicit in the traditional view of character; and it is clearly motivated by the ideological position embedded in structuralist theory, as Culler points out:

> ... the general ethos of structuralism runs counter to the notions of individuality and rich psychological coherence which are often applied to the novel. Stress on the interpersonal and conventional systems which traverse the individual, which make him a space in which forces and events meet rather than an individuated essence, leads to a rejection of a prevalent conception of character in the novel: that the most successful and living characters are richly delineated and autonomous wholes, clearly distinguished from others by physical and psychological characteristics. This notion of character, structuralists would say, is a myth.[2]

As Culler goes on to say, the structuralists are right to insist upon the ideological motivation behind this myth. But if the 'rich and autonomous' character is the 'recuperative strategy of another age', nevertheless we should be aware also of the ideological, historical and philosophical determinants of the 'faceless protagonists of modern fiction' themselves.[3]

At first glance the structuralist position may seem reductive or too strenuously codified; this is particularly so when we place it alongside the traditional version of character, such as that identified with Henry

James. In addition to denying that character is subordinate to plot (in his often repeated questions—'What is character but the determination of incident? What is incident but the determination of character?') James describes the creation of character also as a more mysterious process. For James, character is less dependent on 'function' than either Propp or Todorov suggest:

> I have always fondly remembered a remark that I heard fall years ago from the lips of Ivan Turgenieff in regard to his own experience of the usual origin of the fictive picture. It began for him almost always with the vision of some person or persons, who hovered before him, soliciting him, as the active or passive figure, interesting him and appealing to him just as they were and by what they were. He saw them, in that fashion, as *disponsibles*, saw them subject to the chances, the complication of existence, and saw them vividly, but then had to find for them the right relations, those that would most bring them out; to imagine, to invent and select and piece together the situations most useful and favourable to the sense of the creatures themselves, the complications they would be most likely to produce and to feel.[4]

Here the assumption of the uniqueness of the individual is the stimulus for the creative interest in character. This is true even though James admits that his intuition of a rich interiority requires the invention of 'chance', of 'complications' and 'situations' (that is, a plot) in order to 'bring the character out'.

James' approach to character may be 'bourgeois individualism' but it does pertain to the way we, as readers, experience character in fiction. Unexamined as the process is in traditional theory, we *do* read character through analogies to the world; and although we know that narratives are holistic structures, as readers we do tend to relate to them by way of their parts rather than their wholes. Most often, and where at all possible, we receive characters as 'people'; as Chatman points out, 'the contemplation of character is the predominate (sic) pleasure in modern art narrative'.[5] Chatman sounds very like Henry James when he argues that this contemplation occurs at some distance from the text: 'We recall fictional characters vividly, yet not a single word of the text in which they came alive; indeed, I venture to say that readers generally remember characters that way.'[6]

Clearly, while realist and individualist assumptions about character can permeate even the most 'contemporary' of formulations, contemporary revisions of these assumptions have not yet produced a convincing or comprehensive alternative position. Neither of the approaches I have referred to deal effectively with *all* methods of characterisation in fiction; so traditional theory may deal more sympathetically with fiction which focusses on the individuated self, while the novels of

Robbe-Grillet may seem peculiarly barren to the critic looking for Henry James.

Crucially, however, just as the conception of the self is the central area of argument between the two theoretical approaches to character, the choice of a particular mode of characterisation may be determined by a particular view of the self. For example, it can be argued (if oversimply in such a bald formulation) that an interest in and representation of 'psychological essences', through the kind of characterisation associated with nineteenth-century fiction, is traceable to a view of the self that is romantic and individualist. Alternatively, the rejection of such a mode of characterisation is a rejection of an ideology which invests faith in the primacy of the self, and a recognition of the kinds of contingencies that effect the withdrawal of the hero from twentieth-century narrative. There is thus an historical and ideological nexus between modes of characterisation in fiction on the one hand and the ideology of the self articulated in the culture which produces that fiction on the other.

The application of this principle to the representation of character in Australian narrative is provoked by the fact that it is customary to connect Australian writing with its history. The coincidence, in the writing and in the history, of notions both of egalitarianism and of the 'democratic theme' is often pointed out. This, in turn, depends upon the assumption of a connection between egalitarianism, democracy, and individualism. The connection is situated historically in the Australia of the 1890s and within the literary tradition in the work of Lawson and Furphy. So one would expect this sort of coincidence, if indeed it has been accurately described, to have produced fiction which 'matches' it—which employs, in other words, a Jamesian conception of character to give a detailed, individuated, representation of the self.

This is not what happened. Instead, paradoxically, the literature most clearly identified with an individualist ethos (Lawson and Furphy) is that which most clearly also prefers events to personality, the community to the individual. In Lawson and Furphy characters are used as setting rather than as expressions of the self. (Similarly, in film, the dominance of documentary realism results in the representation of characters as 'types', their distinguishing marks deriving from that aspect of Australian life for which they act as metonyms.) Lawson and Furphy both exploit the proliferation of single-dimensional but 'colourful' characters in order to present a sense of the kind of community in which the characters exist. Brian Matthews refers to this in his discussion of Lawson's 'world' by talking of the characters as being 'submerged' within that world.[7] Matthews thus recognises the modernity of *While the Billy Boils*. Such formal strategies as Lawson employs are modernist, moving towards the more conventionalised less individuated use of character as a function of plot—the structuralists' view of character. This does not mean that Lawson is a proto-structuralist; but it does mean that his mode of characterisation reveals a scepticism about individualism and the uniqueness of the self. In his fiction,[8] an intrinsic individuation and interiority of character tends to be 'submerged' into its social, external determinants. This brings into question the whole accuracy of the connection normally made between Lawson's (and Australia's) 'democratic' sentiments, also between the notions of individualism and Australian nationalism.

The assumption that Australianism involves a 'strange blend of individualism and interdependence'[9] is both familiar and current, despite the fact that such an idea is a prime target for renovation as an account of our tradition as a whole. That this position may be both unconvincing *and* orthodox is revealed by the parallel existence of an alternate orthodoxy—one which does note the ways in which our literature tends to prefer the community to the individual (hence the 'strange blend of ... interdependence'). Tom Inglis Moore claims that our writers tend to depict social groups rather than individuals. He refers to the occupation groups of shearers and teamsters in a writer such as Furphy as being presented with an approach that is 'communal, not individual'.[10] (Interestingly, this is connected to what Moore calls a social consciousness, which leads to demands for equality—something one presumes comes from notions of individualism.) Joan Kirkby in her comparison of Australian and American poetry also notes the rejection of the primacy of the self and the displacement of personality in much of Australian poetry.[11] And D. R. Burns approaches the problem from another perspective in *The Directions of Australian Fiction 1920–1974*:

> The description of the work a man does and of the play of nature
> compensates, in some measure, for the lack of complexity in the characters.
> Or perhaps the characters tend to lack complexity in themselves because the
> authors are intent upon defining them in terms of their relationship to
> nature or the work they must do. There is some move towards the
> development of more complex characters in recent times... But this
> movement doesn't comprise a mainline direction. The Australian novelist
> who wants to study such complexities may look abroad towards the older
> societies of Europe. There, typically, the expatriate Australian character
> learns that, contrary to the ethical teachings of the Australian State School
> system, a single person may be not a One but a Many.[12]

Presumably, by 'complexity' Burns means a psychological complexity, a more individuated essence. This is seen as a foreign mode of characterisation in Australian literature—one lying outside our ideology. The limits of such theorising of this subject is revealed in Burns' next sentence when he invokes, without any sense of contradiction, the 'philosophy of the pioneering times' which is typically individualist and independent. The two orthodoxies—one proclaiming the centrality of the independent individual and the other his submersion in our fiction—seem to coexist unproblematically in critical accounts of Australian characterisation.

Any discussion of the democratic theme in Australian fiction needs to recognise how our version of the democrat can manifest itself simply (if paradoxically) in an anti-individualist trope—the fear of difference. Veronica Brady refers to the philosophical limits of Australian egalitarianism when she talks of the sense of equality in Furphy remaining at the level of 'sentiment', which 'tends to give way under the pressure of economic, political or social necessity'.[13] Lionel Trilling, with much less provocation from his literature than an Australian critic could find, wondered if the egalitarian ideals of the American colony had discriminated against singularity of character. American fiction could well be eliminating difference through the exertion of a levelling influence on the representation of 'richness of character':

> I think that if American novels of the past, whatever their merits of intensity and beauty, have given us very few substantial or memorable people, this is because one of the things which makes for substantiality of character in the novel is precisely the notation of manners, that is to say of class traits modified by personality.[14]

Notions of difference and of individuality do seem to be compromised by the democratic theme; in a comparison of the representation of the 'singular character'—as emblematic of individuality—in the literature of the two colonies, however, it becomes clear that Australian literature's commitment to that individual is, at the least, equivocal.

The singular individual, richly endowed with indicators of difference, survives in fact in much Australian fiction in essentially peripheral roles—such as those filled by the array of characters in *Such is Life* (the signifiers of its ethos). Where there is difference in Lawson's stories, it can indicate victimhood (the cook in 'The Shearing of the Cook's Dog'), madness or eccentricity ('The Bush Undertaker'), or a kind of constitutional unsuitability for communal life (Giraffe in 'Send Round the Hat', who is eventually consigned to the care of his sweetheart and thus banished from Lawson's world for good). Where the singular individual occupies the centre of the novel, as in Richardson's fiction, he derives little benefit from his individuality. Indeed, Richard Mahony's singularity, denoted finally through his inability to adapt to a social structure and its harsh economic realities, is precisely the attribute which renders him vulnerable to rejection by the very community he wishes to enter. If we were to consider how a traditional American writer might deal with such a character, an appropriate parallel might be Roger Chillingworth in *The Scarlet Letter*. Both men are physicians, ageing prematurely, disappointed and ill; both are viewed by their society as somehow infernal and odd. Yet, in Hawthorne's novel, it is Chillingworth's difference which gives him his power, his privileged position in the small community of Salem. The comparison thus uncovers very different results. No doubt this is due to the establishment of a type of singularity within American fiction that depends upon a very different myth of the individual in relation to the society. While perhaps it is strained in one way, the comparison also suggests that where American fiction defers to difference as an expression of individuality which is to be respected, for its part the Australian version as constructed in our fiction sees in difference, and thus individuality, an implied criticism; and so it reacts with suspicion and resentment. This can manifest itself in one of at least two ways: either through the thematic exploitation of the difficulties placed before an individuated character (which we have dealt with in the preceding chapter) or through the eschewal of individuation in the representation of character itself.

Within Lawson's fiction, a central location for an investigation of the tradition's production of character is in the use of the literary convention of mateship. Both the mode of characterisation and the convention deserve inspection. The literary convention of mateship, as Patrick Morgan establishes, is not at all what it appears to be:

> Mateship purported to describe a complete and genuine personality; in reality it accepted the visible and less important part of the personality as the whole thing. The unreal and discardable display was taken to be the essence, and the atrophied central core and lack of firm identity were ignored. When Lawrence wrote that Australians were 'marvellous and manly and independent on the outside' we recognise that as a description of mateship. But whereas Lawrence was critical, the Australian community applauded and recommended such behaviour. By mid-century, types such as Jack Meredith, in *My Brother Jack*, were the society's culture-heroes. In the tradition of self congratulation, the shift of emphasis to the outside was accepted as real. In other words, both the mateship exponents and the mateship promoters were taken in by their own propaganda—they wanted to regard the disguise as the real thing. In addition, an attempt was made to retroject this mateship veneer back into earlier Australian history, and to link it up with the silent, and more admirable, bushman characters of nineteenth century outback fact and fiction.[15]

The retrospective link that Morgan notes in the fiction is most pertinent here. I do not wish to argue for an easy identification of Lawson, the author, with his narrators; or for a seamless union between Lawson's own authorial view of the convention of mateship and the view of the communities that he describes; nevertheless there *is* a nexus between Lawson's own representation of character on the one hand and the literary convention of mateship on the other. The common element in both is the lack of individuation in Lawson's representation of the self—something which is also to be found in the conception of the personality embodied in the practice and myth of mateship.

The link is clear in Lawson's story, 'Telling Mrs Baker', where he recounts the tale of two bushmen who are obliged to see the wife of their dead mate and explain the circumstances of his death. Unfortunately, the mate has died of the horrors brought on by repeated binges—primarily at the instigation of a 'flash barmaid', 'one of those girls who are engaged, by the publicans up-country, as baits for chequemen'. While the fact that he has been ensnared in such a fashion absolves Bob, the mate, from some guilt, nevertheless his brother Ned feels that the wife should be spared the shame of knowing the true cause of her husband's death. Accordingly, Jack and Andy go through the charade of convincing Mrs Baker that her husband died of some kind of illness. Mrs Baker accepts the story, although her 'Sydney sister'—more astute than your bush girls—has suspicions. When the sister is privately informed of the real facts and the reason for concealing them at the story's end, she responds warmly:

> 'I want to thank you for her sake,' she said quickly. 'You are good men! I like the bushmen! They are grand men—they are noble. I'll probably never see either of you again, so it doesn't matter', and she put her white hand on Andy's shoulder and kissed him fair and square on the mouth. 'And you, too!' she said to me. I was taller than Andy, and had to stoop. 'Good-bye!' she said, and ran to the gate and in, waving her hand to us. We lifted our hats again and turned down the road.[16]

This ending clearly endorses the mates' behaviour because of their essential kindness to Mrs Baker. Yet, early in the story, it is implied that the fictional account of Bob Baker's death is invented in order to protect not so much the living woman but rather the memory of a dead mate:

> 'Why not let her know the truth?' I asked. 'She's sure to hear of it sooner or later; and if she knew he was only a selfish drunken blackguard she might get over it all the sooner.'
> 'You don't know women, Jack,' said Andy quietly. 'And, anyway, even if she is a sensible woman, we've got a dead mate to consider as well as a living woman.'[17]

The 'dead mate' prevails and Bob Baker's name is protected. 'Telling

Mrs Baker' seems a clear example of honour being kept among mates and a testimony to the strength of the links forged in the Australian bush.

But it need not be. For it is complicated by the fact that Bob is a liar, a drunkard, and a thief, while Mrs Baker is (according to Andy) 'a good woman', 'one of the right stuff'. Even the good things possible to say about Bob before he takes to the drink—that he was a 'jolly, open-handed, popular man'—are undercut by the narrator's sceptical 'which means that he'd been a selfish man as far as his wife and children were concerned, for they had to suffer for it in the end.'[18]

In fact the only way in which this story can be read without offence *is* through the acceptance of the literary convention of mateship. Mateship is the principle which justifies the narrator and his friends' subterfuge; it is the sole indicator of any relationship between the three men which might give the subterfuge an affective dimension; and it is the 'noble' and 'good' acknowledged by the sister, thus providing the scale of values embedded in the ending. It is our endorsement of the convention of mateship which allows us to ignore the complicating moral and personal contingencies outlined in the previous paragraph. We can do this inevitably because of a neglected but crucial aspect of the convention—one that I wish to highlight here and which is its insistence that individual characteristics do not cancel out the loyalties contracted through work and association in the bush. In short, what makes mateship possible is not the authenticity of the particular relationship. Its primary attribute is rather the *negation* of individuality or even specificity of character. The naturalness of the institution of mateship is never questioned, but is continually reinforced and applauded.

Lawson's frequently ironic detachment from the subjects of his observation usually protects him from a charge of direct advocacy; yet the convention and the institution of mateship is clearly supported in his fiction. Even such characters as Steelman, who exploits the bonds of loyalty to selfish advantage, are not seen as flaws in the institution; Steelman's cunning manipulation of his victims is allowed to appear as if deserving of some reward. Notably, Steelman preys on ideological turncoats—married men in the cities. The one most put out by Steelman's operations tends to be the victim's wife. Her claims on her husband are secondary to those of Steelman as the mate:

> The married victim generally had neither the courage nor the ability to turn him out. He was cheerfully blind and deaf to all hints, and if the exasperated missus said anything to him straight, he would look shocked, and reply, as likely as not: 'Why, my good woman, you must be mad! I'm your husband's guest.'[19]

While the narrator stops short of recommending the behaviour, the first sentence quoted invites the reader to believe that, since Steelman is more of a prankster than a parasite, his friends might actually deserve his harrassment because they lack the 'courage' to turn him out.

'The Union Buries Its Dead' is one of the most complex of Lawson's stories and can be subjected to a number of different readings. Nevertheless, while the relation between the narrator, the implied author, and the ideology of the bush in the story is under constant negotiation during the tale, both Lawson's narrator and Lawson the implied author are finally unconvincing in their attempts to undercut the bush legend. The narrator may dismiss the figure of the 'heart-broken old mate' as sentimentally conventional; but he himself expresses an equally sentimental satisfaction in the phlegmatic acceptance of mortality which emerges as a binding agent within the community. The Australian version of that self-regarding toughness Leslie Fiedler labelled the 'higher Masculine sentimentality'.[20] It is endorsed when the point of view of the narrator and the more equivocal point of view of the implied author combine to create the story's final effect: a definitively joyless celebration of solidarity among bush workers.

As is the case with Bob Baker in 'Telling Mrs Baker', the fact that no-one knows the dead man in 'The Union Buries Its Dead' (he is insistently referred to as 'the stranger') does not discharge the survivors from completing the rituals of honouring a 'dead mate'. In this instance, of course, it is clear that the rituals do not honour the individual:

> The dead bushman's name was Jim, apparently; but they found no portraits, no locks of hair, nor any love letters, not anything of that kind in his swag—not even a reference to his mother; only some papers relating to Union matters. Most of us didn't know the name until we saw it on the coffin; we knew him as 'that poor chap that got drowned yesterday'.[21]

The dead man's only distinguishing characteristic is his relation to the community—his membership in the Union. There isn't 'even a reference to his mother', and his name, it turns out, is assumed. What is being acknowledged and celebrated through the ritual of attending the burial is its source—the convention of mateship itself. In this story and others, the convention functions in order to provide solidarity—community—rather than opportunities for self-definition. And it is the structure of this community that Lawson is most generally interested in, so that his characters typically provide points of entry to the values of that community rather than becoming objects of interest in their own right.

To generalise from Lawson's example, the Australian commitment to certain kinds of independence masks a basic suspicion of difference and of individuality. This manifests itself in a particular mode of characterisation which sees character as overwhelmingly the product of social and ethical determinants, of interest primarily for the purposes of moving the plot, providing a setting, or creating a world. While this is not the only strategy of characterisation employed in Australian fiction, it does run in a steady line through Lawson, Furphy and Herbert, and it is traceable in more contemporary work such as Ireland's *The Unknown Industrial Prisoner* or *The Glass Canoe*, and Rodney Hall's *Just Relations*.[22] The fact that this strategy (together with its connection with mateship) rarely occurs in contemporary women writers indicates that it is a major narrative strategy for our male writers in particular. But it does occur in narrative modes other than those of prose fiction; for instance it is clearly operative in our films and our ballads.

There is a film adaptation of 'The Union Buries Its Dead'; it is one of three stories about mateship in Cecil Holmes' *Three in One* (1957). In the film, the focus on the mates rather than the dead man is even less equivocal than in the original story. Rex Rienits' script appropriates the title 'Joe Wilson's Mates' for the story—Joe Wilson now having turned out to be the dead man's name. While the mystery which Lawson builds up around the man does not give him any individuation but does still allow him the possibility of some kind of identity, Holmes' film simply uses his death as an opportunity for examining mateship in action. In *Three in One*, the dead man's union card is passed very slowly from hand to hand, treated with the reverence and awe of a dead body. The camera follows the card's progress around the circle with absolute seriousness, in order to establish the idea of membership to the community as the most important, almost religious, of qualities. The mates themselves are represented in the way we are used to in Lawson: 'colourful', lively bush characters, with collections of all the jolly and interesting traits that thrive, presumably, in the bush. The characters either have definite social functions—the landlord, the union representative—or quirks of behaviour which connect them to particular stereotypes—the teller of tall tales, the spiv from the city, the swagman. The film swamps the viewer with local colour; much of the longest sequence takes place in the pub, and it begins with a couple of tall tales to establish the community's richness and humour before lurching into renditions of 'Flash Jack from Gundagai' and 'Click Go the Shears'. Given the amount of time that all this occupies in a twenty-minute narrative, the songs and yarns must be seen as important agents in establishing the strength and authenticity of the bush community. The individual all but disappears in this film as the community of bush mates is celebrated at length. And the slightly nihilistic implications of Lawson's original story are all but buried in what John McCallum in his introduction calls 'an amusing commentary' on the values of the bush.

Earlier Australian films take on the responsibility of documenting Australian community life almost habitually, even in the most melodramatic of plots such as that of *A Girl of the Bush* (1921). In *A Girl of the Bush*, minor characters (such as the Chinese cook) are introduced by way of a description of their function in the community rather than in the plot. Such 'flat' characters—ones used as indicators of social setting, group customs, community values and beliefs rather than as particularised articulations or transformations of any of these—are very much in evidence also in the films made during the 1970s revival. One of the consequences (we shall examine the others later on) of that period's dominant mode of documentary realism was to subordinate interest in character to interest in social process, and to subordinate interest in narrative to interest in observation.

Documentary realism is a form which radically discounts individual problems and contradictions by placing them within a larger historical frame. Apparently objective and unmediated, it contains many of the formal possibilities of the quasi-yarn which initiates us into Lawson's world. Many of the early films of the revival used the camera as the spinner of the yarn; they adopted a slice-of-life approach which submerged characterisation: *Sunday Too Far Away, The Picture Show Man, F. J. Holden, Newsfront, Caddie,* even *Picnic at Hanging Rock,* while not all obvious contenders for such a description could be argued to reveal this characteristic. *Sunday Too Far Away* is a particularly relevant film to approach after the discussion of Lawson—since it, too, is a celebration of a dying social/occupational group as a model of social relations. Moreover, we can see in it the same kind of attack on difference, the same kind of exclusion of women, and the same deference to the values of the community rather than to those of the self.

Sunday Too Far Away's construction of a documentary frame to enclose its characters sacrifices Jack Thompson's individualising portrayal of Foley, the gun shearer nearing the end of his prime. Foley is collapsed back into his occupational group, the shearers in the early 1950s. The use of end-titles to place the film in history and to deny its fictional structure makes Foley simply representative rather than an intrinsically interesting or important character. Apparently, this formal preference for the documentary mode is also responsible for the disappearance of the sub-plot involving the education of Michael Simpson, the young rouseabout who barely features in the final edition of the film.[23] The film's subject is finally the occupational group, and its values are communal rather than personal.

As with Lawson's treatment of the bush, and as with Furphy's treatment of his itinerant occupational culture, the method of the film is to stitch episodes together to document a model of social organisation which is to be admired. The shearers in *Sunday Too Far Away* continually define themselves by establishing what they are *not*, by providing us with a list of the positions which they will not hold and the responsibilities which they will not accept. The definition of the group, as in Lawson, becomes a crucial subject. Continually the shearer's society is being compared and preferred to that of others—for instance, the cockie's, whose life is ruled by money rather than by skill, and the scabs, who may have the skill but lack the sense of honour and solidarity. The world of the city, as revealed by Foley's experiences in the fish market and Old Garth's failure to find his son in the vast metropolis of Melbourne is also to be despised. Fiercely proud of their calling, the shearers view any deviation from their codes with suspicion, as an indication of a withdrawal from the authentic. Barry, who reads continually and writes letters to his wife, is put down in ways reminiscent of Lawson's treatment of both difference and of women;[24] the men's response to Barry's letter writing is simply to attack him—'ya queer or something? What the Bloody hell's wrong with you?' Moreover, Foley's attempt to get out of shearing fails, and is regarded by the film as a case of *hubris*; the shearing shed, mythologised visually as a place of epic endeavours, is his true context. It is in this place of work that the only differences that matter (those of levels of skill and achievement in shearing) are articulated. The film provides a limited view of individuality, and indeed Foley has to learn to accept his loss of even that degree of individuation.

The bonds which structure the community of *Sunday Too Far Away* are just like those which structure the world of 'The Union Buries its Dead'. There is a sense of obligation and honour which dominates the first half of the film as the men are forced to weigh the difference between honour among mates and the legal definition of the term. The final words of the film establish honour as the motivation behind the nine-month-long strike, the beginnings of which the film aims to document. Following the end-titles relating the shearers' victory is the coda 'it wasn't the money so much, it was the bloody insult'. The construction of this sense of honour and solidarity is accomplished through strikingly effective community scenes—the reunion of the shearers at the beginning of the shed with the barrage of stories and communal lore, the response to Foley's pathetic attempt to warn off the scabs ('that was pissweak'), and the way in which their dealings with Tim, both mate and boss, scrupulously protects the group regardless of the feelings of the individual. As this solidarity is established, a sense of the richness of the culture which it binds together is also established, making it very difficult to resist seeing the shearers as some kind of ideal.

For *Sunday Too Far Away*, as for *Such is Life* or *Joe Wilson's Mates*, this is the central interest. The proliferation of colourful characters on the screen only serves to provide us with points of entry to the structure of the community; they do not invite us to examine the nature of or the motivation behind their membership in that community. Just as in 'Telling Mrs Baker', it is assumed that working together is sufficient cause for the bond of mateship, so that the naturalness of the convention in the story is assumed just as easily in the film.

In *Sunday*, the subordination of Foley is largely the result of the film's documentary form. There are, however, a number of ways in which the deflection of interest from character to setting, from plot to social structure, manifests itself in Australian feature films. The Ocker comedies, from *Alvin Purple* (1973) to the more penetrating *Don's Party* (1976), are perhaps the most obvious examples of the reduction of individuation by means of the representation of social types as material for comedy. However, in a wide range of Australian films with much more ambitious objectives, characters still appear simply as the result of their social and ethical determinants rather than as 'themselves.' In *Gallipoli* (1982), character suffers from the film's stylistic shotgun wedding as documentary realism is awkwardly conjoined with romance. The heroes, Frank and Archy, are provided with the most minimal personal definition: Archy is from the bush, Frank is from the city, and both are professional runners. As representatives of Australian youth going to war, they are given no detailed social context but exist in a nationalist limbo—heroes in waiting, ready to be the symbolic indices of the futility and waste of Gallipoli.

In a significant number of Australian films the major characters are *events* rather than people: the shearer's strike in *Sunday*, the axe murders in *The Chant of Jimmie Blacksmith*, the history of the 1920s and 1930s in *Between Wars*, Gallipoli in *Gallipoli*, and the newsreel view of events in *Newsfront*. In those films, the characters are there simply for the events to act upon them; and their individuality resides purely in their readiness to indicate their vulnerability when confronted by the events. Peter Weir's films provide particularly clear examples of this. Weir displaces interest in character with interest in setting—the atmosphere which enhances the potential significance of the events in his films. Characters, with one or two exceptions, are not seen as intrinsically interesting subjects in themselves. Accordingly, his films are dominated by forces lying outside the character's control: *The*

Cars That Ate Paris (1974) turns on the bizarre structure of the community of Paris; *Picnic at Hanging Rock* (1975) on the mysteries of the disappearances at the Rock; *The Last Wave* (1977) on the apocalyptic tidal wave approaching Sydney; *Gallipoli* (1981) on the myth of that battle; and *The Year of Living Dangerously* (1983) on the fall of Sukarno in Indonesia. Weir's interest in people, like Patrick White's, is essentially very abstract—and he consistently places his characters within a natural or apparently natural cycle of events about which they can do nothing, except just register their vulnerability or bewilderment. In both *Picnic* and *The Last Wave* it is nature itself that is the irresistible force, while in *Gallipoli* and *The Year of Living Dangerously* it is history represented as nature that cannot be controlled.

When one thinks of Weir's films it is his images rather than his characters that one remembers: the cars in Paris, Miranda's frozen wave as she mounts the Rock, Gulpilil holding the secret stone in David Burton's dream in *The Last Wave*, or the first view of the 'ghostly fun-park' of Gallipoli. (Only Billy Kwan, in *The Year of Living Dangerously*, seems to have any individuated existence.) Partly this is due to Weir's habit of submerging his characters in settings while using them as metonyms for that setting. The opening of *Gallipoli* is typical: we have a series of close-ups on Archy's face, thereby individualising him and announcing interest in him; however, the cut to the long shot of the surroundings—and their startling emptiness—establishes the setting itself as the most interesting factor. The delay in providing us with this setting only serves to emphasise its impact. Immediately after this the titles are imposed on the screen. They immediately situate the film in history and in Western Australia, and the narrative begins.

Weir represents character in two basic ways. His treatment involves either a complete denial of specificity—as in the case of the girls who disappear with Miranda in *Picnic* (they are simply adolescent, pubescent, and repressed by their middle-class environment in the school) and of *The Last Wave*'s use of Aboriginals (they simply stand as metonyms for their entire culture by virtue of the simple exploitation of black faces)—or else it involves a limited degree of specificity. The latter method arises in order to reveal what happens to the individual in the face of circumstance, nature, or history (the three terms are almost synonymous to Weir). Interestingly, Weir's 'study of mateship' —*Gallipoli*—does both. And thus *Gallipoli* incorporates similar assumptions about mateship to those which we find in Lawson. Frank, the dark one, is given more specificity than any other character—certainly more than Archy, who is the film's assumed norm and is representative of the first mode of characterisation mentioned. Frank moves from his earlier specificity to a less individuated mode as the film develops. Initially, he is seen just as a working-class boy and part of a close-knit group of mates who are bound by work. Frank, however, teams up with Archy; and so he finally asks to be transferred, in effect, out of his class—and into the elite Light Horse ('it's got a bit of class' because it only 'takes toffs and farmers' sons'). Frank's attempt at upward mobility is thus given the alibi of mateship, even while it is simply swapping his earlier group of mates (seen by the film as being less attractive than Archy) for another. This runs counter to his individuality, which resides rather in his working-class background and his personal reasons for joining up—he wants to 'come back an officer' and is hoping to avoid 'being pushed around the rest of my bloody life'. As with Lawson's mates, then, it is Frank's 'difference' that is the first casualty of his mateship with Archy. For the film, Frank has no personal function beyond this point; from then on he is there simply to register the loss at Archy's death.

In *The Year of Living Dangerously*. Billy Kwan's difference is seen finally as a kind of obsession. Weir portrays Kwan's act of protest against Sukarno as produced by an insane desperation. Kwan's ability to work and his fine understanding of the culture are both sacrificed to his individuating characteristic—his need to believe in his heroes, and his pattern of living through other people. Billy is an example of that mode of representing individuality as a characteristic that renders one vulnerable in the face of events (like Giraffe in Lawson's 'Send Round the Hat', or the hatter in 'No Place For a Women'). In contrast, Miranda's 'victimhood' in *Picnic* emerges from an heightened sensitivity to the rock and to the sense of her own fate, delivered to the audience by the obscure premonitory remarks which she makes at the beginning of the film. But even this individuality is limited, as it emerges not so much from her character as from her 'nature'. Similarly, David Burton's premonitions of disaster in *The Last Wave* (which is his only individuating characteristic) is only a natural 'gift'—one which has been transmitted genetically to him through his connection with an ancient Mayan race who once visited Australia. His gift, more than Miranda's, seems to render him helpless. He is only able to predict, but not change, the future. And he finds himself in a maze of superstition and belief that he cannot escape or influence. Leaving the slight silliness of the plot (the Mayan connection in particular) aside, David Burton becomes in his special knowledge both an agent and a victim of the apocalypse. His individuality of experience only serves to exacerbate his awareness of mortality.

As we move from Weir's work to the large number of other films dealing not so much with discrete events but with broad historic trends, the subject matter becomes increasingly explicitly Australian history rather than the individuated experience of Australians. The problem in such films is frequently one of constructing characters as recipients of that history who are sufficiently individualised to dramatise its impact; the dominant convention of characterisation can make it very difficult for directors to present even the particularity of victimhood economically and convincingly. In examples of 1970s period dramas such as *The Irishman* and *The Picture Show Man*, where the events which dominate the plot are simply the demonstration of the slow expiry of a way of life or an occupation (but the two tend to be synonymous in such representations of the past), the leading characters are presented as merely 'colourful' eccentrics. It is their sheer mannerisms and habits that are the signifiers of their difference as well as their anachronistic status. The functions which they serve are quite comparable to Furphy's proliferation of single dimensional characters in *Such is Life*: they are there purely for their interest as cinematic 'events' rather than as meaningful instances of individual life. Early bush comedies such as *On Our Selection*, as well as the period drama, also typically employ this technique in their minor characters.

More importantly however, and as is the case also in Lawson, in order to fill the gap left by their mode of characterisation, many Australian films actually *exploit* the nationalist myths of individualism and independence. Films such as *Breaker Morant* or *Gallipoli* are, like Lawson's stories, outstanding examples of the conflation of nationalism, of mateship and of the myth of individualism. Gaps in the substantiality of character are filled by means of the insertion of the nation; and characterisation is made to enact a consensus not on the basis of what constitutes the *individual* experience of Australia but on the basis of what constitues the common, *unindividuated* experience of Australia. So 'Australianism' in a character in film is often used as a substitute for (and paradoxically as a signifier of) individuality and authenticity. The assertion of the nation's individuality is then transferred to those who feel enclosed within that identity. For instance, Bryan Brown's Handcock in *Breaker Morant* is the archetypal anti-authoritarian Australian (while also serving as Breaker's loyal lieutenant) whose most individualised expression is the letter to his wife which is sealed with the words, 'Australia for ever'. Handcock's subjectivity and his nationality completely merge into each other. Brown's special function as an actor is precisely to provide both the physical representation of the individual and the signification of national character, thus opening up the possibility of both personal and nationalist identification. Brown's combination of the typical and the individual enables him, in common with many other actors such as John Ewart and Bill Hunter, to act as an icon of Australian-ness:[25] The constant fulfilling of this function by the Australian actor immediately reveals how important is his role, and that of the 'star' in the construction of the Australian character in the Australian film.

Richard Dyer's work is important here. For it too focuses on the star's performance as a signifying function, which may be separate from and different to the written character within the film script. Stars, Dyer says, are signs.[26] Since one can conceptualise a star's *total* image (as distinct from the particular character that he or she plays in a film) the casting of a particular actor has important repercussions on the kind of effect that the characterisation will have. The casting of John Wayne, for example, was always determined by what *he* signified; the inscription of a particular version of Americanism is always clear in his face, voice, and mannerisms. So it is with local examples such as Bryan Brown—whose appearance in *Winter of Our Dreams* (in the role of a weak and self-deluding intellectual) created a complete confusion in many reviewers' and audiences' minds about the total meaning of the film. This was simply because the film did not seem to fully incorporate Bryan Brown's meaning as a sign. On the other hand, the casting of Jack Thompson as Clancy in *The Man From Snowy River* meant that the character scarcely needed to be written at all. Thus the effect of the star is not only on the total signification of their character in a film, but also on the quality of the characterisation. And if stars can be seen as 'types' then they must to some extent be flat and representative rather than rich and individuated. And yet their 'star status' does carry with it the potential to impose their own particularity on the type, by association. Dyer introduces the notion of 'transcendence',[27] whereby stars may transcend the social type which they are meant to represent and thus invest it with individuality. Clearly, there are limits to this effect if the film is to be deciphered by its audience, but it does mean that a character which is 'flat' in the script can be invested with a kind of individuality by the particularly 'signifying' actor.

As iconic representations of recognisable social types, film stars thus have deep ideological meanings. 'One of the types that stars embody is the type of the individual himself,' says Dyer; 'they embody that particular conception of what it is to be human that characterises our culture.'[28] Thus, it is hardly surprising that there are very few prominent male actors in the Australian film industry who do not actively denote Australianism as a primary signifying function: by being both typical and individual they assist in the leakage between national and personal identity which we have been describing. Not only do such marked 'Australians' fill many of the minor roles in our films—John Meillon, John Ewart, Bill Kerr, and even Chips Rafferty come to mind, here—but they can also fill central roles in full-length features. Len Maguire's (Bill Hunter) experiences in *Newsfront*, for instance, are meant to be representative of those of the whole country; his life is seen with the documentary eyes of a camera which is more interested in detailing *Australia*'s loss of innocence than that of the character himself. Indeed the characterisation is completely proscribed by the imposition of dates, titles, still photographs and newsreel footage; and Hunter's ability to make ordinariness recognisable as such greatly assists the process.

The 'type of the individual' which emerges from the analysis of the Australian star—in the faces of the Bryan Browns and Jack Thompsons—may be available to us through semiotics. Our task here, however, has been to examine the type of the individual which is implied in the operation of a specific mode of characterisation in Australian narrative. The ideological implications of the aspects of that mode as discussed above need underlining. The lack of individuation in character clearly reflects a lack of faith in the concept of individualism within the Australian context; and that lack of faith is also observable as an implicit ideological component in the mode of documentary realism (realism itself will be addressed in the last chapter). Hence the suspicion of the possibilities of meaning, which is a thematic of our fiction. In film, the dominance of documentary realism reflects a general withdrawal from narrative as a way of shaping or constructing meaning from experience. This withdrawal operates in favour of the invocation of history, as something within which the individual is more or less totally submerged. And it expresses a point of view which is in the final analysis a denial of all ideological positions, a refusal to admit the political construction of experience. The ideology of selfhood which produces such forms and such strategies of characterisation is one, therefore, which undermines all perception of the supposed radical potential of the nationalist myths of independence and individualism. That such a perception is still commonly expressed points to the effectiveness of these myths in being able to naturalise themselves and their own versions of history. So it is to the function of these nationalist myths and to their particular formation in Australian narrative that we turn next.

NOTES

1 See Roland Barthes', 'Introduction to the Structural Analysis of Narratives', in *Image-Music-Text* (London: Fontana, 1977), pp.79–125.
2 Jonathon Culler, *Structuralist Poetics*, p.230.
3 ibid. p.231.
4 'Preface' to *The Portrait of a Lady* (Harmondsworth: Penguin, 1963), p.vi.

5 Seymour Chatman, *Story and Discourse: Narrative Structure in Fiction and Film* (London: Cornell University Press, 1978), p.113.
6 ibid. p.118.
7 'Henry Lawson's Fictional World' in Leon Cantrell (ed.) *Bards, Bohemians and Bookmen* (St Lucia: University of Queensland Press, 1976), p.199.
8 Even though the short story form inhibits development of character, and comparisons between the level of complexity in a novel and a story would have to include many qualifications, the view of what *constitutes* charcter in Lawson, in comparison to other writers of fiction, can be outlined.
9 W. F. Mandle, *Going It Alone* (Melbourne: Penguin, 1980), p.8.
10 *Social Patterns in Australian Literature*, pp.10–11.
11 (Sydney: Hale and Iremonger, 1982), pp.7–8.
12 (Melbourne: Cassell, 1975), p.3.
13 *A Crucible of Prophets*, p.52.
14 'Art and Fortune' in *The Liberal Imagination* (London: Mercury, 1961), pp.262–3. These remarks clearly draw on a realist preference, and exclude Ahab, Natty Bumppo, and so on.
15 'Hard Work and Idle Dissipation: The Dual Australian Personality' *Meanjin*, Vol.41, No.1 (Autumn, 1982), p.35.
16 *Henry Lawson: Short Stories and Sketches 1888–1922*, ed. Colin Roderick (Sydney: Angus and Robertson, 1972), p.424.
17 ibid. p.418.
18 ibid. p.415–16.
19 ibid. p.208.
20 *The Return of the Vanishing American*, pp.169–88. Fiedler is referring to Hemingway, among others.
21 ibid. p.84.
22 An earlier version of this material speculates about the connection with Patrick White. 'Mateship, Individualism, and the Production of Character in Australian Fiction', *Australian Literary Studies*, Vol.11, No.4, (October 1984) pp.447–57.
23 For an account of the problems of focussing the film—on Foley, on Michael, or on the strike—see David Stratton's account in *The Last New Wave* (Sydney: Angus and Robertson, 1980), pp.99–105.
24 Tim Rowse has noted the connection between women and difference in *Australian Liberalism and National Character*: 'female influence in the culture is often taken to amount to a destructive obsession with status and difference', (p.208).
25 Susan Dermody and Elizabeth Jacka, in their forthcoming book, *The Screening of Australia*, (Currency Press), have advanced this idea.
26 'Stars as Signs', in *Popular Television and Film*, pp.236–69.
27 ibid. p.245.
28 ibid. pp.244–5.

5 *Representing the Nation*

As this study proceeds, the representation of 'the nation' becomes increasingly important. It provides the alibi—that of the harshness of the Australian context—for the lowering of the threshold of personal expectations as discussed in Chapter 2; it is the object of the arguments around the image of convictism which are outlined in Chapter 3; and it provides the supporting mythology for the convention of mateship and the representation of character within the models which have just been discussed in the previous chapter. In other words, those Australian fictions which are able to represent themselves as national do so by drawing on the available myths and discourses of national character and identity; and so these myths and discourses—and the ideological tasks which they are able to perform—are necessary objects of study in any account of the narratives of the Australian culture. If, as the last chapter argued, our nationalist myths are not unmediated reflections of history but transformations of it, then they must work to construct a very specific way of seeing the nation.

This way of seeing the nation is dependent upon a relatively narrow range of myths—primarily those attached to the radical nationalist icons of the bushman and the digger. Even Australia II's victory provoked references to Gallipoli, and one would be hard pressed to name contemporary versions of 'the Australian' that have the cultural currency of the bush legend, the legend of the 1890s. In film and fiction it is this legend that provides the paradigms for the representation of nationalism. In this chapter therefore we will examine its dominance, its occurrence in contemporary film, and its ideological function.

Although the ideology of nationalism is most customarily discussed in its relation to hegemony, it is not always seen in this way. It can be viewed as a positive, resistant ideology (as it is by Vance Palmer) which provides the terms for an authentic assertion of identity in order to establish political independence; or else it can be enclosed within an evolutionary model of cultural development which sees nationalism as the index of the end of colonialism and the beginning of the transition to cultural maturity, to the utterances of an unselfconscious 'adult' national voice.[1]

In contemporary theory nationalism is most often seen critically. Its consensual function enables it to obscure differences and divisions that may well need to be recognised and addressed, and its power to establish the overriding priorities for the culture has extensive possibilities. As Patrick Wright points out, the 'nation' acts within the culture as a 'ground for the proliferation of other definitions of what is normal, appropriate or possible'.[2] If the maintenance of hegemony depends upon the winning of assent and upon the regular mobilisation of consensus, then the idea of the nation is an important medium through which this consensus can be drafted. The idea of the nation is thus a target of Marxist critiques of culture which emphasise the political nature and effects of the construction of national identity.[3] Within such constructions, it is argued, minorities are marginalised; and divisions or conflicts within society are minimised in deference to the overriding, accepted priorities of the nation which unite the people. As the national character is valorised, the discourses of nationalism therefore tend to become areas occupied by those interests seeking to centre themselves within the culture. A selective history of this process in Australia is given in Tim Rowse's *Australian Liberalism and National Character*, and a number of other authors have traced the fortunes of the discourses of nationalism through political affiliations as divergent as the Australian Labour Party and the Country Party.[4]

In Australia, the discourses of nationalism are drawn almost exclusively from the mythologised past, specifically the radical past—the time when Australia was represented as the 'social laboratory of the world', its commitment to democracy manifest in the secret ballot and in votes for women, and its essential character being seen to reside in the organic, egalitarian society of the bush communities.[5] That the myth of Australia's radicalism and egalitarianism can survive the contradictions of one's everyday experience reveals how effectively it has been mythologised. The representations of the past in film, fiction, fine art and television tend to propose a continuity between nineteenth-century Australia and the present that is unquestioned despite its inconsistency with aspects of contemporary life. The relationship is narrativised as a story which reaches its end in the present. The typical depiction of the authentic Australian in the past is that of the common man of authentic values, who is constantly oppressed and victimised by British imperialism or by authority generally. Both the romanticising of the figure of the bushranger or the mythologising of the democratic spirit of Eureka are examples of this. And the net effect of such a representation of the national character in the past is to declare that the struggles depicted as necessary for that character need not be continued into the present; that, for us, the struggle is over; and that the battles fought for Australia in the past have borne fruit in the conditions which we now enjoy. As Patrick Wright puts it in his discussion of the construction of the 'national past' in Britain:

> [This construction] makes it possible to think of historical development as complete, a process which finds its accomplishment in the present.
> Historical development is here conceived as a cumulative process which has delivered the nation into the present as its manifest accomplishment. Both celebratory and complacent, it produces a sense that 'we' are the achievement of history and that while the past is thus present as our right it is also something that our narcissism will encourage us to visit, exhibit, write up and discuss.[6]

The representation of Australia's radical and formative past, then, is not only available to the left-wing radicals who might see themselves as the inheritors of the tradition, but also to more conservative elements within the culture who would see this version of the past as justifying the present. Indeed, representations of the past seem, in film for instance, especially acceptable to the establishment critics and other guardians of culture—and certainly the eulogising of the past is for them preferable to the treatment of the present.

The key issue in talking about the role and nature of the presence of nationalism in Australian narrative is thus not so much the range of meanings made available but the fact of the dominance of one set of terms, one body of myth or discourse, as the accepted mode of *representation* of the meaning of the nation. The myth of the Australian legend in Australian writing has been dealt with elsewhere;[7] further, the conditions which determine the production of feature films are much more likely to encourage the use of nationalist myths than the conditions of production of literary fiction. In the next section of this chapter, then, we will examine the role of nationalism in some Australian films.

In *Australian Liberalism and National Character*, Tim Rowse adapts a Raymond Williams aphorism to local use by maintaining that there 'are in fact no Australians. There are only ways of seeing people as Australians'.[8] There are not very many of these, however; and Rowse's study reveals just how malleable the dominant ways of 'seeing people as Australians' are: radical myths of national identity have been consistently appropriated by conservative ideologies in order to cloak divisions within the structure of Australian society. Richard White, too, insists that there is no 'real' Australian waiting to be uncovered;

'a national identity', he says, 'is an invention'.[9] Since this study has interested itself in representation as the product *and* the manufacturer of cultural meanings, the point is acceptable; nevertheless it is worth remembering that such inventions of national identity are not simply cultural templates to be employed, with automatic success, by various groups. That the message has been 'sent' is no guarantee that it has been received. Further, definitions of national identity are sites of struggle; the definitions are never static or 'fixed'. Nevertheless, the specific terms of the particular 'invention' are of some cultural importance.

What is most immediately apparent about the Australian construction of national identity is that the particularities of the 1890s version of nationalism have outlasted most of the political and social conditions which produced them without losing their potential for signifying Australian-ness. Their presence has also been accepted as an index of cultural maturity in a number of representational media. The single most representative character, the figure of the battler, probably occurs first in Lawson,[10] as does much of the mythologising of the harshness of the land and its amelioration by the model community of 'mates'; and it is the convincing assertion of such Australian types through an Australian 'voice' in Lawson, Paterson and Furphy that produces the first recognition of an Australian literature. With such writers, Australian literature is seen to 'come of age', to mature. Similarly, in accounts of Australian painting, the longed-for break with the European tradition is seen to arrive with the Heidelberg School, whose restricted pallets caught the authentic colours of the Australian landscape and whose work actively mythologised the very same world explored by the writers. The work of Tom Roberts and Frederick McCubbin, in particular, mythologised the bush, the itinerant bush workers, the shearers, the landscape dominanted ethos of the country, and worked within the visual equivalent of realist prose; hence Robert Hughes' assessment of Roberts and his contribution to the maturation of Australian fine art:

> Roberts's imagination runs parallel to the prevalent tone of Australian writing in the nineties. His virtues of mateship, courage, adaptability, hard work and resourcefulness are the very ones Lawson celebrated in his short stories, and Joseph Furphy described in *Such is Life*. Their use indicates a growing sense of cultural identity. These virtues were thought distinctively—even uniquely—Australian.[11]

Frederick McCubbin is seen in a similar context:

> His admiration for mateship . . . ballooned into a near-religious mystique by 1905, when he painted *The Pioneers* in the manner of an altar triptych,

showing the hard life, struggle, resourcefulness, achievement and death of the early settlers, and even supplying a vision of the future in the last panel.[12]

As the conservative reaction against the modernist threat from Europe then stifled Australian painting for a long period (during the 1920s and 1930s) Australian painters suffered a sense of increasing irrelevance. Yet their emergence from this and their successful claiming of a prominent place within the national character soon occurred, by way of Sydney Nolan's and of Russell Drysdale's reworking of the same mythic material. Nolan's depiction of the landscape (his isolated stick figures dwarfed by it) and his romantic narrativisation of the legend of Ned Kelly enabled what looked like abstract paintings at first glance to be read by way of the codes of the 1890s definition of nationalism. Drysdale's work is less challenging, providing in such paintings as 'The Drover's Wife' direct reference to Lawson, and his efforts constitute a simple up-dating of the images of Roberts and McCubbin.

It is not just Australian literature that announces its distinctiveness by incorporating this particular mode of representation as a convention—a convention, it must be stated, that by no means dies with Lawson but that can be seen at work even at the end of such a non-realist work as Peter Carey's *Bliss*.[13] It seems as if other art forms must do the same. Although the specific meanings which are generated by the use of these 1890s codes, the interests which they serve and the ideologies which they produce may vary, this set of terms and body of myth thus still remain as the definitive signification of Australian-ness; and their invocation has hegemonic potential.

Australian cinema is no exception to the rule. John Tulloch has more than adequately charted the treatment of the bush legend in the early film industry in Australia, and he has also indicated the ways in which this cinematic treatment drew on the literary sources and put the myth to hegemonic use.[14] In the early films, what is often striking about the use of the myth as a way of enfolding audiences within the narrative is its transparent arbitrariness. For instance *A Girl of the Bush* (1921), a lively melodrama of love and betrayal in the back-blocks, seems not to require its frequent exploitation of documentary titles detailing Australian life. The film nevertheless opens with the verse from Dorothea MacKellar's 'My Country'; however, it relates the poem to the rest of the narrative ideologically rather than thematically—in order, that is, to establish the film as an Australian tale and therefore one of interest to us all. Ken Hall's *On Our Selection* (1932) opened with a gratuitous 'Bushland Symphony' of bush bird calls which the audience greeted with cheers of recognition.

In more recent times, we have seen a spate of nationalistic films

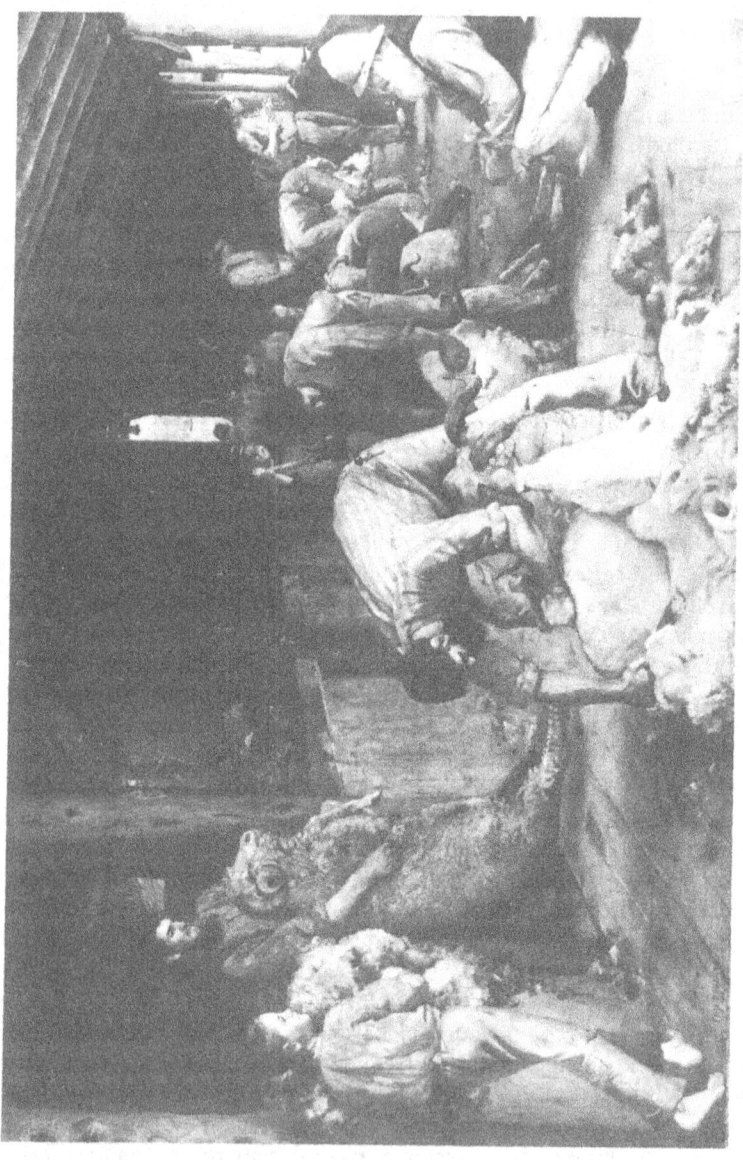

Representing the nation 113

Icons of the Australian character: the classical overtones of the painting give way to the naturalism of cinema, but the image is the same. *Left*: Tom Roberts (1856–1931) 'Shearing the Rams' (1890) (*National Gallery of Victoria*) and (*above*) Jack Thompson as Foley in 'Sunday Too Far Away' (1975). (*Still courtesy of the South Australian Film Corporation*)

emerging from the industry. The nationalism is now more sophisticated than the kind involved in the films identified with Chips Rafferty, or in those films which attempt to make populist tales of country life in the 1950s (films which were formally different, but equally naive) such as Cecil Holmes' *Three in One* (1957) and Anthony Kimmins' *Smiley* (1956). Nevertheless, the construction of Australian-ness through reference to these earlier representations is no less common. Russell Boyd has talked of using Tom Roberts as a guide to getting 'the light of the Australian countryside' in *Picnic at Hanging Rock*, and sees the achievement of this as a 'coming of age'; Gill Armstrong used Roberts and McCubbin in the design of *My Brilliant Career*, and the influence of Roberts' shearing paintings is clear in both *The Chant of Jimmie Blacksmith* and *Sunday Too Far Away*.[15] These may not be seen as nationalist films; but such works as *Breaker Morant*, *Gallipoli*, *The Man From Snowy River*, or *Phar Lap* certainly demand to be seen as nationalist texts, the mode of their nationalism—again—that of the 1890s. This has been recognised: one reviewer describes *Breaker Morant* as nationalist to the point of 'jingoism'; *Gallipoli* advertised itself as the film which will make you 'proud to be Australian'; and Banjo Paterson's powerful celebration of the Australian virtues, the poem of 'The Man From Snowy River' becomes, in Max Harris' phrase, the 'logo' of the film.[16] In particular, the Lawson-Furphy brand of nationalism in fiction includes not only a set of definitions of Australian cultural identity, but also a major strategy for measuring that identity against the English, and valorising those aspects of our national character which depart from English values and loyalties.[17] And the two 'war' films, *Breaker Morant* and *Gallipoli*, make direct use of this strategy.

In *Breaker Morant* the execution of Morant and Handcock is seen as a racist act; the features which define the characters as Australian (Morant is seen as Australian, despite his birthplace, and the three central characters encapsulate the various positive formations of the Australian—the larrikin, the worldly misfit from Europe, and the innocent) are precisely those which incite the British to destroy them. They are represented to us as individualist, independent, resistant to authority, and determinedly iconoclastic. British and Australian values are directly contrasted through the most unequivocal of structures—the courtroom drama. The conventional roles of the innocent and the guilty, the gaoler and the convict, are neatly and characteristically inverted so that the Australian convicts are seen, yet again, as honest and courageous while their English persecutors are treacherous and cowardly. The simplicity of the equation sits awkwardly with the film's considerable moral ambiguity, but, true to the tradition of the battler, the audience's identification with the Australians develops in proportion to the film's establishment of their position as underdogs, outmanoeuvred by the system.

The English in *Gallipoli*, while contained within a less unequivocally nationalist narrative context, are equally stereotyped—monocled and parading on camels when they are not sending our boys into the battle zones to provide cover for their own troops. Peter Weir represents the English in Egypt with the crude nationalism of an 1890s *Bulletin* cartoon, and while this is not central to the film's purpose it is an important moment for the film's relationship with its audience because it proffers an invitation for them to indulge their preference for the Australians by finding the English ridiculous. The anti-English attitude modulates easily, as it does in our history, into a general suspicion of authority. In both films, the paradigm of authority—bureaucratic force aligned against human vulnerability—is English. The Australian versions of authority tend to tacitly condone the larrikin, independent and undisciplined behaviour of the troops; the Breaker allows his subordinates to address him as Harry and is the 'acceptable' version of authority who participates in his troops' 'unmilitary' but understandable revenge on the Boers, while in *Gallipoli* Australian officers incite the riot that disrupts the mock battle in training. The avuncular Major Barton (Bill Hunter, whose iconic function we have already referred to) actually renounces his authority in the suicidal last attack; and declaring that he will not ask his men to do anything he would not do himself, he dies with them. So that the only recommended authority is, paradoxically, an egalitarian one.

The basis for the social structure assumed under this egalitarian principle is mateship. The bond between Morant and Handcock is an obvious example of the automatic 'me, too' mateship. As they are marched off to their execution Morant and Handcock are asked if they have a religion. Morant replies that he is a 'pagan'; Handcock asks him what that is, and the answer—that a pagan is someone who does not believe in a Divine being who controls all—satisfies him. 'I'm a pagan, too', then says Handcock; and it is the separation of their values from the civilised and effete values of the English (not their paganism) that is once more celebrated. *Breaker Morant*, however, unlike *Gallipoli*, is capable of at least intimating the existence of a more radical and political bond between men than that of nationality or mateship. Despite Stephen Crofts' claim to the contrary,[18] the film does suggest that the Australian soldiers are lackeys to an imperialist power whose interests are intrinsically opposed to theirs. Morant's suggestion that they are fighting on the wrong side—against 'farmers' like themselves—is a critique of the system itself. To see a greater brotherhood between the Boers and the Australians than between the Australians and the English is to go beyond nationalism to a more

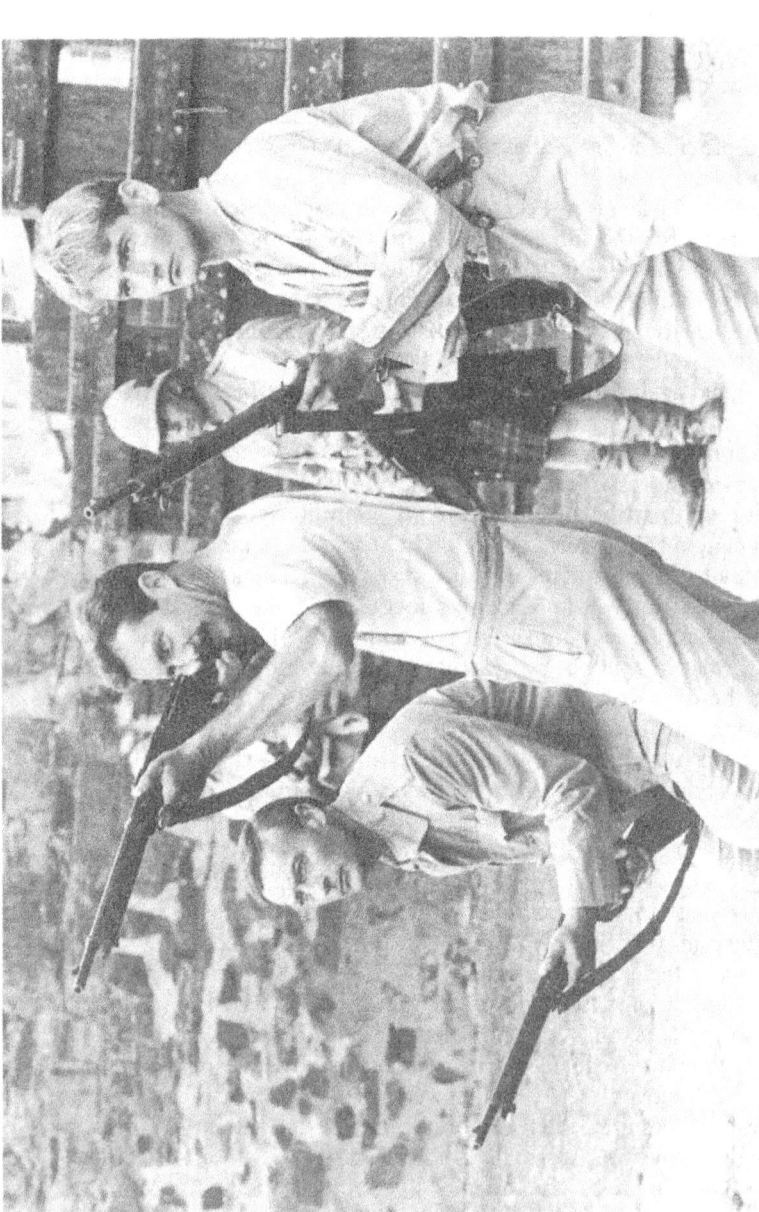

Bailing out the Empire: Morant (Edward Woodward), Handcock (Bryan Brown) and Whitton (Lewis Fitzgerald) break the monotony of prison to repel a Boer attack in 'Breaker Morant'. (Still courtesy of the South Australian Film Corporation)

political understanding of the social structure, and it is a perception that *Gallipoli*, in contrast, is unable to reproduce in its depiction of the classless Australians and their upper class English officers.

In both *Gallipoli* and *Breaker Morant* the nationalism is sufficiently woven into the narrative to make it a good point for reviewers to retrieve and display. In *The Man From Snowy River* the nationalism is so pronounced that it produces a backlash. Probably the most nationalistic film that has been produced since the beginning of the 1970s revival, *Snowy River* was, ironically, attacked for selling out to American values. Unlike *Gallipoli* and *Breaker Morant*, it is unashamedly populist; it selected an American star to play not one but two Americans; and, stylistically, it flies in the face of the critical preferences current in the Australian film culture. *The Man From Snowy River* is all plot, it seems, developing at a breakneck pace and with ruthless economy in a style more reminiscent of the golden years of Hollywood than the Australian 'renaissance'. It is enthusiastically romantic—and since the romantic fiction of the nineteenth century, and the ballads of Paterson and Gordon, romance does tend to have disappeared from Australian narrative traditions. Despite its debts to Hollywood, the film is constructed, as Tom O'Regan has pointed out,[19] in order to appeal to as wide a section of the Australian population as possible; and it deliberately uses the specific terms of Australian nationalist myths in order to set up an alternative tradition of frontier romance, an Australian genre that is different in meaning to the American Western. This particular meaning of the film has been approached from a number of positions: Jack Clancy has described it as an allegory of cultural independence from the twin threats of English and American imperialism,[20] but since it is still so frequently seen as a 'sellout' of Australian values, it is worth outlining why in my view *Snowy River* is such a vividly nationalist film.

Unlike the two films discussed so far, the version of Australian identity articulated in *Snowy River* is not dependent upon a comparison with England; apparently the makers were confident enough of their idea to concentrate on the Australian's relationship with his own land. That confidence is clearly evident in the visuals; the camera is exuberantly active, swooping and soaring among the mountain scenery in a celebration of the landscape that is brash and naive. The harshness and indomitability of the landscape, so clearly caught by Russell Boyd's blinding vistas of reflected light in *Gallipoli*, is here presented simply by its scale—the screen is packed with busy horizons, shot from cranes and helicopters. The result is a vision of a land that is awesome but not unimaginable, inspiring affection and a qualified optimism as befits the romantic form.

Although the film carries the same keynotes of mateship, of egalitarianism and of the bush ethos which we find in Paterson's poem, it is in the depiction of the relationship with the land that it is most faithful to the poem and the most nationalistic. The land is tough, dangerous and beautiful. Jessica sees this when she is trapped on the cliff in the storm: 'It changes so fast,' she says; 'one minute it's Paradise, the next it's trying to kill you.' Accommodation within this murderous Paradise is the goal which the hero, Jim Craig, pursues. His acceptance of the challenge that the landscape presents differentiates him from the squatters in the valley below, while his affinity with the bush horses invests his quest with hope by connecting him with the film's strongest metaphor for the spirit of the land. Jim and Jessica meet through a staged demonstration of his familiarity with horses (he teaches her a rope trick that the villainous station horse breaker, Curly, spends the rest of the film trying to master) and he reaches what the film defines as manhood by matching the bush horses on their own terrain. His respect for the 'colt from Old Regret' is the clearest example of his harmony with the Australian version of nature, and it is important that he trains the horse by 'gentling it' rather than by dominating it.

This is the thematic substance of the film and it is central to the nationalist myth and the ideology of the invented Australian; ours is not, like the American, a myth of the imposition of the individual on the land—of the politics of conquest; ours is a myth of accommodation and acceptance which admits the impossibility of conquering the land and merely recommends a manner of survival by learning to live in partnership with it. In what it means to be a 'man' in *Snowy River*, we have an Australian transformation of the individualistic ethic of the American Western; in this country the 'man' is not the toughest one, but the one who can accept and live with the priorities of the land. Jim's success is rewarded with the love of Jessica, whose family background typifies the range of alternatives that Jim rejects—the values and ways of the city and an exploitative attitude to the land. Jessica, too, rejects these—as the daughter of 'Matilda' she is anything but the archetypal civilising female. Through their union the film offers us a conventional romantic resolution, but also a paradigm of existence in harmony with the land justifying the nostalgic sense of acceptance which also underlies Paterson's poem.

Admittedly, *The Man From Snowy River* is atypical of nationalist films for a number of reasons. First, its camp, even witty, awareness of its own myth-making activity separates it off from the myth itself. This enables the representation of Clancy of the Overflow, for example, to be perceived as a work of romantic invention in which the audience is asked to collaborate. Importantly, *Snowy River* is received as fiction as well as history. Second, the film also uses its romantic form to present an optimistic and positive image of Australian existence. It is not necessary to 'win' as much as Jim Craig does in order to produce a satisfying articulation of Australian-ness. Indeed, in the follow-up film, *Phar Lap*, the doomed horse with the oversized heart becomes the type of the Aussie battler whose very talent results in his death. The film begins with that death, so that it eliminates expectations of transcendence immediately; and only afterwards do Phar Lap's battles against the predictably upperclass, Anglocentric and clubbish racing officials follow. Again, the process of definition is one of establishing differences between Australian and foreign values. *Phar Lap* represents its 'hero' as the victim of the struggle between, on the one hand, the Australian turf officials with their need to protect their privileged structure from infiltration and, on the other, the commercial imperatives of the American owner. Like Australia, Phar Lap is the subject of colonisation by European civilised values and American capitalism. Phar Lap is the champion of the working man in the film (although the 'class struggle' is implicitly depicted as free enterprise versus monopoly rather than labour against capital) but his death is not a triumphant one. Despite his defiant victory in the Melbourne Cup, his death is made, by the very structure of the narrative, inevitable.

As *Phar Lap* reveals, the nationalist discourse can be much more than just egalitarian; it can also naturalise certain proletarian values, whereby the authenticity of a working-class, unsophisticated way of life is preferred to those civilised values which are seen to be both the regrettable objectives of the Australian ruling class and the hallmarks of foreign, (particularly British) domination. The general type of the battler is the alternative to this—but he too is partly defined by the subordinate position that he occupies within society. As Wilkes points out in his discussion of the battler in Lawson:

> To deserve the title, a battler is not required to exert himself against a hostile world; he has only to occupy a lowly place in it. So in Lawson even the failures may come to seem honorific through their apartness from the privileged and the affluent.[21]

As Wilkes goes on to say, the battler and the larrikin become inverted heroes. Their class position and their consequent powerlessness can be seen as indices of their value, because these characteristics are indices also of their Australian-ness. The ideological effect of this will be examined later in this chapter, but it is clearly related to the legitimation of the politics of subordination as described in Chapters 2 and 3.

If nationalist constructions do support existing social and economic conditions—by naturalising and romanticising the battler, for instance, in order to disconnect the figure from a class position—this is not necessarily *all* that they do. Indeed, the case of *Snowy River* suggests that genuinely populist films—even nationalist ones—seem to have subversive potential. The notion of 'popularity' is open to several constructions; one can see it simply in terms of large scale commercial success, while another can see it as a resistant, subversive expression of the needs of a subordinated class.[22] Popular art, in this second formulation, is a rejection of the dominant bourgeois ideology, and such a view of the popular could explain some of the critical response to *Snowy River*. Certainly there seems to be a class motivation behind the critical reaction in the press, since its box-office success is in inverse proportion to its critical evaluation. It was called a 'tragedy', a 'costly, awful mess':

> Using 'clues' from the poem, the scriptwriters, John Dixon and Cul Cullen, have cobbled together a tenuous, puffed-out soap-operatic story about love and hate in the high country. I don't know what their brief demanded, but the evidence of the film suggests that the story was written to accommodate a number of commercial considerations—indeed that the script itself was little more than the realisation of a marketing plan.[23]

The references to commerce, to 'marketing', and to soap opera, seem to expose the film's 'crass commercialism', its lack of 'quality', as its weakness rather than as its thematic or ideological substance. While the film may indeed hold subordinated positions within its thematic, its rejection of 'quality' and its unashamed populism are also ideological. Like the ocker comedies, *Snowy River* attacks the dominant notions underlying the 'Australian film' (what Susan Dermody calls the AFI genre, typified by *Picnic* and *My Brilliant Career*[24]). Thus it is culturally important in that it establishes a connection between commercial success and a successful rejection of those pretensions towards high art which enclose most depictions of the Australian type. In a country where Lawson's populism is qualified by his perceived skill as a realist writer; where Tom Roberts' proletarian romanticism is acceptable since his oil paintings are clearly intended for gallery walls, *Gallipoli*'s intentions towards high art can be much more easily accepted than *Snowy River*'s populism:

> *Gallipoli* is the best film I've seen this year. The best film from anywhere. Nothing I have seen has moved me so much. Nothing has had the thematic virtue of *Gallipoli*.[25]

Clues to the basis of this judgement lie in its cultural cringe ('the best film from anywhere') and in its use of 'thematic virtue' (which merely indicates approval of the film's ideological position—anything but progressive). Despite the invocation of standards of excellence, this response is to approve the film's conservative, naturalising treatment of Australian history; so that it is not only the middle-brow nature of *Gallipoli*'s formal representation of the nation that protects it from the attacks directed at the vulgarity and crass parochialism of *The Man From Snowy River*. (Interestingly, the 'parochial' film did much better business overseas than its 'quality' competitor.)

Thus the meanings carried by nationalist discourse are not simple or self-evident. Certainly, the function of nationalism in a 'quality' film and the exploitation of it in a 'soap opera' is affected by the form: in the quality film, the high art, universalising, codes effectively cloak the political dimension of nationalism, by enabling the essentially egalitarian or proletarian myths to be connected with their opposite, the universalising and civilising notions of value. And so the discourses of nationalism are made acceptable. But this does not apply where the populist form articulates the mythic content in a different fashion. Even if one does not see populist art in Brechtian ways—as ultimately revolutionary—but (as Stuart Hall does) as a site of constant struggle between the dominant trying to contain the subordinate, and the subordinate attempting to resist this containment,[26] *Snowy River* does seem to resist containment sufficiently to alarm part of our film culture. One is tempted to examine *Snowy River* for oppositional content, for the ways in which it subverts hegemonic constructions of property or progress, in order to account for the response. But even without doing this, the conservative reaction to the film suggests that although nationalism does normally serve an hegemonic function, its articulation through popular representational forms provides it with the potential for recovering class divisions and for challenging the dominant points of view of the culture.

The historical connection between popular forms and the nationalism of the 1890s is a close one, and has not gone unnoticed. Indeed, the establishment's suspicion of, and reaction against, nationalism's discursive formations has probably contributed to nationalism's success in maintaining its sense of being oppositional and resistant—and even proletarian. Certainly there is a long history of Eurocentric, conservative attacks on nationalism—particularly in Australian literary criticism. There, the attacks are not framed in explicitly political terms but rather as disinterested and academic concern at the anachronistic and 'inappropriate' nature of these discourses for a civilised, developing, urban culture. Usually proceeding from the same elitist high culture position which Docker saw as controlling the Australian literary tradition, the anti-nationalist argument tends to resist the dominance of the egalitarian, rural, secular myth as one that is parochial, backward looking, and lacking in refinement. There is a sense that as a description of the 'real' Australia the nationalism of the 90s is inaccurate, and that as a description of the desired Australia it is unacceptable. Nationalism is an ideology and its cultural function is not to define Australia as a real entity but to represent Australia as an ideological construction. This is not often recognised in literary criticism. In *The Stockyard and the Croquet Lawn*, Wilkes complained about the unquestioned dominance of this mode of nationalism, 'other significant manifestations of it having been overlooked'.[27] We hear echoes of H. P. Heseltine, twenty years earlier, insisting that the myths embodied in Lawson's work were anachronistic: 'if all Lawson and his tribe can offer is mateship and proletarian protest', wrote Heseltine, then 'they must regretfully, even painfully, be relegated to the past'.[28] Judith Wright, while dismissing Paterson's ballads as 'colonial heroics', regrets the currency of the myth which his poems, among others, have created. Sounding just like the reviewers of *Snowy River*, she grudgingly accepts that the versions of heroism depicted in Paterson's poems have 'built themselves slyly into our characters'; but this, she continues, is a 'dubious legacy' which may take us 'another century to outgrow'.[29] Ann Hutton, too, talks of the archaic forms of nationalism in film, and asks for a 'cinematic identity more appropriate' to our age.[30]

Just as contemporary film critics prefer the nationalism of *Gallipoli* because it clearly has high art pretensions to that of *Snowy River* (which is populist), so Wright, Wilkes and Heseltine imply that there is better art upon which we might build our national ideologies. Apart from assuming that we can *choose* such things (as we can, apparently, choose the works which form our literary canon) this position also assumes that one can fix a nexus between artistic quality and cultural impact: what is seen as the meretriciousness of Paterson's poetry or of George Miller's film marks them out as threats to the culture—and so it immediately disqualifies them as important references to, and representations of, a central body of myth in our culture; and thus finally it is made to 'invalidate' that body of myth.

This kind of reaction against the cultural force of the myth of the 1890s and against more contemporary descendants (such as ockerism) is a strategy of containment. It is motivated by the elitist notion that popular art should not be part of our cultural capital. Further, it arises because cultural myths are seen in the most literal sense; that is, it is assumed that they can be 'disproved'. Behind Wilkes' often admirable and useful re-reading of Australia's cultural development, and behind Heseltine's seminal correction of orthodox accounts of our literary tradition, a notion clearly works that the 'Lawson-Furphy' tradition dominates our perception of the past by some kind of mistake. The received idea is wrong, and so let us correct the received idea. What

Heseltine saw as a distorted version of Australian writing, Wilkes sees as an historically incomplete version of Australian cultural development. Underlying Wilkes' approach is the assumption that the myth of the bushman, for instance, is available to empirical challenge. Yet it is widely accepted that the Australian of the 1890s was no more the mythologised figure produced by the nationalism of the 1890s than we are now.[31] The myth of the bushman was as much an urban invention as a rural fact, but its centrality to representations of Australia remains unaffected by the invocation of historical truth.

The view that the 'truth' matters here is itself mistaken. Our version of national character is not unmediated. History does not simply provide the environmental conditions from which certain dominant modes of behaviour naturally emerge. Rather, the culture is formed *both* by history and its representations. Representation is a discursive mediation which occurs between the event and the culture and which contributes to the construction of national ideologies. The articulation of these ideologies is the work of constellations and alliances of groups or interests which appropriate, transform and mythologise the specific terms of the legend as part of the labour of producing and determining meaning. The dominant version of Australian nationalism which some groups hope to 'outgrow' is not dominant because most Australians 'lived' it, or because it is an unmediated reflection of social conditions at any one point in time. Rather, it is dominant because it is currently accepted as the construction, the mode of signification, of nationalism in Australia. It provides the repertoire of representational codes, the discourses through which Australians currently agree to represent themselves and their country. Its importance is not finally as a reflection, or as a refraction, of the past, but as a construction of the present (fully enclosed within and mobilised by it.) As Jameson reminds us, 'our readings of the past are vitally dependent upon our experience of the present'.[32]

With this in mind, it is to the function of the specific terms of Australian nationalism that we should now direct our attention. Reactions such as those described above do, at least, reveal an intuitive awareness of the possible implications of the unquestioned dominance of these terms—their inherently regressive, reactionary nature. Despite the oppositional possibilities provided by such populist texts as *Snowy River*, the specific terms of the Australian legend characteristically offer a bogus plausibility for stasis, for acceptance. It does this by enclosing such an attitude of acceptance within the characterisation of the Australian type, as the legacy and achievement of the national past.

The key to the hegemonic function of nationalist discourse is the way in which it valorises Australian-ness as the privileged, desired term. This enables, for instance, even the worst aspects of Australian existence to be represented more or less naturalistically, with the proviso that these aspects be enclosed within a connotative framework which celebrates them as definitely Australian rather than explores them for opportunities of renovation. So, as Stephen Crofts protests, *Breaker Morant*'s convincing depiction of the cultural dependence of Australia upon Britain is used simply to celebrate the underdog's subjection ... by establishing it as an icon of Australian-ness—of 'manliness, comradeship and sardonic dignity'.[33] I have already pointed out that the depiction of the landscape does this too. Indeed, the nationalist invocation of 'Australianness' not only naturalises the conditions I have described but also treats them honorifically, as objects worthy of celebration.

Although we have not looked at the historical development of the bush legend in any detail (Tulloch, Rowse and McQueen all cover this in various ways that complicate the environmental determinism of Ward[34]) many accounts of nationalism in Australia point to the way in which its terms are appropriated and exploited by dominant interests. Amanda Lohrey's statement on this is characteristic:

> It's directly related to the judicious pruning of the Australian Legend to fit establishment ideology and the suppression of the potentially most vital part of it [unionism].[35]

Lohrey goes on to quote Jack Lindsay's claim that the 'falsification of the national character in terms of outdated attitudes is a mask for the deeper distortions of our reality'. Such accounts see the workings of hegemony as accomplished more by conspiracy than through 'cultural leadership', in Gramsci's phrase. Certainly, the displacement of our radical tradition into the past through the myths of the 1890s *is* an efficient way of keeping it there, yet it would be too simple to assume that only the dominant sections of Australian culture see this displacement as being in their interest. To suggest that one can separate oneself from the construction of national character is to excise one of the major ways of making meaning out of experience within that culture. Nationalism is a way of celebrating those aspects of national character which are current, and the celebration is one in which it is very difficult not to participate.

However, the political effect which Lohrey and Lindsay refer to is recognisable: that the celebration of this specific version of the national character has political consequences is made clear by Stephen Crofts. Crofts points to the problem which is inherent in 'heroizing' such portraits of the battler and the larrikin as we find in *Breaker Morant*:

... the promotion of the underdog, of the Aussie battler, brings the 'Australian character' perilously close to gallows humour. These are the traits which enlist sympathy for our heroes, which ensure a good laugh at corrupt authority, but which do nothing to challenge the real bases of that authority. This is close to the philosophy of 'She'll be right, mate'. To heroize the three lieutenants' doomed defiance is to make a jingoistic virtue out of a set of characteristics whose effect is to perpetuate the ruling order.[36]

My only addition to this would be to stress that this perpetuation of the ruling order is not simply the effect of the nationalist myth, but its essential function.

The myth of nationalism rooted in the 1890s operates as a discourse through which narrative can naturalise a grim and static view of the powerlessness of the individual within the Australian context—without for all that appearing in any way to proscribe or rule out other views of Australian experience, or without appearing to suggest that the endurance of that experience is anything but honourable. Nationalism, while appearing to act in a celebratory manner that could qualify or even negate the thematic patterns and ideological structures which I have examined in this study, in fact naturalises exactly these patterns and structures. The difference is that its account of the Australian predicament is represented as positive. The cultural significances are inverted by enclosing them within a discourse of national character, which is then privileged as the ultimate defining feature and celebrated wherever it is found as the ultimate value. As such, the nationalist myth provides us with a signal example of the operation of ideology in narrative, the ways in which conflicts and differences within Australian experience are 'resolved' by the simple invocation of the nation.

That this may not be the whole picture, however, is something of which I am aware. The vitality of nationalism—its connection with populist forms, and the continual struggle for its colonisation—suggests that it has elements within it which may be subversive. The disparity between the various opinions of *Snowy River* implies the existence of important divisions around what constitutes an Australian film—a topic which is itself usually enclosed within the discourse of nationalism. Certainly the existence of such divisions makes it necessary to admit possibilities of change, and to recognise the fact that the 'dominant' which I am describing is only able to maintain its dominance through a continual struggle against opposition. The concentration in this study on dominant patterns inevitably leads to potentially monistic conclusions, tending to funnel all aspects being considered into a single pattern. To concentrate on one area in an attempt to establish its importance is legitimate. However, to conclude this study without some account of other, possibly contradictory, models of

126 *National fictions*

Australian experience in our narratives would be to unnecessarily circumscribe the point of view of the study. Thus I now want to entertain the proposition that there may generally be more complicating factors surrounding the generation of meaning in Australian narrative than the ones which I have so far considered.

NOTES

1. *The Legend of the Nineties*; Heseltine's 'The Australian Image: The Literary Heritage'.
2. 'A Blue Plaque for the Labour Movement? Some Political Meanings of the National Past', in *Formations of Nation and People* (London: Routledge and Kegan Paul, 1984), p.47.
3. Exemplary would be the account of ideology and hegemony given in Stuart Hall's 'The rediscovery of ideology: the return of the Repressed in media studies', in Gurevich et al. (eds) *Culture, Society and the Media*, pp.56–90.
4. Amanda Lohrey, '*Gallipoli*: Male Innocence as a Marketable Commodity', *Island Magazine*, 9/10, (March 1982), pp.29–34.
5. A. A. Phillips, *The Australian Tradition* would be the central example of this approach.
6. op. cit. p.52.
7. The account of Ward, Phillips, Palmer, and the argument with these positions presented in McQueen, Wilkes, Wilding and others provides the context I have in mind. There seems to be little need to restate the radical nationalist position or the arguments against it.
8. p.257.
9. *Inventing Australia*, p.viii.
10. Wilkes, *The Stockyard and the Croquet Lawn*, p.87.
11. Robert Hughes, *The Art of Australia* (Ringwood: Penguin, 1970), p.59.
12. ibid. p.68.
13. I have in mind the invocation of the figure of the 'bushman' at the novel's end.
14. *Legends on the Screen*.
15. *Cinema Papers*, 10, centrefold; *Cinema Papers*, 15, p.249; Sue Matthews, *35 MM Dreams*, p.141.
16. Jack Clancy, 'Breaker Morant' *Cinema Papers*, 28 (August–September 1981), p.283; Max Harris, 'Banjo Would have Hated it' *Weekend Australian Magazine*, (27 March 1982), p.7.
17. Wilkes, p.2.
18. 'Breaker Morant Rethought: Eighty Years On The Culture Still Cringes' *Cinema Papers*, 30, (Dec.–Jan. 1980–81), pp.420–1.
19. 'Ride The High Country: In and Around *The Man From Snowy River*' *Filmnews*, (September 1982.)
20. 'Parents and Orphans', *Cinema Papers*, 42, (March 1983), pp.50–2.
21. p.87.
22. See Tim O'Sullivan et. al. *Key Concepts in Communication* (London: Methuen, 1983), pp.174–6.
23. John Hindle, 'Galloping Soapie in the High Country' *The National Times*,

(28 March–3 April 1982), p.40. It is worth noting that sections of the press more comfortable with popular art (*Cinema Papers*, 38, pp.261–2, and *Rolling Stone*, 352, pp.63–4) were more impressed by the film.
24 With Elizabeth Jacka, forthcoming, *Screening Australia*.
25 John Hindle, 'The Best of the Year', *The National Times*, (August 16–22 1981), p.33.
26 'Notes on Deconstructing the Popular' in Samuel, R. (ed.) *People's History and Socialist Theory* (London: Routledge and Kegan Paul, 1981).
27 p.2.
28 'The Literary Heritage', p.87.
29 *Preoccupations in Australian Poetry*, p.82.
30 'Nationalism in Australian Film', p.153.
31 R. M. Crawford, for one of many possible examples, 'The Birth of a Culture' in *The Australian Nationalists*, p.34–5.
32 Frederic Jameson, *The Political Unconscious*, p.11.
33 ibid. p.420.
34 *Legends on the Screen, Australian Liberalism and National Character*, and *A New Britannia*, are the works I have in mind.
35 op. cit. p.34.
36 op. cit. p.420.

6 *Complications and Conclusions*

The problem of change, of the way in which hegemonic systems can be opposed and altered, has constantly dogged Marxist theory. The standard criticism of Althusserian models of cultural production, for instance, is that the process of overdetermination seems too comprehensive; the effect of such models, it is claimed, is to deny the dialectical process of history.[1] The tendency in Marxist theory to construct a model of a total system (which we can see in Michel Foucault's work for instance) is problematic. The most important of the problems which arise is the tendency to 'eliminate any possibility of the *negative* as such, and to reintegrate the place of an oppositional or even merely critical practice and resistance back into the system as the latter's mere inversion'.[2] The *Screen* debate on realism and the 'progressive text' over the BBC series *Days of Hope* falls into this category, as it rules out the possibility of realism ever being used for other than bourgeois, hegemonic ends.[3] This present study, too, may seem to concentrate overmuch on the totality of the system, denying change. Therefore, before concluding, it is important that we acknowledge some of the other possibilities in Australian narrative as a way of opening out at least some areas for change. In so doing, we also reinforce the theoretical admission of difference within the culture, between particular readings of narrative, and between narratives themselves.

Film and fiction have so far been treated as contributors to a larger system, the emphasis having been placed on their similarities rather than their differences as narrative forms and as generators of meaning. Yet the application of developmental models to the study of film and fiction in Australia reveals important differences. At the simplest level, it is possible to see Australian fiction at a point now (in 1986) as composed of a wide variety of styles and conventions, and as composed of a number of individualised voices whose utterances resist being pulled back into the general pattern. Most critics would find it difficult to see contemporary film in this way. Instead, the search for

Complications and conclusions 129

homologies between Australian film and fiction inevitably leads one to the fiction of fifty years ago—the period in which Australian fiction was slowly emerging from the double shadow of nationalism and the cultural cringe to focus attention on contemporary Australian life. If cultural forms necessarily 'mature'—as the evolutionary model has it—then Australian fiction must now be at a later stage of maturity than Australian film. An inference from this, if it was acceptable, would be that Australian film has ahead of it the same kind of development and individuality that Australian fiction could be argued to enjoy at the present. However, the forms *are* different; they are the product of very different industries and although they both serve the function of narrative they do so by providing very different forms of pleasure for their audiences. To see contemporary Australian cinema as having so far 'failed' to produce its Patrick White or Peter Carey is to misunderstand the conditions which determine the development and the language of the two media.

Further limitations of this kind of developmental view—and I admit to having argued it elsewhere myself[4]—lie in the fact that it depends upon a progressive model of history that not only asserts the inevitability of change but also connects that change with progress. This present study does not rest on such a model of history, although I do recognise the usefulness of such approaches in explaining the recurrence of particular modes and thematics across a range of very different media and representational forms. What an historical survey can reveal is not simply the evolutionary course of a medium or its messages. Here, such a survey is useful in that it reveals the existence of narratives of a different kind to those so far discussed. Thus this sort of survey makes it possible to see how the incidence of oppositional, critical stances towards the dominant structure has fluctuated. In other words, it reveals the more dialectical movements within the body of Australian narrative.

Two separate areas of development in contemporary film and fiction, in particular, suggest possibilities of narrative form and meaning that are not necessarily homologous with the account that I have given so far: in the first place, we have the increasingly critical focus on urban, social and political subjects in Australian film; and in the second place, the formal influence of fantasy, metafiction and 'fabulation' in Australian fiction. These two areas, while perhaps not the only two which one could choose, do remind us of the possibilities of change at the same time as they provide possible complications to the conclusions of this study.

Treatment of bush subjects dominates the film industry of the 1920s and 1930s. The subsequent movement into more contemporary urban dramas (in the 1930s and 1940s) was associated with the Australian industry's attempt to make more Hollywood-styled 'international' movies in order to survive. The superficiality of these films' examination of Australian contemporary life means we do not have a strong tradition of films which deal seriously with contemporary realities. It is the use of history, and the *construction* of contemporary Australian life through the representation of the past that is the dominant mode in our film tradition—and this sort of treatment is becoming once more dominant in the current productions of the television mini-series. During the revival of the 1970s, there was only a handful of films which concerned themselves with contemporary urban life on a level which could be called critical or analytic. With the significant exception of Bert Deling's *Pure S* and perhaps Esben Storm's *27A*—neither of which gained widespread release—we would have to look to the ocker comedies such as *Stork* (1971) or else to the quartet of scripts by literary writers, *Libido* (1973). The release of Michael Thornhill's *The FJ Holden* (1977) and John Duigan's *Mouth to Mouth* (1978) stand out as rare examples of attempts to describe and capture the problems of contemporary urban and suburban existence in Australia. Thornhill's film was not generally well received, although it documents the rituals of teenage life in Sydney's western suburbs with accuracy and affection and allows its world to retain a sense of authenticity while revealing its essential deprivation. Susan Dermody's *Cinema Papers* review recorded her elation at the film's 'use of its material'; and she also noted the critical nature of its depiction of suburban life:

> ... the lives we look at are teeming with details and impulses; yet they are resoundingly empty, uninhabited spaces, unaware of the possibility of conscious action altering the pattern of existence.[5]

It is a familiar thematic, and Rod Bishop and Fiona Mackie also refer to it by discussing *FJ Holden* as a film which projects the image of the battler, struggling against 'oppressive environments'.[6] The film does, to some extent, celebrate the life it documents—as its reception indicates (it did not do well in city theatres but was extremely successful in the drive-ins, doing 90 per cent of its business there).[7] However, *FJ Holden* does not simply naturalise its subject. The emotional constriction of the characters, the poverty of communication between them, stand out rather as images of oppression and of the diminution of possibility; and despite the humour and vitality of the film these images linger. And yet the film is not as committed an attack on Australian society as Thornhill's earlier *Between Wars* (1974), where similar principles of conservatism and conformism came in for more political analysis.

Mouth to Mouth is a more critical film. Although it occasionally does romanticise the predicament of the unemployed—notably in the last shots of Carrie walking past the dream-filled windows of city stores, with the romantic song lyrics underlining her personal love problem— the film is still a genuine stylistic departure from the norms which had been set in Australian cinema. Unlike Donald Crombie's lyrical treatment of the urban slums of the depression in *Caddie*, John Duigan's depiction of the world of the four young unemployed characters in contemporary Melbourne is anything but affectionate. *Mouth to Mouth* was shot by Tom Cowan—whose camera work in *Pure S* was largely responsible for its savage effect on its audience. Although less confrontational than *Pure S* and less unpleasant to watch, *Mouth to Mouth* also presents us with a world which is filled with wreckage—building sites, litter-filled tenement backyards, neglected houses, abandoned buildings, railway yards with rusting rolling stock, shattered families ... and also the aspirations of the main characters. The lighting is insistently dim, the few daylit exteriors operating as much needed relief from the claustrophobic effect of the rest of the film. The world of the unemployed is seen as separate from that of the normal middle-class Australian, even though it is ruled by the same images of success. The attempt to gain entry into this normal world dominates the four characters' lives; and their dependence on its definition of a useful life is underlined in various ways: Carrie's efforts are stimulated by her envy for the surroundings enjoyed by her clients, and her need for a romantic relationship with Tony; Tim and Serge's attempts to find work punctuate the film as regular reminders of the cycle of hope and frustration which dominates their lives.

Duigan's view of the Australian context is consistent with that outlined in the second chapter, and it presents the promises of Australia as an ironic, impossible joke for these young people. A sign over Jeanie's bed in the abandoned warehouse (if that is what it is; significantly, its previous function is never made clear) promises 'satisfaction as big as our land'. It refers to her emotional generosity, of course— but it also emphasises the improbability of any other forms of satisfaction ever being allowed them, while ironically underlining the characters' progressive marginalisation within a society that has no place for the unemployed even as it creates them. Even liberal principles are seen as a luxury, as the demonstration outside their squat is given the ambience of a family picnic. The extent of the callousness with which society can treat its victims is established in the gratuitous murder of the old man, Fred, who has cared for Carrie when she needed help, and in whom she recognises her own possible fate. There is little that is romantic about the world of the film; it is visually grainy and dark, and thematically grim; the characters' relationships are born out of desperation, out of the need for companionship in times of stress. *Mouth to Mouth* is not as anarchic or aggressive as *Pure S*, but it *is* more aware of the political construction of its subjects' lives.

On its release, *Mouth to Mouth*'s departure from the existing precedents was noted: Jack Clancy wrote in *Cinema Papers*: 'We have not seen anything like this in Australian films', and he commended its 'combination of compassionate observation, social concern and behavioural truth'.[8] The film was the first of its kind to suggest the usefulness of documentary realism (although its enclosure within this convention is qualified by such factors as the rapid cutting pattern) when applied to the excluded forms of Australian life, to those aspects of existence which are not part of the consensual view of the Australian way. The disconnection of documentary realism from representations of the past is thus the significant achievement of *Mouth to Mouth*.

Critiques of realism argue that it is a form which privileges one organising view of the real, which the reader accepts in order to make sense of the narrative. Consequently realism is a form which is incapable of expressing criticism—of producing a contradiction which, while remaining unresolved, would still oblige the viewers to think for themselves.[9] This position has been argued, as mentioned earlier, in relation to the political progressiveness of the BBC's leftist reconstruction of labour politics in the television series, *Days of Hope*. Such a position might also qualify our sense of *Mouth to Mouth*'s progressiveness; however, while realism may be a more bourgeois, naturalising form than the 'interrogative text' (which questions the natural views of reality) there is still doubt as to how legitimately we can 'read off' the ideology of a film—or any text—from its choice of form.[10] If realism *is* able to privilege its view of history, then it may *also* have the potential to propose an oppositional or alternative view of history which is itself naturalised by the form. *Mouth to Mouth* is realist in form, yet its conception of Australian life is not entirely contained within dominant constructions. The disjunction between its view and the dominant views is mediated by the form, so that *Mouth to Mouth* exploits its documentary style to express opposition. Rather than simply naturalising existing social conditions, *Mouth to Mouth* attempts to interrogate them. It does this by forcing us to recognise the existence of a form of life which is produced by basic divisions within Australian society, but which is denied by that society.

Although *Mouth to Mouth* stands slightly outside the patterns of representation as outlined in this study, its meaning is still consonant with that exposed in our third chapter. The film is significant, however, in suggesting new uses for the dominant formal conventions and in opening out new areas of subject matter. As we continue into the 1980s, the incidence of films dealing with contemporary urban Australia and with particular, often marginalised, sections of that context, increases. For instance, migrant experiences occupy Paul Cox's *Kostas* (1979) and Michael Pattinson's *Moving Out* (1982); the obsessive relationships of the subcultures of Carlton and Fitzroy dominate the film version of Helen Garner's *Monkey Grip* (1981); the gap between the worlds of the middle class and of the streets is again John Duigan's subject in *Winter of Our Dreams* (1981); the structures of oppression and exploitation link the worlds of the small-time criminal and the aspiring model in Don McLennan's *Hard Knocks* (1980); and David Pattins' documentary style provides a case study of a day in the life of a VD clinic in *The Clinic* (1983).

These are not radical but popular films which may collectively imply the renovation of the filmic representation of life in Australia by their enfranchising of new, potentially oppositional, class and gender positions. *The Clinic* is remarkable for, among other things, depicting the main character as normal, well-balanced, admirable *and* homosexual; the diagnosis of Sam's attempt to transcend her criminal background and her gender in *Hard Knocks* is presented from a point of view which is uncompromisingly critical of the society in which it takes place. The realist visual style toughens up the point of view of *Monkey Grip*: the 'true romance' voice-over threatens to send the film into the most mawkish of modes, despite its trendy setting, but it is rescued by its visual depiction of the grimmer aspects of the life within the urban subculture.

Although the dominant conventions in such films are still those of realism, they are often put to uses which challenge the viewers' comfortable expectations—which asks them to question rather than to comfortably 'know'. *Hard Knocks* juxtaposes 'before' and 'after' images of the main character in order to set up expectations of the gradual unfolding of a 'rags to riches' success story, of the reformed criminal who becomes the successful model. But these expectations are eventually revealed to be naive. The end of the film has Sam under attack from those who wish to exploit her in the modelling world; from her friends from the prison who resent her attempt to break out of her criminal context; and from the police who refuse to see her as anything but a criminal. We are strongly encouraged to identify with Sam in her entrapment (more than we are with Lou in *Winter of Our Dreams*, for instance) and the dominant emotions aroused by the film are those of frustration and anger.

The argument about the progressive, critical and oppositional potential of realism (which is by no means over) may thus require a special application in so far as the history of Australian film is concerned—

One of the new directions in contemporary Australian cinema: Alyson Best and Norman Kaye in Paul Cox's 'Man of Flowers' (1983). (*With kind permission of Paul Cox*)

since realism here has been so closely connected with representations of the past, and since contemporary life has occupied so little of the screen. Within such a tradition, and given the established convention of realism's signification of historical truth, the realist depiction of non-consensual views of life which construct the identification between the viewer and the characters living that life may well be interrogative, proposing rather a critical analysis of Australian society. It is also clear that the formal break from realism can carry with it the potential for dislodging the viewer from a comfortable position of knowing and accepting—a position that is related to both the narrative and the world that it represents. The value of dislodging the viewer from this position, and the expansion of the ability to shock and confront which results, is readily apparent in Hayden Keenan's *Going Down* (1983). Initially *Going Down* is reminiscent of *Pure S*, but its realist form gradually evolves into comic fantasy, into an exhilarating riot of invention. Its style is aggressive and confrontational (when on its first run in Sydney, those passing the cinema were harangued by a man who warned them not to see the film, because 'it will damage your mind') and in some scenes shocking, but its omnivorous appetite for the life that it represents is irresistible. Formally, *Going Down* is a signal reminder of the value of departing from the established norms and practices. The film begins with two lengthy handheld shots which take us through the rooms of a seedy communal house, recording the ephemera of the characters' world in documentary, if rapid, fashion. As the film develops, the objective, documentary use of the camera diminishes, and the tempo of the cutting increases. The range of images and content widens, and any residually realist conventions are finally exploded in the high comedy of the journey to the airport. The level of invention and artifice is gradually revved up through this film, foregrounding its function as a display and celebration of the medium and of its ability to transform the real.

The formal possibilities exploited in *Going Down* are also apparent in formal features which have been noticeable for some time in Australian fiction—although this is not to argue that the two trends are necessarily related. However, it is certainly true that the realist style is no longer dominant in contemporary Australian fiction. The seeds of realism's demise lie in the 1950s and particularly in the novels of Patrick White. Thematically, White challenged the natural and agreed 'truths' about existence. Formally, his infiltration of an essentially poetic, metaphoric coherence into his fictions complicates what is otherwise a realist style and enables him to offer rare suggestions of 'transcendence'.[11] White's use of fable as a structural convention has been noted—and fable is a universalising alternative to realism.[12] Fable proposes the lack of cultural difference between human societies in order to focus on those common, metaphysical principles which are seen to be immanent in all human existence. In White, this process can be almost reactionary, but more radical exploitation of the possibilities of formal invention has now become common. In younger writers, the foregrounding of the manipulation of language and of 'fabulation',[13] (that is, the creation of narratives which depend less on their referential dimension than on the arbitrary construction of stories and worlds for their own sake) has become important. The influence of American fabulists such as John Barth, Kurt Vonnegut, and Tom Robbins—writers whose work is inherently individualist—can be seen in the prominence of verbal style in much contemporary fiction and in the increasing application of black humour—which, importantly, operates as a signifier of resistance rather than of acceptance.

Peter Carey's work is a key example of this trend. His novel, *Bliss*, depends more on the metaphorical felicities of its inventions than on sharp social observation, although its world is by no means totally removed from our own. *Bliss*, like many of Carey's shorter pieces, has a definite nationalist tinge. It depicts Australia as being colonised by 'the Americans'; in this process, the natural indigenous remnants of Australian life are the good, and the 'imported shit' is the bad. The novel's relation to the conventional myths of Australian existence, however, is ambivalent. On the one hand, the novel sets up the condition of the archetypal 'Good Bloke', Harry Joy, who seems to represent all the Australian virtues:

> Harry Joy was not particularly intelligent, not particularly successful, not particularly handsome, and not particularly rich. Yet there was about him this feeling that he belonged to an elite and for no good reason (none that Bettina could see) he was curiously proud of himself.[14]

This summary of the 'middling standard' could, if supported, be open to the kind of criticism that Crofts directs at *Breaker Morant*. However, in *Bliss* we see the powerlessness behind it:

> He had known the quiet superiority of being a Good Bloke. But beside this there was a nagging doubt that something was missing from him, that he suffered an impotence. For instance, when he saw a chair raised above a head in a movie he felt excitement and resentment that this passion was denied him. When Bettina became angry he felt a jealousy. When she threw a plate, he envied her. (160)

By the novel's end, Harry Joy has taken a different direction, and the novel rebuilds the familiar figure of the bushman in order to mythologise the condition into which the hero has escaped:

> He did not become a leader or a strange man with a long white robe, not a shaman, a magician or a priest. He was a bushman. He was a bushman in the way he stood with one leg out and the back of his wrist propped on his hip. He dug holes, used flooded gum trees to outgrow and conquer the groundsel weed; he won Clive's respect by the energy with which he helped at the mill, where they cut packing case timber from blackbutt and sold it to pineapple farmers in the world outside. (277)

There are important differences between Carey's bushman and Lawson's—no mateship, for one thing—but the novel's primary resolution does move towards the pantheism of the idyll in nature. It is, fortunately, more complex than this, for Harry has other ways of making meaning.

In *Bliss*, the role of story, of fiction itself, is essential to the creation and communication of meaning. The stories of Vance Joy, and later of Harry Joy, have the magical properties of myth. And what they offer are alternative meanings and alternative values to those of the society. The novel's style, foregrounded as an invention rather than as a reflection of the real, is consonant with the thematic assertion of the necessity for reinventing reality. A strong tradition of metafiction[15] (which is fiction proposing the fictiveness of both fiction and reality) exists in the United States and can be examined in such writers as Vonnegut, Robbins and Barth, as well as in the more elaborate South American fabulists such as Marquez. These writers see their role as resisting even the discourses through which fiction normally deals with reality —so as to assert instead the priority of the self over its social and ethical context. One of the characters in *Slaughterhouse Five* tells a psychiatrist that he will have to come up with 'some new lies' if he wants people to go on living—and Vonnegut and others seem to accept this challenge as one which confronts the writer too.[16] By working within this tradition, *Bliss* inevitably proposes an existentialist, or absurdist, alternative to realism—which is that of exploiting the resources of the self to construct reality.

This proposition is largely responsible for the optimistic and even magical conclusion to the novel, which places the narrative in the specific context of legend. Although superficially similar, the return to the land at the end of *Bliss* can be seen to have different implications to the endings of *Voss* or *To the Islands*: Harry Joy may find his resolution in the land, but this is not a discovery necessarily intrinsic to the natural world—rather, it is made possible by the ways of inventing meanings which this alternative social structure can value. If this new formulation is convincing this is because the novel manages to separate itself from the conventional use of the land as an alternative image of society.

A conventional use of the alternative of nature would also seem to be implicated in the ending of David Malouf's *An Imaginary Life*. Despite its setting on the fringes of the Roman Empire, *An Imaginary Life* is a novel which can be seen to refer to and derive from Australian experience in detailed ways; its resolution of the problem of exile in the antipodes by submersion in the land has a long lineage in Australian narrative. Yet there is a more positive, less resigned sense of acceptance at the end of *An Imaginary Life* than in most Australian fiction. Ovid's death in nature is not so much an acceptance of defeat or a signifier of accommodation as a kind of reconciliation between the poet and those sources of life which he has hitherto regarded as beneath his civilised attention. What Ovid learns in *An Imaginary Life* is not simply how to accept his own defeat in death, but how to live 'authentically', and thus he can eventually face death as simply another of those changes for which he must be ready. Unlike much of the fiction discussed in the third chapter, the knowledge won in this novel is implicitly existentialist. Ovid chooses to 'belong to this place now. I have made it mine. I am entering the dimensions of my self.'[17]

Like *Bliss*, *An Imaginary Life* foregrounds its style and its status as fiction. Its language is not that of the realistic novel or of history; it is the language of legend and myth. It has an elegaic and impressionistic quality, its clauses looping together to connect and complicate the impressions which they register. Although the novel draws much of its significance from the construction of analogies with contemporary

Australia, the world which it represents is the product of fantasy.

The thematic influences of existentialism and of individualism, and the stylistic influence of fantasy and black humour, are more in evidence in Australian fiction now than at any previous point. They are not, however, the only modes in which we encounter the depiction of the 'authentic' life, which bases itself on a firm conception of the subject and of the context. Patrick White's 'tale of survival',[18] *A Fringe of Leaves*, presents an uncharacteristically optimistic portrait of its main character, Ellen Roxburgh, and of her gradual development to free herself from the social and ethical constraints around her. The ending of that novel may not present her suggested union with Mr Jevons as a romantic solution, but neither is her ability to make independent assessments of her situation that of a victim. At the end of *A Fringe of Leaves*, as at the end of *The Tree of Man*, life goes on; the difference is that its continuity is not symbolised by the cycle of the seasons and the permanence of nature, but by the sheer resilience which sustains the protagonist.

In narratives which seem able to propose critical reformulations of the dominant structures, the foregrounding of the individual style of the narrative—visual, verbal, structural—is important. The foregrounding of style can have a confronting, individualising effect, challenging the reader's ability to make sense of the text's view of the real. Realism presents itself as natural, as not a style at all; and in it there is a minimum of mediation between the material and the reader. The adoption of styles which attack, oppose or fracture realist expectations carries with it considerable potential for giving to the point of view of the text a putative sense of autonomy, by reducing its referential dimension and dramatising its role as fiction. This reduction of the referential dimension is less possible in film than in fiction—even the film version of Carey's *Bliss* (1985) is more naturalistic than the novel—and the movements described have different ideological determinants in the two media. However, both the use of fantasy and black humour in fiction and the film's appropriation of clearly generic narrative styles—in *Mad Max* (1979), *Starstruck* (1981) and *The Man From Snowy River* (1982)—currently share the potential to dislodge the reader and to create space for alternative constructions.

Hebdidge has talked of the style of subcultural groups—the dress and the music of punk—as offering 'gestures of refusal'; the display of membership to a subculture in clothing, behaviour, rituals and so on is to Hebdidge a 'form of resistance in which experienced contradictions and objections to ... ruling ideology are obliquely represented in style'.[19] Although it is possible to see such gestures as recognitions of the impossibility of any other form of defiance, there is within

Hebdidge's view a reminder of the continual immanence of change within culture—an immanence of change which must qualify any description of dominant patterns such as the ones we have detected here. As Hebdige points out, the emphasis on 'integration and coherence at the expense of dissonance and discontinuity'[20] can be misleading. Nevertheless, the foregrounding of style in literary fiction does not automatically serve analogous functions to those he sees in subcultural behaviour; style is, after all, connected with those individualist myths of the artist that are universalising and privileging, and one is wary of drawing too many conclusions from the marginal movement that we are discussing.

It does remain true, however, that the dislocating effects of American black humour are customarily talked of as strategies of resistance—of assertions of the self against society—and as a denial of those established systems of meaning which frustrate the imperatives of the romantic, individualised, American version of the self.[21] As such, American black humour infers very different models of the relation between self and society than those characteristic of Australian fiction. Its appropriation by Australian writers, together with the use of fantasy, has the potential of shading the primary tones which I have used to paint the landscape of the Australian narrative. In film, also, the foregrounding of satire, pastiche, and intertextual references that celebrate the fictional status of *Goodbye Paradise* (1982), or else the explosion of documentary realism into absurdist fantasy in *Going Down*, or again the deliberately elitist inscription of the film-maker as artist in Paul Cox's films (which motivates Cox's obsession with visual style)—all these have similar potentialities, albeit with less homogeneous ideological functions.

These examples present genuine challenges to the dominant structures I have described, but they are challenges which inevitably take place within the frame of those structures. Their importance is neither to be denied, nor over-estimated. The process of their analysis, inevitably draws upon the patterns which I have outlined in earlier chapters. As in the expression of the subculture, the foregrounding of either 'group' or individualised experience is still contained within the general framework of meanings of the culture—which may be the subject of renovation or resistance but which still strives to appropriate these group expressions as its own. So, despite the use of fantasy in Carey's stories for example, their general thematic remains one that is nevertheless entirely familiar. Although Carey's style works at stripping meaning away from rather than naturalising existing meanings, the portrait of the individual which emerges from, say, 'The Fat Man in History', or 'Chance', or 'American Dreams', is one which emphasises isolation, entrapment, and the failure of community.[22] And despite

Cox's universalising, European aestheticism, the characters in *Man of Flowers* (1983) and in *My First Wife* (1984) are given a definitively social lesson in acceptance and endurance. In *Hard Knocks*, the definition of class position literally invokes the stigma of convictism, both in general and in a specific scene—the one where Sam overhears the agency boss calling her a 'convict' (and therefore 'used to screws') while arranging her sexual exploitation with another man.

Not only is it necessary to remind oneself of the large frame within which these apparently contradictory representations are constructed, but one also needs to be aware that what may be represented to the reader or viewer as a critical point of view may operate structurally as a means of naturalising acceptance of existing conditions, of winning assent. The role of 'Australian' humour, for instance, is characteristically seen to act as a goad against hegemonic constructions, exposing contradictions, and undermining the authorities and institutions which control us.[23] This is premisely what American black humour claimed to do, by connecting itself with an individualistic ethic that asserted the priority of the self over the society. American black humour claimed to subvert as well as mock. But instead of doing this, most of the humour within *Australian* narratives turns back on itself, to sugar the pill and ensure the acceptance of powerlessness. A comparison between two 'Vietnam' films made by the two different cultures, *The Odd Angry Shot* (1979) and *M*A*S*H* (1970), immediately demonstrates the difference—both formal and ideological—between the two treatments. The stereotype of Australian humour as wry laughter in the face of adversity is more a description of a mode of *surviving* those conditions rather than an attempt to *subvert* them. Stan Cross's celebrated cartoon depicts two men hanging from a beam projecting from the upper storey of a tall building. The lower of the two men is hanging onto the other's legs, laughing as the other's pants come down—and the caption reads 'For Gorsake, stop laughing, this is serious'. The cartoon can be seen as quintessentially Australian: to laugh at the predicament can be seen as typically Australian, while to suggest that the two men should stop laughing so they can do something about the predicament is not.

A characteristic example of the naturalising process of humour, although drawn from an essentially dramatic narrative, occurs in *Sunday Too Far Away*. At the film's end, Foley has failed to ring the shed and has blown all his money, leaving no prospect of escape. The strikers have gathered to meet the trainload of scabs coming to take their jobs and thus threaten the success of the strike. Most of the shearers stand by passively, but Foley, conscious of his now dubious role as leader, tries to deter the scabs. They ignore him, walking off to the pub while Foley shouts after them with as much dignity as a dog barking at a car. As he turns back to the group, flushed and indignant, one of them says 'That was pissweak'. Foley puts his fist to the man's jaw in mock threat, acknowledging the validity of the comment, and the group dissolves in laughter. Foley's quixotic pretensions are thus cut down to size (it is one of the means by which he is collapsed back into the group) and the group thereby finds some relief in being able to confront their own powerlessness to change the situation. All that is left then is the defiant gesture, the fight in the pub that concludes the film's action. Within the point of view of the film, such humour is not made to appear passive or gallows-like but as admirable, as proceeding from a sense of proportion that is only possible when one is able to detach oneself from the condition of being mocked. The remark's trenchant realism ('pissweak') is seen as a consoling and recognisable Australian virtue. The humour, in other words, enhances the viewer's identification with the shearers by clearly establishing them as the underdogs, and thus it has an important function in the narrative. If it subverts anything, it is the shearers', and by extension the viewers', hopes of ever being able to control their own conditions.

In films which are formally comic, the comedy does not normally operate subversively either. *The Adventures of Barry McKenzie* (1972) lampoons the Australian type in such a way as to make it open to a number of readings. In Britain it confirmed all the popular stereotypes of the 'stage Australian', and exposed it to ridicule; in Australia, it was either seen as terminally vulgar, or as attempting to propose an ocker critique of the English—one in which Bazza becomes a lovable if exaggerated representative of Australianism who succeeds in defining that quality in the most conventional of ways, in opposition to British values. While satiric in mode, the film however is also capable of a celebratory construction, of an affectionate mythologising of the Australian abroad. As such, it would then present an assertion of national identity rather than a critique of it.

A more sophisticated example of this process is the film version of David Williamson's play, *Don's Party* (1976). The transfer to the more intimate medium of film provides the script with greater potential for criticism; the camera's survey of Ray Barrett's cratered and dissolute face, for instance, is capable of generating a more physical sense of failure than is possible from the stage. Yet the more aggressively Australian characters—such as Mac—are positioned against the more civilised, European characters—such as Simon—in order precisely to reconfirm the former's greater authenticity and thus acceptability. Mac's portrait is affectionate, while Simon is enthusiastically routed and his wife offered the definitively masculine version of liberation, going to bed with Mac. As G. A. Wilkes points out in some general comments about Williamson's plays, the writer 'delights in the stereotypes he depicts', and provides no intimation that he has 'spent sleepless nights worrying about the condition of the middle classes or the anti-intellectual quality of Australian life'. The effect of Williamson's plays—and, I would argue, also those films that he has scripted—is 'still celebratory'.[24]

While one can detect ameliorating, progressive or oppositional aspects in Australian narrative by viewing it developmentally, this does not radically qualify the outline of the dominant ideologies evident in the narrative structures examined in this study—although it does remind us that ideology 'leaks'. That there are a number of conflicts and contradictions, and that the possible readings of those texts which support the dominant ideologies are potentially various, is admitted. This is not, in my view, a denial of the validity of the structures which I have outlined, but simply a recognition that they are built in order to integrate and resolve potentially conflicting positions and that these structures are neither monolithic nor permanent.

The theory of narrative which has informed this book is one that insists on the connection between the individual narratives on the one hand and the culture which produces them on the other. Narrative has been seen as serving a function which is analogous to that which Levi-Strauss ascribes to myth. It provides a symbolic resolution to a social contradiction, and is one of the major areas of the labour of representation within the culture, performing the ideological work of 'making things mean'.[25] Narrative thus is an epistemological category, one of the means through which we construct our world. Its relationship to ideology is clear, as Frederic Jameson points out:

> ... ideology is not something which informs or invests symbolic production; rather the aesthetic act is itself ideological, and the production of aesthetic or narrative form is to be seen as an ideological act in its own right, with the function of inventing imaginary or formal 'solutions' to unresolvable social contradictions.[26]

Although one can agree with Stephen Heath in his assessment that the meaning of narrative art in film is not totally reducible to ideology;[27] and although one is aware that the kinds of arguments being made in this study are more valuable for stressing similarities than differences and for enquiring into a large body of writing or film-making rather than into the individual text in either medium—yet the picture of Australian narrative which emerges does carry important suggestions about the nature of the meanings which Australian culture produces for itself.

The pattern extracted in this study may seem a grim one. The view of form and meaning in Australian narrative which I have outlined in the preceding chapters is one which suggests that the commonsense notions of Australian experience (as being harsh but worthwhile, eliciting realistic expectations of a modest level of survival rather than romantic or naive notions of transcending one's physical conditions) and the commonsense notion of the 'Australian type' (as resourceful, tough, possessing an independence and individualism that does not preclude a sense of community and 'mateship') are consoling inventions. The function of these constructions is to encourage assent to a system which consistently privileges the good of the community (however that is represented) over and above the good of the individual—even though the individual characteristically finds these two principles opposed to each other. The level of disaffection with the Australian context which thus marks the representation of the self in narrative is in fact radically inconsistent with the assertion of the value of *authentic* Australian experience—something which marks much, particularly populist, Australian narrative. Thematic representations of the self's powerlessness and isolation are juxtaposed against the idea of one's resourcefulness and commitment to community; and the resolution of this contradiction in favour of acceptance and accommodation is made possible by the effective denial of the contradiction's importance. The ideology of the pragmatic, resourceful self runs completely counter to those very kinds of meaning and power which are represented as being beyond the individual's reach, thus encouraging scepticism about both meaning and power.

Hence the common assumption that scepticism and illusion-puncturing realism are Australian virtues; but this does not usually recognise that the thematic function of these notions in Australian narratives facilitates the doubting of the value of individual effort, the denial of the possibility of change and the qualifying of the strategy of hope. In this commonsense portrait of the Australian self in society, a conservative and comprehensive assent to the prevailing historical conditions is a *defining* element. It is difficult not to see this process of smoothing over contradictions and of naturalising existing conditions as having class implications. If, as Marx asserts, everything is 'in the last analysis' political, and if narrative is (in the words of Jameson) 'a socially symbolic act' and the expression of a 'political unconscious',[28] then the representation of the relation between dominant and subordinate classes in Australian narrative reveals a remarkably well-established and accepted politics of subordination. The figure of the convict itself can be seen as a displacement of class categories; and its celebrated tradition of anti-authoritarianism—with its divorce from the possibility of change—can be viewed as an alibi for impotence.

This book's account of Australian narrative has concentrated on the ways in which a number of strategies of representation converge on a particular meaning. Although this meaning seems to be dominant, it should not be seen to be composed of entirely consistent contributing ideological positions. The way dominant meanings are generated within culture, and their maintenance through hegemony, is complex. Meaning itself is a site of struggle between conflicting interests and constructions. Nevertheless, the study has looked at a significant area of representation within the culture, a major location of the making of meaning. The results may stimulate social or political anxiety. However, this account should not generate such a response, since on the one hand the meanings outlined *are* those which, for good or ill, organise Australian experience in narrative (to attack them as undesirable is simply to enter the arena occupied by the Leonie Kramers) and since, on the other hand, such meanings *are* ultimately political (so that their function as myth and as history does need to be recognised). And of course the meanings are not set in stone. We have already seen instances of resistance to, and changes within, dominant structures in our narratives and the pace of this change—particularly in film—seems likely to accelerate.

The importance of our description of Australian narrative is ultimately related to its usefulness as an account of the culture—even though its width of application beyond the study of narrative is a matter for further study rather than automatic assumption. In this work, all the benefits obtained from viewing Australian culture are suggestive rather than comprehensive. But at least we *can* learn a great deal about Australian culture by examining the function of filmic and literary narratives and the ideological work which they accomplish.

NOTES

1. The account of ideology and the state usually seen as central to Louis Althusser's system is given in 'Ideology and Ideological State Apparatuses' in *Lenin and Philosophy and other essays*, (New York: Monthly Review Press, 1971), pp.127–86. Criticisms of Althusser occur in Docker's *In a Critical Condition*, Belsey's *Critical Practice*, and most importantly, in Terry Lovell's *Pictures of Reality: Aesthetics, Politics and Pleasure* (London: BFI, 1983).
2. Jameson, *The Political Unconscious*, p.91.
3. For a convenient collection of the key articles in this debate, see Bennett et al. (eds), *Popular Television and Film*.
4. 'Travel Books in Disguise: The Australian Novel and Australian Film'.
5. No.13 (1977), p.77.
6. *The New Australian Cinema*, p.161.
7. *The Last New Wave*, p.90.

8 No.16 (1978), p.356.
9 *Popular Television and Film*, p.286.
10 The term, 'interrogative text', is used by Catherine Belsey as the alternative to the classic realist text in *Critical Practice*, Chapter 4. 'The *interrogative* text ... disrupts the unity of the reader by discouraging identification with a unified subject of the enunciation. ... it does literally invite the reader to produce answers to the questions it implicitly or explicitly raises', p.91. The argument against the *Screen* position on realism is in Terry Lovell's *Pictures of Reality*, pp.84–7.
11 The argument of Veronica Brady's *A Crucible of Prophets* takes us in this direction, and it is a well established point of view on White now.
12 Laurie Hergenhan's chapter on *A Fringe of Leaves* in *Unnatural Lives* makes this connection on p.154.
13 The term seems to originate with Robert Scholes' book *The Fabulators* (New York: Oxford University Press, 1967) and it is further developed in the later revision of this book, *Fabulation and Metafiction* (Urbana: University of Illinois Press, 1979).
14 (London: Picador, 1982), p.10. Further references to this novel will appear in parentheses in the text.
15 Accounts of this fiction can be found in Scholes' *Fabulation and Metafiction* and in Tony Tanner's *City of Words* (London: Jonathon Cape, 1971).
16 (London: Panther, 1968), p.71.
17 (London: Picador, 1980), p.94.
18 Dorothy Green, *The Music of Love* (Melbourne: Penguin, 1984), p.42.
19 Dick Hebdidge, *Subculture: The Meaning of Style*, (London: Methuen, 1979), p.133.
20 ibid. p.79.
21 See Tanner's *City of Words*, Richard Hauck's *A Cheerful Nihilism: Confidence and the Absurd in American Humorous Fiction* (Bloomington: Indiana University Press, 1971) or Ihab Hassan's *Radical Innocence* (Princeton: Princeton University Press, 1961).
22 *Exotic Pleasures* (London: Picador, 1981).
23 e.g., John Carroll 'National Identity' in *Intruders in the Bush*, p.214.
24 *Stockyard and the Croquet Lawn*, p.122.
25 Stuart Hall, 'The rediscovery of "ideology": The return of the repressed in media studies', p.64.
26 *The Political Unconscious*, p.79.
27 '*Jaws*, Ideology and Film Theory' in *Popular Film and Television*, p.205.
28 The title, and the thesis behind *The Political Unconscious*.

Afterword

In the opening chapter of this book, I described the critical context within which it was written. Subsequent developments require that these descriptions be updated for this second edition, and so the first task of this Afterword will be to note some of the important work that has appeared in the intervening years. A second task is to deal with, at least briefly, some of the formal and textual trends to develop since the book was first written. The patterns outlined in the preceding chapters are embedded in broad movements in cultural production and, as such, tend to incorporate the numerous differences that occur regularly and systematically within Australian narratives. Consequently, it might seem a little illogical to review contemporary shifts in narrative in this Afterword; any differences that might have arisen would still have to demonstrate their influence and their power to affect the traditions described. Nevertheless, it is understandable that contemporary readers should ask contemporary questions of the book, and so this Afterword addresses such questions. My third objective is to talk about some recent developments in Australian film which do seem significant. More than contemporary Australian literature, contemporary Australian film is the product of an institutional structure with specific and explicit responsibilities for constructing 'national' texts. There are changes within this set of responsibilities now, and arguments about how those responsibilities were met in the past, which relate to the central ideas in this study.

The critical field into which the second edition of this book projects itself is rather different from that which existed when it was being written. Certainly, Australian literary studies is a much more theoretically literate field now than it was in 1984. Probably, the bulk of the credit for this should go to the rich feminist vein within Australian literary studies, which has posed the most sustained and powerful critique so far of the dominant definitions of the Australian literary tradition and the dominant protocols of analysis. Other critiques of this tradition, objecting to its spurious homogeneity, have come from writers dealing with multiculturalism and with regionalism. From each of these positions we have seen a vigorous and challenging body of criticism emerge, although admittedly more through journals and magazines than through full-length studies from mainstream publishers.

In contrast, the publication of literary biography has boomed, producing new forms as a result: Brian Matthews' *Louisa*, for instance, is particularly agile in its dealing with poststructuralist notions of authorship and history.[1] Indeed, one could see the newly theorised interest in the interrelations between Australian writing and Australian culture as expressing itself primarily through the revived interest in biography. Given the importance of the development of an Australian 'canon' within the history of Australian literary studies, on the one hand, and the compromised position 'the canon' in general occupies within poststructuralist theory, on the other, the literary biography provides a particularly strategic avenue for the consolidation of an Australian literary tradition at the moment. The number of books which have stretched the boundaries of the discipline in other directions are few, if impressive in themselves. Paul Carter's *The Road to Botany Bay*, Kay Schaffer's *Women and the Bush* and Bob Hodge and Vijay Mishra's *Dark Side of the Dream*[2] all make distinctive and groundbreaking contributions to Australian historical, feminist, literary and cultural studies.

It has been a slightly different story for Australian screen studies, particularly for discussions of the post-1970s revival. Admittedly, screen studies journals had an increasingly lean time during the latter half of the 1980s; *The Australian Journal of Screen Theory* and the *Australian Journal of Cultural Studies* both folded, for instance, and the current version of *Cinema Papers* is a shadow of its former self. As compensation, however, there has been an explosion of book publishing on Australian film and, to a lesser extent, television. Furthermore, where once the field was dominated by film historiography, the last seven years have produced books dealing with a rich variety of topics and exploring a range of approaches. Foremost among them is Dermody and Jacka's magisterial three volume 'anatomy' of the industrial structure of the revival and the texts it produced; Moran and O'Regan's valuable *Australian Film Reader*, a collection of documents and articles covering the full period of Australian film production, and their edited collection of overview essays, *The Australian Screen*; Cunningham's full-length study of the Australian *auteur*, Charles Chauvel; Bruce Molloy's analysis of the 'social mythologies' in the features produced during the neglected period from the 1930s to the 1950s; and Brian McFarlane's textual evaluation of the films of the revival until 1985 and his comparative study (co-authored with Geoff Mayer) of the British, American and Australian film industries.[3] This list by no means exhausts the useful work published in the last few years. However, even during such a productive period, the number of books which attempt to move outside their discipline has remained limited.

Finally, the most important contextual development to note lies within the field of Australian cultural studies. A relatively new field in 1986, it is now a much more established (if still disparate and contestatory) group of interests and methodologies: its publications have been varied and wide ranging, as suggested by the list of titles published in the series to which this book belongs. Cultural studies has seized enthusiastically the opportunity of interdisciplinarity, continually raiding other fields for material or approaches and occasionally feeding the results of its processing of this material back into the source disciplines. To some extent, cultural studies has moved into the opening vacated by Australian Studies which became gradually less excited by the opportunity for interdisciplinary work as its sphere of influence contracted to the disciplines of literary studies and history.[4] Cultural studies has also benefited from the spaces created within Australian publishing by screen studies and feminism; like them it is widely regarded as a key presence in the 'new humanities' in universities today.

As we move into the middle of the 1990s, it is certainly worth asking whether much has changed in the field of Australian narrative. Is it possible, for instance, to say whether the 'new' women writers of the 1980s have made or are likely to make a significant difference to the Australian narrative tradition I describe in this book? Does the current fashion for less 'Anglo', more multicultural, representations of Australian life in film and television represent a change in common sense definitions of the nation?

One of the constraints on responding confidently to such questions is the need to take 'the long view'. It is very tempting to see the latest sign as a permanent wonder. The hint of multiculturalism, for instance, in such films as *Death in Brunswick* and *Strictly Ballroom*, coupled with television sitcoms such as *Acropolis Now* or theatre revues such as *Wogs Out of Work*, would be exaggerated if read as a general indication of a new readiness to accept multiple Australian identities. Conclusions drawn from apparently related contemporary cultural moments—no matter how vivid or resonant—can be misleading.

My account of Peter Carey's *Bliss* in the previous chapter, for instance, uses his work as a site of difference where one can locate new influences on, and divergent constructions of, Australian identity. The temptation for this reading of his work lay primarily in its relatively flamboyant formal and stylistic characteristics such as his use of the internationalised signatures of fabulation or 'magic realism'. At the time it appeared, *Bliss* offered a fresh and exciting experience for Australian readers. However, Carey's next two novels, *Illywhacker* and *Oscar and Lucinda*, could easily be regarded as an attempt to move back into the mainstream. Both are large episodic sagas, modernist in form, rooted in and commenting on the Australian rural and colonial past. As I have noted elsewhere, [5] *Illywhacker* owes as much to Joseph Furphy as it does to Gabriel Garcia Marquez, while *Oscar and Lucinda* is, in my view, formally and stylistically the least adventurous of Carey's novels. Certainly, these two novels stand in an ambiguous, perhaps even contradictory, relation to Carey's earlier projects. To further indicate the difficulties in establishing homogeneity, even within the work of one author over a short period of time, one would have to say that *The Tax Inspector*, Carey's most recent novel, sits a little uneasily in both of the formal paradigms I have just implied are appropriate for his work.

My answer to queries about the impact of the 'new' women writers, or the influence of multiculturalism in urban genre films, would have to be that it is too soon to tell. This is not to say that there are no signs of change to justify curiosity about their eventual effects. The specific character of any change which might occur, however, is very difficult to predict. For a start, and to use the example of women's writing, our prognosis would be affected by how we constructed the category of 'women's writing': the importance attributed to a feminist politics, for instance, or the choice of authors nominated as representative must exercise an influence on the kind of cultural or political effects ascribed to women's writing. The degree to which women's writing is seen as a unified, homogeneous field is implicated also. The work of Elizabeth Jolley, for instance, seems more profoundly idiosyncratic and thus harder to incorporate into a contemporary 'trend' than that of, say, Helen Garner.

That said, and given that Australia's is such an exorbitantly masculinist narrative tradition, the fact that one must now consider how one defines the field of women's writing is a positive sign of conclusive change. It is hard not to imagine that changes in the versions of subjectivity and identity we accept as Australian must follow. This is not likely to go uncontested, however. The most notorious response to the challenge represented by women's fiction is Gerard Windsor's accusation that Australian publishers and reviewers now actively favour women writers. Windsor's concern is motivated by the perception that male writers seem to have lost their easy dominance of Australian publishing. Opportunities for writing by and about women have expanded and the singularity of the Australian narrative tradition must be fractured, even if only temporarily, by this. Nevertheless, and taking 'the long view', the expansion of the feminist press does seem to have peaked now, and publishers are starting to talk of the market for women's writing being 'saturated'. Such views inevitably construct women's fiction as a trend—corrective and important, but on the wane. One senses the pendulum is swinging back, as if the tradition has no doubt of its capacity to absorb these deviations. The specificity of women's writing and of women's experience in Australia will require continued reiteration and demonstration if it is to revise the definitions of the Australian self constructed through our narratives.

There may be signs of change in an area I have not addressed elsewhere in this book, that of popular fiction. The history of Australian literary production reveals a rich vein of popular melodrama and romance writing in the nineteenth century employing formal structures largely antithetical to those I have concentrated on in this book. That vein ran out and the latter half of the twentieth century witnessed the virtual disappearance of an Australian popular fiction; popular colonial romance has only survived by switching media—from the novel to film to television. Paradoxically, the massive development in the market for Australian literary fiction through the 1960s, 1970s and, to a lesser extent, the early 1980s was accompanied by an almost total evacuation from the field of Australian popular fiction.

There are now signs of a recovery of an audience for Australian popular fiction. Crime fiction, in particular, including feminist crime fiction, has boomed to the extent that it now offers a range of styles and modalities from Peter Corris and Jennifer Rowe at the intellectual end of town to Robert G. Barrett at the macho end. The type of the individual represented in this fiction usually accords with the descriptions mounted in chapters 2 and 3 of this book; Corris's Cliff Hardy strikes me as a very clear example of the paradigm I describe. However, with the development of a new market dominated by internationalised genres which demand strong narrative closure, highly dramatic plots and a significant investment in the agency of the individual over history, one could see the potential for a competing set of discourses to emerge. Certainly, if this development is connected to the 'new diversity' Gelder and Salzman note in their account of contemporary Australian literary fiction, an account which emphasises the field's 'heterogeneity',[6] the prospects for changes to, or multiple variants of, the tradition I have described seem significant.

Fiction, however, enjoys a degree of institutional and industrial autonomy that distinguishes its conditions of production from those of the feature film. The arguments within this book are about the functioning of something like Jameson's 'political unconscious',[7] the culturally produced languages used to construct our film and prose narratives. In the case of film, the conditions under which it is produced are actually rather more 'conscious' and deliberate than Jameson's phrase would suggest; Australian film since the 1970s has been unashamedly and explicitly enlisted in the process of forming the nation. Where the Australian literary critic may be interested primarily in the idiosyncrasies of the individual text, the Australian film critic customarily approaches local film texts as indications of, among other things, national funding policies and trends in the production industry. The funding institutions are as much objects of criticism as the films. Australian literature went through a similar stage when its participation in the production of images of Australian life was vigorously overseen by anxious cultural institutions. Due to its comparatively simple industrial structure, however, and also to its less ambiguous relation to the nation's popular culture, the production of literature was never as thoroughly implicated as film has been in the semi-official process of nation formation.

As we saw earlier in this book, the assumption that Australian film should 'represent' the nation had an effect on the range of generic models considered appropriate. As the furore around *The Man From Snowy River* makes clear, and as a similar controversy around *Crocodile Dundee* also suggests, any film genres that could not be easily adapted to speak with what was regarded as a sufficiently broad Australian accent were suspect. Especially suspect were American, or more correctly Hollywood, genres, the appropriation of which was seen as an unequivocal index of the selling out of the national project. Over the last decade, however, our film industry has continued to produce traditionally nationalist texts *as well as* a significant number of more generic projects: *Crocodile Dundee* exemplifies both sides of this apparent contradiction. In general *Crocodile Dundee* is most notable not for its familiar 'bush myth' nationalism, but for its confident appropriation of Hollywood generic narrative structures.[8] There are sufficient examples of similar appropriations of Hollywood genres now to constitute a trend: the work of Nadia Tass and David Parker (*Malcolm, Rikki and Pete, The Big Steal*), Phil Noyce's claustrophobic thriller, *Dead Calm*, or the most recent Peter Weir film, *Green Card*.

In some of these 'genre' films, the narrative patterns described in this book are transgressed or challenged. *The Big Steal* is not at all equivocal about its moment of narrative closure; it coincides with the moment of sexual union the rest of the film has been deferring. *Crocodile Dundee* and *Crocodile Dundee 2* may have offered possibilities for sequels, but there are no other narrative ambiguities allowed to survive their endings. *Dead Calm* provides us with a spectacular, if bizarre, resolution of its narrative conflict where there is no hint of a residue to sour the taste of deliverance. In these films we may be seeing the first traces of the ideological effects of this new trade in narrative conventions such as a modification of the idea of the individual within Australian fictions. Within such traces we may locate evidence of the difficulty of adapting formal and structural devices from another culture without taking with them some of the meanings they most easily generate. We should also be aware of influences which head in the reverse direction. For example, one might view the curiously ambivalent ending of *Green Card* as a moment where Peter Weir's Australian accent speaks loudly, even discordantly, within an American genre.[9]

It might seem as if the worst fears of those who warned against selling out to the Americans in the 1970s have been realised in the 1990s. Apart from the residual nationalism of the Crocodile Dundee films, the latter half of the 1980s and the first few years of the 1990s has seen Australian film begin to quietly disengage itself from the explicit project of nation formation. The shift has been particularly comprehensive. It is evident in the writings of critics who ask if we, as a culture, have got our money's worth out of the films made;[10] it is evident in changes in rhetoric surrounding the film industry which now increasingly talks of the 'local' rather than the national as its constituency and subject; it is implied in institutional documents produced by bodies such as the AFC which accept the economic rationalist 'user pays' principle by claiming that the industry is justifiable in terms of its economic spin-offs (employment, tourism and so on) rather than its cultural significance; and it is evident in the recent crop of Australian films which, like contemporary Australian fiction, tend to take their locations as read in order to focus the more sharply on specific, individualised stories within them.

Death in Brunswick, *Proof* and *Strictly Ballroom* are not about Australia in the way *Newsfront*, *Caddie* or *The Man From Snowy River* were. Based on this evidence, I have argued elsewhere that we are witnessing 'the end of the national project'—the end of the explicit enlistment of the film industry in the construction of the national culture.[11]

This, of course, does not mean that the films will no longer speak of/from the culture in the ways outlined in earlier chapters. The explicitness of this speaking position, however, its programmatic character, does look like changing. In principle, this is a positive development; certainly, in terms of the diversity of texts and meanings likely to result, the trend is to be welcomed. As I said earlier, some of the most successful Australian films of the last two years—*Proof*, *Death in Brunswick*, *Strictly Ballroom*, *The Big Steal*—complicate the patterns outlined in this study either by their generic structure, their contemporary urban setting or their degree of narrative closure. Certainly it is true of all the above films that where once the mythologies of the past were mobilised as a means of refracting propositions about the nature of the Australian present, these more recent films are directly interested in the richness and diversity of contemporary Australian society. A further textual and ideological diversity is emerging as the dominance of male film-makers and masculine concerns—the bush, mateship, war—is challenged by female writers and directors such as Jane Campion, Jocelyn Moorhouse and Ann Turner. The first feature from Aboriginal film-maker Tracy Moffat is also in production as I write.

The benefits seen to flow from these textual and ideological shifts lend support to the views of those film-makers, critics and administrators who wish to disconnect the industry from the project of 'nationing'. In many of their arguments, the 'local' is offered as an alternative, as a way of combating nationalism's overriding of difference and of emphasising the importance of our films addressing Australians' diverse as well as their common identities. However, there are effects to consider other than the textual. From the point of view of the industry's survival, since the most powerful argument for the industry's continued subsidisation depends upon its role as the cultural flagship for the nation, this disengagement from the rhetoric of nationality is potentially risky. Our films simply will not be produced unless they are subsidised and our governments may not subsidise them if they do not produce returns—either in commercial or cultural capital. So, there is a distinct possibility that the film industry's growing ambivalence about its national responsibilities will erode support for it within government.

For those working within the film culture today, this constitutes a dilemma. Many of the films produced over the last two decades seem to some, at least, of little lasting interest or cultural value. However, to argue this too vigorously outside the industry may well threaten the future of film making in Australia. Furthermore, while many were once prepared to work with the idea of the nation as a strategic weapon in order to win political support for the industry, some are no longer prepared to defend an idea they see as largely responsible for underwriting a conservative, complacent body of films that has failed to sufficiently criticise the culture it represents on the screen. Much of the enthusiasm for the competing idea of 'the local' is due to dissatisfaction with these representations of the nation.

At a critical level, the challenges posed to the industry by Elizabeth Jacka and others have the potential of encouraging more questioning and diverse films. Nevertheless, it is hard to see how the replacement of the rhetoric of the national with that of the local will be of any practical assistance to the industry. Consequently, it seems unwise to abandon even the strategic use of the category of the national as if it were irredeemably tainted.[12] My view, following Benedict Anderson,[13] is that nationalism is immensely flexible. The terms in which it is currently constructed in Australia may be well established, as this study argues, but they are not fixed. While nationalism has proved to be a problem in contemporary screen and cultural theory, and in critical dealings with much Australian film, we don't resolve this by dispensing with the category altogether; nor should we, while we can still contest it and its constitutive discourses. It is one thing to do as I have done in this book, to describe what seem to me the dominant discourses used to construct our national identity within narrative. It is another thing to assume that the battles for control of these discourses are over, or that the terms within which our national identity is produced are in some way finalised.

To conclude with a sign towards the possibilities for change, even in the pervasive and enduring structures outlined in the preceding pages, it is worth noting Iain Chambers' admonition that ' "the nation" as a heterogenous cultural and linguistic unit is not a closed history, something that has already been achieved'. Rather, it is 'an open framework, continually in the making'. Writing from Britain where the 'framework' looks perhaps the least open, Chambers can still suggest that it is possible to 'move out of the mythological tempo of "tradition" into the more fragmented and open discontinuities of histories'.[14] Without underestimating the difficulty in cracking open

Afterword 155

the specific codes of nationalism within any contemporary historical conjuncture, this is a timely reminder of the need to resist the temptation to move the struggle onto less contested territory.

NOTES

1 Brian Matthews, *Louisa* (Melbourne, McPhee/Gribble Penguin: 1987).
2 Paul Carter, *The Road to Botany Bay* (London, Faber: 1987); Kay Schaffer, *Women and the Bush: Forces of Desire in the Australian Cultural Tradition* (Melbourne, Cambridge University Press: 1988); Bob Hodge and Vijay Mishra, *Dark Side of the Dream: Australian Literature and the Postcolonial Mind* (Sydney, Allen & Unwin: 1991).
3 Susan Dermody and Elizabeth Jacka, *The Screening of Australia*, Vols 1 and 2 (Sydney, Currency Press: 1987 and 1988) and *The Imaginary Industry: Australian Cinema in the late 80s* (Sydney, AFTRS: 1988); Albert Moran and Tom O'Regan, *Australian Film Reader* (Sydney, Currency Press: 1985) and *The Australian Screen* (Melbourne, Penguin: 1989); Stuart Cunningham, *Featuring Australia: The Cinema of Charles Chauvel* (Sydney, Allen & Unwin: 1991); Bruce Molloy, *Before the Interval* (Brisbane, UQP: 1990); Brian McFarlane, *Australian Cinema 1970–1985* (Melbourne, Heinneman: 1987) and *New Australian Cinema: Sources and Parallels in British and American Films* (Melbourne, Cambridge University Press: 1992).
4 See my 'Return to Oz: Populism, the Academy and the Future of Australian Studies', *Meanjin*, (1/1991).
5 'American Dreaming: The Fictions of Peter Carey', *Australian Literary Studies*, (12:4, 1986).
6 Ken Gelder and Paul Salzman, *The New Diversity: Australian Fiction 1970–1988* (Melbourne, McPhee Gribble: 1989).
7 Frederick Jameson, *The Political Unconscious: Narrative as a Socially Symbolic Act* (London, Methuen: 1981).
8 See Meaghan Morris, 'Tooth and Claw: Tales of Survival and *Crocodile Dundee*' in *The Pirate's Fiancee: Feminism, Reading, Postmodernism* (London, Verso: 1988).
9 See my 'The Genres are American: Australian Narrative, Australian Film and the Problem of Genre', *Literature/Film Quarterly* (forthcoming).
10 Elizabeth Jacka, 'Australian Cinema: An Anachronism in the 80s?'in Susan Dermody and Elizabeth Jacka, *The Imaginary Industry*.
11 'The End of the National Project?: Australian Cinema in the 1990s' in W. Dissanayake (ed.), *Questions of Nationhood and History in Asian Cinema* (Bloomington: Indiana University Press, forthcoming)
12 I argue this position at greater length in 'The end of the national project'.
13 Benedict Anderson, *Imagined Communities: Reflections of the Origin and Spread of Nationalism* (London, Verso: 1983).
14 Iain Chambers, *Border Dialogues: Journeys in Postmodernity* (London, Routledge: 1991), p.47.

References

The following is a list, largely, of books referred to within the text. Although there are a small number of texts included which are not directly referred to in footnotes, this is not a full bibliography.

There are different bodies of theoretical writing represented here—film, fiction, literary theory, cultural studies theory and so on—but I have not divided the listing into such categories. Given the nature of the study, its interdisciplinary focus, the problems of overlap and cross reference would have made this list of references unwieldy.

Finally, while print texts are listed in the traditional form, alphabetically by author, films have been listed alphabetically by title. The name of the director follows the title and date of release.

NARRATIVES REFERRED TO

Films

The Adventures of Barry McKenzie (1972) Bruce Beresford
Alvin Purple (1973) Tim Burstall
Between Wars (1974) Michael Thornhill
The Big Steal (1990) Nadia Tass
Bliss (1985) Ray Lawrence
Breaker Morant (1980) Bruce Beresford
Caddie (1976) Donald Crombie
The Cars That Ate Paris (1974) Peter Weir
The Chant of Jimmie Blacksmith (1978) Fred Schepisi
The Clinic (1983) David Pattins
Crocodile Dundee (1986) Peter Faiman
Dead Calm (1990) Philip Noyce
Death in Brunswick (1991) John Ruane
The Devil's Playground (1976) Fred Schepisi
Don's Party (1976) Bruce Beresford
The FJ Holden (1977) Michael Thornhill
For The Term of His Natural Life (1927) Norman Dawn

Gallipoli (1981) Peter Weir
The Getting of Wisdom (1977) Bruce Beresford
A Girl of the Bush (1921) Franklin Barratt
Going Down (1983) Hayden Keenan
Goodbye Paradise (1982) Carl Schultz
Green Card (1991) Peter Weir
Hard Knocks (1980) Don McLennan
Heatwave (1982) Phil Noyce
In Search of Anna (1979) Esben Storm
The Irishman (1978) Donald Crombie
Jedda (1955) Charles Chauvel
Kostas (1979) Paul Cox
The Last Wave (1977) Peter Weir
Libido (1973) David Baker, Tim Burstall, John B. Murray, Fred Schepisi
Mad Max (1979) George Miller
Mad Max II (1981) George Miller
Malcolm (1986) Nadia Tass
The Man From Snowy River (1982) George Miller
Man of Flowers (1983) Paul Cox
The Mango Tree (1977) Kevin Dobson
Monkey Grip (1982) Ken Cameron
Mouth to Mouth (1978) John Duigan
Moving Out (1983) Michael Pattinson
My Brilliant Career (1979) Gillian Armstrong
My First Wife (1984) Paul Cox
Newsfront (1978) Phil Noyce
The Odd Angry Shot (1979) Tom Jeffrey
On Our Selection (1920) Raymond Longford
On Our Selection (1932) Ken G. Hall
Phar Lap (1983) Simon Wincer
Picnic at Hanging Rock (1975) Peter Weir
The Picture Show Man (1977) John Power
Proof (1991) Jocelyn Moorehouse
Pure S (1976) Bert Deling
Razorback (1984) Russell Mulcahy
Rikki and Pete (1988) Nadia Tass
The Sentimental Bloke (1919) Raymond Longford
Smiley (1956) Anthony Kimmins
Starstruck (1981) Gillian Armstrong
Stir (1980) Stephen Wallace
Stork (1971) Tim Burstall
Strictly Ballroom (1992) Baz Luhrmann
Sunday Too Far Away (1975) Ken Hannam
Three in One (1957) Cecil Holmes
27A (1974) Esben Storm
Wake in Fright (1971) Ted Kotcheff
Walkabout (1971) Nicholas Roeg
Winter of Our Dreams (1981) John Duigan
The Year of Living Dangerously (1983) Peter Weir

158 *National Fictions*

Print

Anderson, Jessica *The Commandant* (Ringwood: Penguin, 1981)
Boldrewood, Rolf *Robbery Under Arms* (Sydney: Angus & Robertson, 1980, first published in 1888)
Carey, Peter *Exotic Pleasures* (London: Picador, 1981)
—— *Bliss* (London: Picador, 1982)
—— *Illywhacker* (St Lucia: University of Queensland Press 1985)
—— *Oscar and Lucinda* (St Lucia: University of Queensland Press 1988)
—— *The Tax Inspector* (St Lucia: University of Queensland Press 1991)
Clarke, Marcus *For The Term of His Natural Life* (Sydney: Angus & Robertson, 1975, first published in 1874)
Drewe, Robert *The Savage Crows* (Sydney: Collins, 1976)
Furphy, Joseph (Tom Collins) *Such is Life* (Sydney: Angus & Robertson, 1975, first published in 1903)
Hall, Rodney *Just Relations* (Ringwood: Penguin, 1982)
Hardy, Frank *Power Without Glory* (Sydney: Angus & Robertson, 1975, first published in 1950)
Herbert, Xavier *Capricornia* (Sydney: Angus & Robertson, 1938)
Ireland, David *The Glass Canoe* (Ringwood: Penguin, 1982)
—— *The Unknown Industrial Prisoner* (Sydney: Angus & Robertson, 1971)
—— *A Woman of the Future* (New York: G. Braziller, 1979)
Keneally, Thomas *Bring Larks and Heroes* (Melbourne: Sun, 1968, first published Cassell, 1967)
—— *The Chant of Jimmy Blacksmith* (Sydney: Angus & Robertson, 1972)
—— *Schindler's Ark* (London: Hodder & Stoughton, 1982)
—— *Three Cheers for the Paraclete* (Harmondsworth: Penguin, 1969)
Lawson, Henry *Short Stories and Sketches* (ed. Colin Roderick) (Sydney: Angus & Robertson, 1972)
Malouf, David *Child's Play* (Ringwood: Penguin, 1983)
—— *Fly Away Peter* (Ringwood: Penguin, 1983)
—— *An Imaginary Life* (London: Picador, 1980)
—— *Johnno* (Ringwood, Penguin: 1976)
Paterson, A.B. *The Man From Snowy River* (Sydney: Angus & Robertson, 1973, first published in 1895)
Penton, Brian *Landtakers* (Sydney: Angus & Robertson, 1972, first published in 1934)
Richardson, Henry Handel *The Getting of Wisdom* (Melbourne: Heinemann, 1977)
—— *Ultima Thule* (Harmondsworth: Penguin, 1977, first published 1929)
Stead, Christina *The Man Who Loved Children* (Ringwood: Penguin, 1970, first published 1940)
Stow, Randolph *Merry-Go-Round in the Sea* (London: MacDonald, 1965)
—— *To the Islands* (Harmondsworth: Penguin, 1962)
Tucker, James *Ralph Rashleigh* (ed. Colin Roderick) (Sydney: Angus & Robertson, 1952)
White, Patrick *The Burnt Ones* (London: Eyre & Spottiswoode, 1964)
—— *A Fringe of Leaves* (Ringwood: Penguin, 1977)
—— *The Tree of Man* (London: Eyre & Spottiswoode, 1956)

—— *The Vivisector* (London: Jonathon Cape, 1970)
—— *Voss* (Harmondsworth: Penguin, 1960)

Critical and theoretical references

Articles and chapters of books

Althusser, Louis 'Ideology and Ideological State Apparatuses' in *Lenin and Philosophy and other Essays* (New York: Monthly Review Press, 1971), pp. 127–86

Andrews, Barry 'More Sinned Against Than Sinning: A Note on the Convict Legend' in C. D. Narasimhaiah (ed.) *An Introduction to Australian Literature* (Brisbane: John Wiley & Sons, 1982), pp. 166–82

Bishop, Rod and Mackie, Fiona 'Loneliness and Alienation' in Scott Murray (ed.) *The New Australian Cinema* (Melbourne: Nelson, 1980), pp. 153–65

Brady, Veronica 'The Novelist and the New World: Patrick White's *Voss*', *Texas Studies in Literature and Language*, Vol. 21, No. 2 (1979), pp. 169–85

Buckley, Vincent 'Utopianism and Vitalism' in Grahame Johnston (ed.) *Australian Literary Criticism* (Melbourne: Oxford University Press, 1962), pp. 16–29

Burstall, Tim 'Triumph and Disaster for Australian Films', *The Bulletin* (24 September 1977), pp. 45–55

Chatman, Seymour 'What Novels Can Do That Films Can't (and Vice Versa)' in W. J. T. Mitchell (ed.) *On Narrative* (Chicago: University of Chicago Press, 1980), pp. 117–36

Clancy, Jack 'Breaker Morant', *Cinema Papers*, No. 28 (1981), p. 283

—— '*The Man From Snowy River*: Parents and Orphans', *Cinema Papers*, No. 42 (1983), pp. 50–2

—— '*Mouth to Mouth*', *Cinema Papers*, No. 16 (1978), p. 356

Crofts, Stephen '*Breaker Morant* Rethought: Eighty Years on the Culture still Cringes', *Cinema Papers*, No. 30 (1981), pp. 420–1

Cunningham, Stuart 'Australian Film', *Australian Journal of Screen Theory*, Nos 5 & 6 (1978), pp. 36–47

—— 'Australian Film History and Historiography', *Australian Journal of Cultural Studies*, Vol. 1, No. 1 (1983), pp. 122–6

Dermody, Susan 'Action and Adventure' in Scott Murray (ed.) *The New Australian Cinema* (Melbourne: Nelson, 1980), pp. 79–95

—— '*The FJ Holden*', *Cinema Papers*, No. 13 (1977), p. 77

Dutton, Geoffrey, 'Strength Through Adversity', *The Bulletin* (29 January 1980), pp. 130–2

Dyer, Richard 'Stars as Signs' in Tony Bennett et al. (eds) *Popular Television and Film* (London: BFI, 1981), pp. 236–69

Ellis, Bob 'Observations', *Cinema Papers*, Nos 44–45 (1984), p. 61

Fore, Stephen 'The Perils of Patriotism: the combat war film as genre and *Southern Comfort* as generic self-immolation', *Australian Journal of Cultural Studies*, Vol. 2, No. 2 (1984), pp. 40–60

Hall, Stuart 'Culture, Media and the Ideological Effect' in James Curran et

al. (eds) *Mass Communication and Society* (London: Edward Arnold, 1977), pp. 315-48
—— 'The Rediscovery of Ideology: Return of the Repressed in Media Studies', in Michael Gurevitch et al. (eds) *Culture, Society and the Media* (London: Methuen, 1982), pp. 56-89
Harris, Max 'Banjo Would Have Hated It', *Weekend Australian Magazine* (27 March 1982), p. 7
Heath, Stephen '*Jaws*, Ideology and Film Theory' in Tony Bennett et al. (eds) *Popular Television and Film* (London: BFI, 1981), pp. 200-5
Heseltine, H. P. 'The Australian Image: The Literary Heritage' in Clement Semmler (ed.) *Twentieth Century Australian Literary Criticism* (Melbourne: Oxford University Press, 1967), pp. 86-101
Hindle, John 'The Best of the Year', *National Times* (16-22 August, 1981) p. 33
—— 'Galloping Soapie in the High Country', *National Times* (28 March-3 April 1982), p. 40
Hutton, Anne B. 'Nationalism in Australian Cinema', *Cinema Papers*, No. 26 (1980), pp. 97-100, 152, 153
Jacka, Elizabeth 'Australian Cinema: An Anachronism in the 80s?' in Susan Dermody and Elizabeth Jacka (eds) *The Imaginary Industry* (Sydney: AFTRS, 1988)
King, Noel 'Changing the Curriculum: The Place of Film in English Departments', *Australian Journal of Cultural Studies*, Vol. 1, No. 1 (1983), pp. 47-55
Lawson, Sylvia 'Towards Decolonisation: Film History in Australia' in Susan Dermody et al. (eds) *Nellie Melba, Ginger Meggs and Friends* (Malmsbury: Kibble, 1982), pp. 19-32
Levi-Strauss, Claude 'The Structural Study of Myth' in Richard and Fernande de George (eds) *The Structuralists from Marx to Levi-Strauss* (New York: Doubleday, 1972), pp. 164-94
Lohrey, Amanda '*Gallipoli*: Male Innocence as a Marketable Commodity', *Island Magazine*, Nos 9-10 (1982), pp. 29-34
McCabe, Colin 'Realism and the Cinema: Notes on Some Brechtian Theses' originally printed in *Screen* (Vol. 15, No. 2) reprinted in Bennett et al. (eds) *Popular Television and Film* (London: BFI, 1981), pp. 216-35
McLaren, John 'The Image of Reality in Our Writing' in Clemment Semmler (ed.) *Twentieth Century Australian Literary Criticism* (Melbourne: Oxford University Press, 1967), pp. 235-44
Mast, Gerald 'Literature and Film' in Jean-Pierre Barricelli and Joseph Gibaldi (eds) *Interrelations of Literature* (New York: M.L.A., 1980), pp. 278-306
Matthews, Brian 'Henry Lawson's Fictional World' in Leon Cantrell (ed.) *Bards, Bohemians and Bookmen* (St Lucia: University of Queensland Press), 1976
Moore, Catriona and Stephen Muecke 'Racism and the Representation of Aborigines in Film', *Australian Journal of Cultural Studies*, Vol. 2, No. 1 (1984), pp. 36-53
Morgan, Patrick 'Hard Work and Idle Dissipation: The Dual Australian Personality', *Meanjin*, Vol. 41, No. 1 (1982), pp. 130-7

O'Regan, Tom 'Ride the High Country: In and Around *The Man From Snowy River*', *Filmnews*, September 1982
Rowse, Tim and Albert Moran 'Peculiarly Australian—The Political Construction of Cultural Identity' in S. Encel and L. Bryson (eds) *Australian Society* (fourth edition) (Melbourne: Longman Cheshire, 1984), pp. 229-77
Ryan, Tom 'Historical Films' in Scott Murray (ed.) *The New Australian Cinema* (Melbourne: Nelson/Cinema Papers, 1980), pp. 113-31
Stewart, Ken 'Life and Death of the Bunyip: History and the Great Australian Novel', *Westerly*, Vol. 28, No. 2 (1983), pp. 39-44
Taylor, Andrew 'Bosom of Nature or Heart of Stone (Some Thoughts on Australian and American Literature)' in C. D. Narasimhaiah (ed.) *An Introduction to Australian Literature* (Brisbane: Wiley, 1982), pp. 144-56
Thomas, Daniel 'Visual Images' in George Seddon and Mari Davis (eds) *Man and Landscape in Australia: Towards an Ecological Vision* (Canberra: Government Publishing Service, 1976), pp. 157-66
Turner, Graeme 'Mateship, Individualism and the Production of Character in Australian Fiction', *Australian Literary Studies*, Vol. 11, No. 4, pp. 447-57
—— 'Travel Books in Disguise: The Australian Film and the Australian Novel', *Overland*, No. 79 (1980), pp. 19-24
—— 'The End of the National Project: Australian Cinema in the 1990s', in W. Dissanayake (ed.) *Questions of Nationhood and History in Asian Cinema* (Bloomington: University of Indiana Press, forthcoming)
—— 'The Genres are American: Australian Narrative, Australian Film and the Problem of Genre', *Literature/Film Quarterly*, forthcoming
—— 'Return to Oz: Populism, the Academy and the Future of Australian Studies', *Meanjin*, 1, 1991
Wright, Patrick 'A Blue Plaque for the Labour Movement? Some Political Meanings of the "National Past" in *Formations of Nation and People* (London: Routledge and Kegan Paul, 1984), pp. 42-67

Books

Anderson, Benedict *Imagined Communities: Reflections on the Origins and Spread of Nationalism* (London: Verso, 1983)
Barnes, John (ed.) *The Writer in Australia* (Melbourne, Oxford University Press, 1969)
Barthes, Roland *Mythologies* (London: Paladin, 1973)
—— *Image-Music-Text* (London: Fontana, 1977)
Belsey, Catherine *Critical Practice* (London: Methuen, 1980)
Bennett, Tony, Susan Boyd-Bowman, Colin Mercer, and Janet Woolacott (eds) *Popular Television and Film* (London: BFI, 1981)
Bluestone, George *Novels into Film* (Berkeley: University of California Press, 1966)
Bonney, Bill and Helen Wilson *Australia's Commercial Media* (Melbourne: Macmillan, 1983)
Bordwell, David and Kristin Thompson *Film Art: An Introduction* (Reading, Mass: Addison-Wesley, 1979)

162 National Fictions

Brady, Veronica *A Crucible of Prophets: Australians and the Question of God* (Sydney: Theological Explorations, 1981)
Burns, D. R. *The Directions of Australian Fiction 1920-1974* (Melbourne: Cassell, 1975)
Camus, Albert *The Myth of Sisyphus* (Harmondsworth: Penguin, 1975)
Carroll, John (ed.) *Intruders in the Bush* (Melbourne: Oxford University Press, 1982)
Carter, Paul *The Road to Botany Bay* (London: Faber, 1987)
Chambers, Iain *Border Dialogues: Journeys in Postmodernity* (London: Routledge, 1991)
Chase, Richard *The American Novel and its Tradition* (Garden City N.Y.: Doubleday, 1957)
Chatman, Seymour *Story and Discourse: Narrative Structure in Fiction and Film* (London: Cornell University Press, 1978)
Connell, R. W. *Ruling Class, Ruling Culture: Studies of Conflict, Power and Hegemony in Australian Life* (Melbourne: Cambridge University Press, 1977)
Connell, R. W. and T. H. Irving *Class Structure in Australian History* (Melbourne: Longman Cheshire, 1980)
Culler, Jonathon *The Pursuit of Signs: Semiotics, Literature and Deconstruction* (London: Routledge and Kegan Paul, 1981)
—— *Saussure* (London: Fontana, 1976)
—— *Structuralist Poetics: Structuralism, Linguistics and the Study of Literature* (London: Routledge and Kegan Paul, 1975)
Cunningham, Stuart *Featuring Australia: The Cinema of Charles Chauvel* (Sydney: Allen & Unwin, 1991)
Curran, James, Michael Gurevitch and Janet Woolacott (eds) *Mass Communication and Society* (London: Edward Arnold, 1977)
Dermody, Susan and Elizabeth Jacka *The Screening of Australia* Vols 1 and 2 (Sydney: Currency, 1987 and 1988)
—— (eds) *The Imaginary Industry: Australian Cinema in the late 1980s* (Sydney: AFTRS, 1988)
Dermody, Susan, John Docker, and Drusilla Modjeska (eds) *Nellie Melba, Ginger Meggs and Friends: Essays in Australian Cultural History* (Malmsbury: Kibble, 1982)
Docker, John *In a Critical Condition* (Ringwood: Penguin, 1984)
Dowling, William C. *Jameson, Marx, Althusser: An Introduction to the Political Unconscious* (London: Methuen, 1984)
Eagleton, Terry *Criticism and Ideology* (London; Verso, 1978)
—— *Literary Theory: An Introduction* (Oxford: Blackwell, 1983)
Ellis, John *Visible Fictions* (London: Routledge and Kegan Paul, 1982)
Fiedler, Leslie *Love and Death in the American Novel* (rev. edition) (New York: Dell, 1969)
—— *The Return of the Vanishing American* (London: Jonathon Cape, 1968)
Foucault, Michel *Discipline and Punish: The Birth of the Prison*, trans. Alan Sheridan (Harmondsworth: Peregrine, 1979)
Gelder, Ken and Paul Salzman *The New Diversity: Australian Fiction 1970-1988* (Melbourne: McPhee Gribble, 1989)
Green, Dorothy *The Music of Love: Essays on Literature and Life* (Ringwood: Penguin, 1984)

Gurevitch, Michael, Tony Bennett, James Curran and Janet Woolacott (eds) *Culture, Society and the Media* (London: Methuen, 1982)
Hassan, Ihab *Radical Innocence: Studies in the Contemporary Novel* (Princeton N.J.: Princeton University Press, 1961)
Hauck, Richard *Cheerful Nihilism: Confidence and the Absurd in American Humorous Fiction* (Bloomington: Indiana University Press, 1971)
Hebdidge, Dick *Subculture: The Meaning of Style* (London: Methuen, 1979)
Hergenhan, Laurie *Unnatural Lives: Studies in Australian Fiction about the Convicts, from James Tucker to Patrick White* (St Lucia: University of Queensland Press, 1983)
Hodge, Bob and Vijay Mishra *The Dark Side of the Dream: Australian Literature and the Postcolonial Mind* (Sydney: Allen & Unwin, 1991)
Hughes, Robert *The Art of Australia* (Ringwood: Penguin, 1970)
Jameson, Frederic *The Political Unconscious: Narrative as a Socially Symbolic Act* (London: Methuen, 1981)
Kress, Gunther and Robert Hodge *Language as Ideology* (London: Routledge and Kegan Paul, 1979)
Kiernan, Brian *Criticism* (Australian Writers and Their Work Series) (Melbourne: Oxford University Press, 1974)
—— *Images of Society and Nature: Seven Essays on Australian Novels* (Melbourne: Oxford University Press, 1971)
Kramer, Leonie (ed.) *The Oxford History of Australian Literature* (Melbourne: Oxford University Press, 1981)
Lansbury, Coral *Arcady in Australia* (Melbourne: Oxford University Press, 1970)
Leach, Edmund *Levi-Strauss* (Glasgow: Fontana, 1974)
Levi-Strauss, Claude *The Savage Mind* (London: Weidenfeld & Nicholson, 1966)
Lewis, R. W. B. *The American Adam: Innocence, Tragedy and Tradition in the Nineteenth Century* (London: University of Chicago Press, 1971, first published 1955)
Lovell, Terry *Pictures of Reality: Aesthetics, Politics and Pleasure* (London: BFI, 1983)
Macherey, Pierre *Towards a Theory of Literary Production*, trans. Geoffrey Wall (London: Routledge and Kegan Paul, 1978)
McFarlane, Brian *Words and Images: Australian Novels into Films* (Richmond: Heinemann, 1983)
—— *Australian Cinema 1970–85* (Melbourne: Heinemann, 1987)
McFarlane, Brian and Geoff Mayer *New Australian Cinema: Sources and Parallels* (Melbourne: Cambridge University Press, 1992)
McQueen, Humphrey *A New Britannia* (Ringwood: Penguin, 1976)
Mandle, W. F. *Going it Alone* (Ringwood: Penguin, 1980)
Matthews, Sue *35MM Dreams: Conversations with Five Directors About the Australian Film Revival* (Ringwood: Penguin, 1984)
Moore, Tom Inglis *Social Patterns in Australian Literature* (Sydney: Angus & Robertson, 1974)
Moran, Albert and Tom O'Regan *The Australian Screen* (Melbourne: Penguin, 1989)
Morris, Meaghan *The Pirate's Fiancee: Feminism, Reading, Postmodernism* (London: Verso, 1988)

164 National Fictions

Murray, Scott (ed.) *The New Australian Cinema* (Melbourne: Nelson/Cinema Papers, 1980)
Narasimhaiah, C. D. (ed.) *An Introduction to Australian Literature* (Brisbane: John Wiley & Sons, 1982)
Neale, Stephen *Genre* (London: BFI, 1980)
Olderman, Raymond M. *Beyond the Waste Land: A Study of the American Novel in the Nineteen-Sixties* (New Haven: Yale University Press, 1973)
O'Sullivan, Tim, and John Hartley, Danny Saunders, John Fiske *Key Concepts in Communication* (London: Methuen, 1983)
Palmer, Vance *The Legend of the Nineties* (Melbourne: Oxford University Press, 1954)
Pascoe, Rob *The Manufacture of Australian History* (Melbourne: Oxford University Press, 1979)
Phillips, A. A. *The Australian Tradition* (Melbourne: Longman Cheshire, 1958)
Pike, Andrew and Ross Cooper *Australian Film 1900-1977* (Melbourne: Oxford University Press, 1980)
Propp, Vladimir *The Morphology of the Folk Tale* (Austin: Austin University Press, 1975)
Reid, Ian *Fiction and the Great Depression: Australia and New Zealand 1930-1950* (Melbourne: Edward Arnold, 1979)
Rimmon-Kenan, Shlomith *Narrative Fiction: Contemporary Poetics* (London: Methuen, 1983)
Rowse, Tim *Australian Liberalism and National Character* (Malmsbury: Kibble, 1978)
Saussure, Ferdinand de *Course in General Linguistics*, trans. Wade Baskin (London: Peter Owen, 1960)
Schaffer, Kay *Women and the Bush: Forces of Desire in the Australian Cultural Tradition* (Melbourne: Cambridge University Press, 1988)
Schatz, Thomas *Hollywood Genres* (New York: Random House, 1981)
Scholes, Robert *The Fabulators* (New York: Oxford University Press, 1967)
—— *Fabulation and Metafiction* (Urbana: University of Illinois Press, 1979)
Sinnett, Frederick *The Fiction Fields of Australia* Cecil Hadgraft (ed.) (St Lucia: University of Queensland Press, 1966)
Stratton, David *The Last New Wave: The Australian Film Revival* (Sydney: Angus & Robertson, 1980)
Tanner, Tony *City of Words* (London: Jonathon Cape, 1971)
Todorov, Tzvetan *The Poetics of Prose* (Oxford: Blackwell, 1977)
Trilling, Lionel *The Liberal Imagination* (London: Mercury, 1961)
Tulloch, John *Legends on the Screen: The Narrative Film in Australia 1919-29* (Sydney: Currency Press, 1981)
—— *Australian Cinema: Industry, Narrative and Meaning* (Sydney: Allen & Unwin, 1982)
Walker, David *Dream and Disillusion* (Canberra: Australian National University Press, 1976)
Wallace-Crabbe, Chris (ed.) *The Australian Nationalists* (Melbourne: Oxford University Press, 1971)
Ward, Russell *The Australian Legend* (Melbourne: Oxford University Press, 1958)
White, Richard *Inventing Australia* (Sydney: Allen & Unwin, 1981)

Wilkes, G. A. *The Stockyard and the Croquet Lawn: Literary Evidence for Australia's Cultural Development* (Melbourne: Edward Arnold, 1981)

Williams, Raymond *Marxism and Literature* (Oxford: Oxford University Press, 1977)

Wright, Judith *Preoccupations in Australian Poetry* (Melbourne: Oxford University Press, 1965)

Wright, William *Six Guns and Society* (Berkeley: University of California Press, 1975)

Index

Aboriginals, representation of, 26–8, 70, 101
Adventures of Barry McKenzie, The, 141
All the Rivers Run, 29
Althusser, Louis, 81, 128
Alvin Purple, 100
Anderson, Benedict, 154
Andrews, Barry, 61–2 *passim*
Australian cultural studies, 148
Australian Film Reader, 147
Australian film studies, 3–5, 147
Australian humour and naturalisation, 140–2
Australian Journal of Cultural Studies, 147
Australian Journal of Screen, 147
Australian literary studies, 2–3, 146
Australian Screen, The, 147

Barrett, Robert G., 150
Big Steal, The, 152, 153
Between Wars, 51, 100, 130
Bliss (film), 138; (novel), 111, 135–7, 149
Brady, Veronica, 3, 52, 74, 83
Breaker Morant, 103, 114–15, 124–5
Bring Larks and Heroes, 31, 51, 59, 67–8, 80
Bryan Brown, 103
Burns, D.R., 46, 91
Burstall, Tim, 79

Caddie, 37–40, 51, 153

Campion, Jane, 153
Carey, Peter, 111, 135–6, 139, 149; 'The Fat Man in History', 'Chance', 'American Dreams', 139
Cars That Ate Paris, The, 101
Carroll, John, 83
Carter, Paul, 147
Chant of Jimmie Blacksmith, The (film), 70–1, 114; (novel), 29, 49, 51, 59
characterisation in Australian narrative, 87, 105; in fiction, 93–7; in film, 100–3; as icons of Australian-ness, 103–5; as ideology, 104–5; modes of representation, 87–105; theory of, 88–90; view of the self, 90
Chatman, Seymour, 89
Chambers, Iain, 154
Cinema Papers, 147
Clancy, Jack, 117, 132
Clarke, Marcus, 26
Clinic, The, 133
Commandant, The, 51
convictism in Australian narrative, 51–2, 62–75; Hergenhan's view, 60–1; history, 60–1; as ideology, 75–6, 81–4; as metaphor, 60
Corris, Peter, 150
country versus city in Australian narrative, 28 *see also* nature and society
Crocodile Dundee, 151
Crocodile Dundee 2, 152

Crofts, Stephen, 124, 125
Culler, Jonathon, 88
Cunningham, Stuart, 34–5, 147
Dark Side of the Dream, 147
Dead Calm, 152
Death in Brunswick, 153
Dermody, Susan, 71, 130, 147
Devil's Playground, The, 51, 71–2, 75
Discipline and Punish, 60, 69, 75
Docker, John, 2–3, 21, 26, 54–7, 121
documentary realism, 98, 105, 132–4
Don's Party, 75, 100, 141
Drysdale, Russell, 111
Dyer, Richard, 16, 104–5

Eagleton, Terry, 14, 33, 82
Ellis, Bob, 58, 78
Ellis, John, 7
existentialism in Australian narrative, 79–80
film criticism and literary criticism, 13–16
film and fiction as narrative, 17–19
film and literature, formal differences, 16–17

FJ Holden, The, 98, 131
For The Term of His Natural Life (film), 61; (novel), 59, 61–5, 68
Fortunes of Richard Mahony, The, 59, 75
Foucault, Michel, 60, 69, 75, 81
Fringe of Leaves, A, 138
Furphy, Joseph, 83, 90–2, 97, 99, 110, 149

Gallipoli, 100–2 *passim*, 114, 115
Garner, Helen, 149
Gelder, Ken, 151
Getting of Wisdom, The (film), 59, 71, 73–5 *passim*; (novel), 73–5
Girl of the Bush, A, 98, 111
Going Down, 134–5
Goodbye Paradise, 139
Gramsci, Antonio, 83, 124
Green Card, 152

Hall, Stuart, 6, 121

Hard Knocks, 133, 140
Heath, Stephen, 142
Hebdidge, Dick, 138–9
Heidelberg School, 26, 110; influence on film, 112
Hergenhan, Laurie, 20, 60–1, 82
Heseltine, H.P., 3, 25, 26, 28, 30–1, 122
Hodge, Bob, 147
Hutton, Anne B., 79, 83, 122

Illywhacker, 149
Imaginary Life, An, 137–8
individual in Australian narrative, 21–2, 59–84, 105; in comparison to America, 76–8; in films of Peter Weir, 101; history, 78; image of the battler, 119; as a national type, 103–5
individualism in Australian narrative, 99; democracy, 90; ideology, 105; mateship, 93–7; nationalist myth, 90–1; 'type of the individual', 103–5
In Search of Anna, 59, 75
Irishman, The, 29, 103

Jacka, Elizabeth, xiii, 147, 154
Jameson, Frederic, 123, 144, 145, 151
Jolley, Elizabeth, 149

Kiernan, Brian, 3, 25, 28, 30–1, 33, 46, 51, 79
King, Noel, 4, 15
Kostas, 133

Landtakers, 43–6
Last Wave, The, 101, 102
Lawson, Henry, 26, 90–1, 93–7, 110; 'The Shearing of the Cook's Dog', 92; 'The Bush Undertaker', 26, 92; 'Send Round the Hat', 92; 'Telling Mrs Baker', 94–5; 'The Union Buries its Dead', 96
Lawson, Sylvia, 5, 28
legend of the nineties, 25–6, 29; cultural currency of, 107–23; ideological function of, 123–5

168 National Fictions

Levi-Strauss, Claude, 9, 18, 19, 35–6, 142
literary criticism and film criticism, 13–15
Louisa, 147

Macherey, Pierre, 33
McCabe, Colin, 5, 14
McFarlane, Brian, 5, 148
Mad Max, 78, 138
Mad Max II, 78
Malcolm, 152
Malouf, David, 60
Man From Snowy River, The, 49–50, 59, 112, 117–21, 138, 151, 153
Man of Flowers, 140
Man Who Loved Children, The, 51, 75
Mango Tree, The, 29
Marquez, Gabriel Garcia, 149
Mast, Gerald, 15
mateship, literary convention of, 93–100
Matthews, Brian, 90, 147
Mayer, Geoff, 148
Merry Go Round in the Sea, 75
metaphysics and ideology, 81–3
Mishra, Vijay, 147
Moffat, Tracy, 153
Molloy, Bruce, 148
Monkey Grip, 133
Moore, Tom Inglis, 28, 30, 91
Moorhouse, Jocelyn, 153
Moran, Albert, 147
Mouth to Mouth, 51, 75, 130–2
Moving Out, 133
My Brilliant Career, 29, 51, 71, 114
My First Wife, 140

narrative and culture, 8–9, 18–20, 75–8, 142
narrative closure, 71–5, 78, 79, 105
narratology, 5–6
nationalism, xiii, 105; in Australian film, 109–21; conservative critiques, 121–2; ideological function, 108–21; myths, 107–8; in opposition to Britain, 112–13; representation of, 107–23
nature and society in Australian narrative, *see also* country and city; centrality of the land, 32; culture into nature, 34–5; ideology, 33–5; myth, 35–7, 50–2; traditional views, 25–31
Newsfront, 34, 51, 100, 153
Nolan, Sydney, 26, 111

Odd Angry Shot, The, 140
O'Regan, Tom, 117, 147
Oscar and Lucinda, 149

Palmer, Vance, 25, 28, 107
Parker, David, 152
Phar Lap, 114, 118–19
Picnic at Hanging Rock, 29, 101, 102, 114
Picture Show Man, The, 103
Pike, Andrew and Ross Cooper, 3
Power Without Glory, 5
Proof, 153
Pure S, 130, 131

Ralph Rashleigh, 61
Reid, Ian, 3, 28, 31, 32, 51
Rikki and Pete, 152
Road to Botany Bay, The, 147
Robbery Under Arms, 25
Rowe, Jennifer, 150
Rowse, Tim, 108, 109
Ryan, Tom, 57–8

Salzman, Paul, 151
Savage Crows, The, 75
Scarlet Letter, The, 93
Schaffer, Kay, 147
Schepisi, Fred, 70
Schindler's Ark, 68, 75
Seven Poor Men of Sydney, 51, 61
Sinnett, Frederick, 78
Smiley, 114
stars as signs, 104–5
Starstruck, 138
Stir, 51, 59, 62–6
Strictly Ballroom, 153
style in Australian film, 79; contemporary directions, 130–5; in Australian narrative, 138–9

Such is Life, 92, 100, 103
Sunday Too Far Away, 29, 51, 75, 98–100, 140–1
Taine, H., 30
Tass, Nadia, 152
Tax Inspector, The, 149
Three Cheers for the Paraclete, 51
Three in One, 97–8, 114
To the Islands, 26, 28, 49
Tree of Man, The, 49, 50
Tulloch, John, 3, 5, 7, 15, 28, 29, 36, 111
Turner, Ann, 153

Ultima Thule, 46–9
Unknown Industrial Prisoner, The, 51, 68–70, 75

Vivisector, The, 51
Voss, 26, 28, 49, 50, 59, 75

Wake in Fright, 29, 40–3
Walkabout, 75
Weir, Peter, 100–2, 152
White, Patrick, 28, 135
White, Richard, 33–4, 109–10
Wilkes, G.A., 32, 121–2, 141–2
Williamson, David, 141–2
Windsor, Gerard, 150
Winter of Our Dreams, 75, 104, 133
Woman of the Future, 51
Women and the Bush, 147
Wright, Judith, 25, 122

Year of Living Dangerously, The, 101, 102